T0295492

REGULATORY FAILURE AND RENEWAL

CARLETON LIBRARY SERIES

The Carleton Library Series publishes books about Canadian economics, geography, history, politics, public policy, society and culture, and related topics, in the form of leading new scholarship and reprints of classics in these fields. The series is funded by Carleton University, published by McGill-Queen's University Press, and is under the guidance of the Carleton Library Series Editorial Board, which consists of faculty members of Carleton University. Suggestions and proposals for manuscripts and new editions of classic works are welcome and may be directed to the Carleton Library Series Editorial Board c/o the Library, Carleton University, Ottawa K1S 5B6, at cls@carleton.ca, or on the web at www.carleton.ca/cls.

CLS board members: John Clarke, Ross Eaman, Jennifer Henderson, Paul Litt, Laura Macdonald, Jody Mason, Stanley Winer, Barry Wright

Regulatory Failure and Renewal

*The Evolution of the Natural
Monopoly Contract*

Second Edition

JOHN R. BALDWIN

Foreword by Stanley Winer
Introduction by Ian Keay

Carleton Library Series 260

McGill-Queen's University Press
Montreal & Kingston · London · Chicago

© McGill-Queen's University Press 2022

ISBN 978-0-2280-1181-1 (cloth)
ISBN 978-0-2280-1182-8 (paper)
ISBN 978-0-2280-1245-0 (ePDF)

Legal deposit first quarter 2022
Bibliothèque nationale du Québec

First edition published by Minister of Supply and Services Canada, 1989
Printed in Canada on acid-free paper that is 100% ancient forest free
(100% post-consumer recycled), processed chlorine free

Funded by the   Financé par le
Government   gouvernement | Canada
of Canada   du Canada

We acknowledge the support of the Canada Council for the Arts.

Nous remercions le Conseil des arts du Canada de son soutien.

Library and Archives Canada Cataloguing in Publication

Title: Regulatory failure and renewal: the evolution of the natural monopoly contract / John R. Baldwin; a new edition with a foreword by Stanley Winer and an introduction by Ian Keay.

Names: Baldwin, John R. (John Russel), 1945- author.

Series: Carleton library series ; 260.

Description: Second edition. | Series statement: Carleton library series; 260 | Includes bibliographical references.

Identifiers: Canadiana (print) 20220150648 | Canadiana (ebook) 20220150869 | ISBN 9780228011811 (hardcover) | ISBN 9780228011828 (softcover) | ISBN 9780228012450 (ePDF)

Subjects: LCSH: Government business enterprises—Canada. | LCSH: Government business enterprises—Law and legislation—Canada. | LCSH: Government corporations—Canada. | LCSH: Trade regulation—Canada. | LCSH: Conflict of laws—Government business enterprises—Canada.

Classification: LCC HD4008 .B35 2022 | DDC 338.6/20971—dc23

Contents

Foreword to the New Edition

The Carleton Library Series and McGill-Queen's University Press are pleased to present John Baldwin's study of the evolution and regulation of public enterprise in Canada. This work was originally written for the Economic Council of Canada (ECC) and published by the Government of Canada in 1989. It is one of many excellent background studies that emerged from the research programs of the ECC over its thirty-year history. A new introduction to the volume by Professor Ian Keay of Queen's University, commissioned by the editorial board of the Carleton Library Series, explains why this work is of contemporary relevance to public policy in Canada. The purpose of this foreword is to reacquaint readers with the ECC, which was disbanded by the government in 1992 after it published its annual review of 1991, *A Joint Venture: The Economics of Constitutional Options*. This study suggested that the separation of Quebec from Canada might not have catastrophic consequences. It is obvious why it was not well received by the federal government amid the national debates that led to the 1995 referendum in Quebec.

The Economic Council was established by the federal government in 1963 in the aftermath of the publication of the *Final Report of the Royal Commission on Canada's Economic Prospects* in 1957. The council itself – headed by eminent economist John Deutsch and including twenty-five people representing business, labour, agriculture, and the consumer movement – was structured along European lines, stressing consensus building rather than competition among major economic sectors. It was given a professional staff of economists and funds to permit the commissioning of studies by outside experts. The ECC was charged with studying and advising the government on issues of importance to the medium- and longer-term economic development of the country and with encouraging "maximum" cooperation between labour and management to that end, among other goals.[1]

The council's first annual review, published in 1964, was 213 pages in length and was accompanied by thirteen background studies by individual authors. This substantial body of work was typical of the council's depth of analysis of contemporary medium-term issues. In all, the ECC prepared twenty-eight annual reviews of similar length, each backed by special studies as well as by forecasts produced using its own large-scale, Keynesian econometric model called Candide.[2] A few of these reports, such as its eleventh, on social indicators, were ahead their time.

As Harry Johnson observed in his review of the council's first annual report,[3] there was a possibility that it would pose challenges to the dominance in economic matters of the Department of Finance and other central agencies. Under its second chair, Arthur Smith, this prediction proved to be correct. The ECC began to evolve into a policy-advising or planning agency rather than purely a research institute. The result was a certain tension or conflict with the policy and planning centres of power set up by the new Trudeau government in the early 1970s, culminating in Smith's early resignation.[4] Subsequent chairs (André Raynauld, George Post, Sylvia Ostry, David Slater, and Judith Maxwell) found a different balance between short-run, and medium- and longer-term problems and issues acceptable to the governments of the day. Some underlying tension remained, however, until the last annual review, which proved fatal.

The Economic Council of Canada filled a gap in policy analysis in Canada, a bridge between multi-year royal commissions and single papers on narrowly defined topics. It produced both an annual review focusing on medium-term economic and social issues and, every three years or so, an extensive analysis of a more general issue that synthesized a number of commissioned studies along with work by ECC staff. Special studies included substantial reports on innovation and jobs, the service economy, poverty, the social and economic impacts of immigration, Canadian natural resources, regional economic development, the Newfoundland economy, fiscal federalism, regulation, and the role of government in society. Some individual background studies emerging from this research program have been widely circulated, or, like the Baldwin study, they deserve to be, though sadly there does not appear to be a central online repository of ECC studies.[5]

There is nothing like the Economic Council in Canada today. There are now several active, well-established think tanks producing excellent policy-relevant research on specific topics from a variety of perspectives. Also, the government-funded Parliamentary Budget Office scrutinizes aspects of current federal budgets. The Finances of the Nation project has recently begun to enlarge the scope of analyses of public finance issues available online. But these organizations do not have the ability to focus all of their resources on one issue – such as the regulation of the Canadian economy, economic growth, inequality, or climate change – for two or three years using a substantial team of highly paid researchers. The Social Sciences and Humanities Research Council has expanded and now finances multi-year academic research projects. But policy-relevant research on the Canadian economy is not suffciently rewarded in academia because applied papers on Canadian economic policy issues are hard to place in the better international journals. Still, from time to time, longer studies on Canadian public policy issues do arise. The Mowat Centre at the University of Toronto, for example, produced some extended studies from an Ontario perspective for about a decade but ran out of funding in 2018.

There is a case to be made for re-establishing an organization like the ECC that has a mandate and the resources to study medium- and longer-term economic issues of concern to Canadians (perhaps with a somewhat wider disciplinary scope than the ECC had). Absent a substantial increase in philanthropy in Canada, such an agency will have to be funded publicly. In that case, it will be important to deal with the problem of how an agency that is funded by tax dollars can remain independent and, importantly, avoid self-censorship, when it is in competition with planning and policy centres of power within government and produces work that will inevitably be seen at some point to be critical of the direction taken by the government of the day. This is a difficult and ongoing problem that deserves further consideration.

In the meantime, the reader is invited to turn to Ian Keay's new introduction to *Regulatory Failure and Renewal,* and then to enjoy John Baldwin's interesting book.

Stanley L. Winer
Canada Research Chair Professor in Public Policy Emeritus, Carleton University

Notes

I want to thank, without implicating, Judith Maxwell, Norm Leckie, and Jody Mason for help in the preparation of this foreword.

1 Section 9(i) of the *Economic Council of Canada Act.*
2 In the interests of full disclosure, I note that my first job after graduate school involved putting my dissertation on government budget constraints into the Candide model.
3 Harry G. Johnson, review of *First Annual Review: Economic Goals for Canada to 1970,* by the Economic Council of Canada, *Journal of Political Economy* 73, no. 4 (August 1965): 410–12.
4 This history is well described by Richard Phidd in his extensive analysis of the ECC: "The Economic Council of Canada: Its Establishment, Structure, and Role in the Canadian Policy-Making System, 1963–74," *Canadian Public Administration* 18, no. 3 (December 1975): 337–525.
5 But see the following website where many ECC publications are to be found: https://publications.gc.ca/site/eng/search/search.html?st=1&e=0&f=0&ssti=on&ast=economic+council+of+canada&cnst=&adof=on&hpp=10&psi=1&rq.ssp=-5.

Introduction to the New Edition
Ian Keay

Natural Monopolies and Regulatory Instruments in Canada

In the first decades of the twenty-first century – more than 150 years after the earliest franchise contracts were negotiated between Canadian governments and privately owned utility companies, and thirty years after the Economic Council of Canada published John R. Baldwin's *Regulatory Failure and Renewal: The Evolution of the Natural Monopoly Contract* in 1989 – the federal government still holds a controlling interest in more than forty crown corporations. The provinces and territories in Canada own at least 150 more firms. These public enterprises typically operate in industries prone to the formation of what economists call "natural monopolies," including pipelines, power generation, municipal water systems, transportation, broadcasting, and telecommunications. This tendency towards public ownership in Canada is very different from the approach adopted by the federal government in the United States, which, despite overseeing a macroeconomy ten times the size of Canada's, controls only thirty-three publicly owned enterprises.

Although there is a long history of public ownership in Canada, crown corporations cannot be viewed as a relic of an earlier age. The use of public ownership as a policy instrument to regulate natural monopolies is clearly a live issue across federal and provincial jurisdictions in Canada. Consider as contrasting examples, the federal government's acquisition of the assets of the Trans Mountain Pipeline in August 2018, and the Ontario provincial government's privatization of the electricity generating assets of Ontario Hydro through the late 2010s. The federal government's decision to acquire and operate pipeline infrastructure, and the provincial government's decision to divest itself of electricity generating stations, were distinctly different policy responses to similar underlying pressures, including the presence of mounting tension across the political spectrum, and ongoing protests and legal proceedings founded on concerns about environment degradation and the violation of Indigenous rights. In both cases, negotiations aimed at resolving these challenges became protracted, costly, and eventually untenable. What these examples confirm is that in the contemporary Canadian policy environment, public ownership is clearly more than just a historical curiosity, it continues to be a viable and widely called upon benchmark policy instrument.

Pipelines and electricity generation are examples of goods and services that we all consume on a daily basis that require extensive, complex, and product-specific delivery networks. Huge sums of money must be invested to build and maintain networks of rail lines, over-head and underground cables, pipes and pipelines, and cell phone towers. Because it cannot be easily converted to other uses, the capital invested in these networks is often long-lived and irreversible. As a result, most products that rely on extensive delivery networks are produced by industries with exceptionally high entry costs and "increasing returns to scale."

The more units a firm produces – its scale of production – the lower its per unit entry costs will be. When entry costs are high, only firms that produce on the largest possible scale will be able to lower their per unit costs to a profitable level. Increases in the scale of production, therefore, are associated with increasing returns, in the form of falling per unit costs. For industries with the most expensive delivery networks, it may only be possible to get per unit costs low enough if a single firm supplies the entire market. To economists this type of industry is known as a natural monopoly because the fundamental characteristics of the economic environment – the size of the market, and the cost to build and maintain the delivery network, for example – dictate that only a single monopolistic firm that can spread its entry costs over the entire market demand, will be able to stay in business (Braeutigam 1989).

Natural monopolies tend to be more prevalent in environments with relatively small markets, and large building and maintenance costs for delivery networks. Canada is a big country with a small domestic market, at least relative to it largest trading partner, the United States, and the domestic market in Canada is dominated by consumers living in geographically dispersed urban-industrial centres. The Canadian landmass covers nearly 25 per cent more square kilometres than the continental United States, but the Canadian macroeconomy and the total population of the country are only about the size of the state of California. On average, therefore, the density of the Canadian market is low. However, what is perhaps a little more surprising is that Canada has long been, and continues to be, a remarkably urban and industrial place. As Keay and Lewis (2018) point out, since at least the 1890s the proportion of Canadians living in cities has been roughly the same as the urban population share in the US, and although manufacturing output per capita has been concentrated in natural resource intensive industries, it was still considerably higher than some countries we typically consider heavily industrialized, such as Germany and France, while being nearly as high as the global manufacturing leaders, including the US and Britain.

Resource intensive manufacturing production that takes place in an environment with dense, but widely dispersed urban markets, necessarily requires extensive, complex and very expensive delivery networks. These networks are responsible for high entry costs that must be spread over relatively low levels of aggregate domestic demand. As a result of these factors, there has long been a tendency to form natural monopolies in Canadian utility industries, including pipelines, municipal water systems, and electricity, telecommunication and transportation networks (Baldwin 1975).

Because natural monopolists have no competitors, in an unfettered market they can reduce variety, quality, and environmental protection, all while charging prices above their marginal costs. This means that these producers can extract monopoly rents – profits in excess of a "normal" return on investment – from consumers, which in turn reduces the value of market transactions and results in what economists refer to as "deadweight loss." Deadweight loss is every bit as undesirable as its name suggests. Both consumers and producers benefit from market transactions, but when natural monopolists degrade service standards and charge prices over their marginal costs, consumers well-being is reduced, typically by more than the total profits earned by the monopolist, and society as a whole loses as deadweight losses mount.

To reduce deadweight loss, governments must intervene in markets characterized by natural monopolies. The total well-being of society can be increased if service standards are enforced and natural monopolists' tendency to raise prices over marginal costs is restrained. This type of regulation involves a redistribution of monopolists' rents, thereby creating winners from this process – typically consumers – and losers – typically the monopolists. Government intervention, therefore, reduces inefficiencies associated with the unfettered behaviour of natural monopolists, but the incentives inherent in the redistributive process open the door for a different sort of inefficiency. Specifically, inefficiency associated with regulation can include what Baldwin refers to in *Regulatory Failure and Renewal* as "government opportunism." Unlike the profit-seeking opportunism exercised by natural monopolists, government opportunism need not be associated with corruption or the search for monetary gain, but it is associated with the search for political influence and control.

A wide range of policy instruments can be used to regulate natural monopolies, and these instruments lead to different redistributive patterns, and different levels and forms of inefficiency. In general, Canada's social, political, and economic environments have been institutionally secure, mature and sophisticated. However, the division of power that defines the federal system of governance in Canada opens the door for idiosyncratic provincial (and therefore municipal) policy making, which has lead to the adoption of a wide range of regionally distinct regulatory responses to the formation of natural monopolies.

One of Baldwin's key insights in *Regulatory Failure and Renewal* is the recognition that the economic history of Canada presents us with nearly ideal conditions for the study of the regulation of natural monopolies. The size and dispersed nature of Canada's urban-industrial markets, the resource intensity of its production, the federal-provincial division of powers, and Canada's long-standing institutional maturity, combine to make economically important natural monopolies common, and the range of regulatory interventions nearly comprehensive. Baldwin exploits the Canadian historical context as the basis for a detailed exploration of the remarkably diverse instrument choices adopted across Canadian jurisdictions by regulators striving to manage the economic rents arising from the formation of domestic natural monopolies.

As the need for regulation was becoming acute during the late nineteenth and early twentieth centuries, the institutional and economic environments characterizing Canadian provinces and cities shared more similarities than differences. However, within these environments a wide variety of policy tools, in a myriad of styles and forms, were tried, often discarded, and sometimes revived. For Baldwin, this variation and fluidity in an otherwise institutionally stable and mature economy, provides a wealth of finely detailed historical evidence. He documents how this evidence reveals an important role for the transactions costs – the costs of search, negotiation and enforcement, for example – that are bourn by market participants in their effort to acquire and process information. Transactions costs are shown to have acted as a trigger for regulation, a determinant of instrument choice, and a factor affecting the long run consequences of regulators' policy decisions. In addition to his analysis of the historical evidence, Baldwin identifies lessons that arise from that evidence with the help of an explicit theoretical structure describing the causal forces linking transactions costs to policy outcomes.

From the perspective of the late 1980s when *Regulatory Failure and Renewal* was first published, the policy relevance of a structural interpretation of the key causal connections, and the articulation of lessons learned from the history of Canada's efforts to regulate natural monopolies, was obvious. More recently in the early twenty-first century, these same connections and lessons remain just as relevant in Canada as municipal, provincial, and federal governments struggle with a long list of regulatory challenges in the presence of natural monopolies, including the need to fund network expansions for intra-urban transport, privatize electricity generation, and justify the public ownership of trans-continental pipelines. The stakes may be even higher when we consider the growing need to regulate natural monopolies in international markets for products such as water, carbon, or information.

Baldwin shows us how differences in transactions costs across jurisdictions, industries, and environments motivate not only the adoption of interventionist policies, but how they affect the choice of instrument, and the effects of regulation on prices, profitability, government revenues, enforcement outcomes, and industrial structure. The cost of information, and the impact of transactions costs on markets dominated by natural monopolies, are starkly illustrated in late nineteenth and early twentieth century Canadian economic history, but their economic and regulatory effects have not dissipated over time or across space.

Baldwin's historical analyses of Canadian utility industries, including railway lines, municipal water works and transport systems, electricity generation, transmission and distribution networks, and long-distance and local telecommunication systems, reveal a riot of heterogeneity across the combinations and permutations of franchise contracts, regulatory agencies and public ownership that evolved in Canada between Confederation in 1867 and World War II. Baldwin's case studies are great fun to read, but the economically important strands in each narrative are never lost in the historical detail, and sharply defined common themes emerge.

Shifts in economic and technological conditions introduced incentives to renegotiate long-standing franchise contracts between local, provincial or federal governments, on one hand, and private utility firms on the other. Where these shifts were frequent and large, as they were through the late nineteenth and early twentieth centuries in Canada, and where the market tends strongly towards natural monopoly, the pressure to regulate and redistribute rents was high. Baldwin evokes Oliver Williamson's (1971, 1981) models of firm formation to support his view that the regulatory instruments chosen by governments depend critically on the size and distribution of the transactions costs that are present. Transactions costs rise with the extent of information asymmetry that exists among market participants. The linchpin to Baldwin's argument is the recognition that where the judiciary's ability to constrain government opportunism is limited and the rewards for opportunism are high, mistrust and uncertainty will be present, information asymmetries will rise, and transactions costs can quickly become unmanageable. In these settings, similar to what Williamson observed for vertically integrating firms, successful negotiation between market participants – governments, consumers, and utility companies – may not be possible. Expropriation and public ownership may be necessary to remove the distinction between regulators/consumers and producers, thereby eliminating any information asymmetry and "internalizing" transactions costs within a single entity – the crown corporation.

Legal constraints on government opportunism can stem from constitutional authority, as in the United States, or from potentially more tenuous and discretionary common law precedent and tradition, as in Canada. The reward for opportunism can flow from quirks in the division of power across jurisdictions, a "taste" for public ownership of capital, populist demands for redistributive policies, or even something as simple as the geographic distribution of population, market activity, and resource endowments. Where the constraints on opportunism are relatively weak and these rewards are high, ongoing expropriation risk faced by private capital may be so high that US-style, arms-length regulatory agencies will become bogged down and ineffectual. In that case, negotiation can still succeed, but only if transactions costs are internalized through the expropriation of private capital and formation of a publicly owned enterprise.

Canada's history of regulating natural monopolies confirms that the conditions under which franchise contracts fail and regulatory agencies become ineffectual, are not ubiquitous by any means, but they are more common in Canada than in the US – two countries that shared many economic and institutional similarities during the decades surrounding the turn of the twentieth century. Baldwin points out that it was not some cultural distinction leading to a proclivity for public ownership in Canada, exceptional demands for redistributive policies, nor even the underlying market conditions that led to a greater reliance on public ownership in Canada. He sees the key difference stemming from the protections, or the lack thereof, offered to private property in the constitutions of the United States and Canada.

In the US, the courts have interpreted the fifth amendment of the constitution, which guarantees "just compensation" for government expropriation of private property, to be a requirement for "fair-return-on-fair-value." With regard to the regulation of natural monopolies, this has come to mean that governments can limit and redistribute monopoly rents, but if private capital is seized to facilitate public ownership, compensation must cover the present value of the entire stream of returns that could be earned with that capital. In Canada, the constitution does not explicitly protect private property, but precedents established in common law have come to form a "constructionist approach" to expropriation. This approach allows for the possibility that private capital can be expropriated without fair-return-on-fair-value, but only if the legislature has explicitly acknowledged that the potential for expropriation may exist. In short, governments in Canada do not face binding legal constraints on expropriation without "fair" compensation, and the risk of this expropriation opens the door for opportunistic behaviour by Canadian governments. Government opportunism, in turn, raises the transactions costs associated with contracting between governments and private capital owners. These transactions costs determine the ease with which franchise contracts can be settled, or arms-length regulatory bodies can effectively engage in negotiations with natural monopolists.

The key point in Baldwin's analysis of instrument choice in the regulation of Canada's natural monopolies – the point that transcends the specific historic and geographic context of his study – is that transactions costs matter, and transactions costs are critically dependent on information asymmetries stemming from the legal protections provided for private property. Baldwin uses a theoretical framework that borrows from models that describe the role played by transactions costs in industrial organization and firm formation. Detailed analyses that use approaches common in the fields of economic history, and law and economics provide evidence, narrative detail, and policy context that can be understood within the structure of his theoretical framework. Case studies delving into the regulation of Canadian railways, water systems, urban transport networks, telecommunication systems, and electricity generation, transmission and distribution, are rich in historical detail, but from these studies Baldwin focuses on the common themes – instrument choice, transactions costs, and opportunism – that reveal themselves. These themes have not lost any of their relevance since *Regulatory Failure and Renewal*'s initial 1989 release. The forces leading to the formation of natural monopolies in industries with high entry costs due to the complexity of their delivery networks, and the incentive to regulate prices and service standards for these producers, have not disappeared. In Canada and internationally, effective regulation of the production and distribution of economically vital goods and services, including petroleum, water, carbon, electricity, and information, is necessary to maintain sustainable economic and political systems.

In the remaining sections of this introduction some context characterizing the economic and institutional realities of the late 1980s and early 1990s, at the time Baldwin first published his study, is provided. A more detailed overview of the model and historical case studies, emphasizing the heterogeneity in the relevant environments and policy outcomes, and the common underlying themes, is presented. To wrap up, a brief discussion of the persistent relevance of Baldwin's analysis concludes.

Context and Motivation: Natural Monopolies in Canada at the End of the Twentieth Century

When *Regulatory Failure and Renewal* was first published as a research study for the Economic Council of Canada in 1989, the federal government was in the midst of a divestiture phase that involved the privatization of publicly owned firms, including what were at that time some of the most iconic crown corporations in Canada (Boardman and Vining 2012). Air Canada, for example, was privatized in 1988, Petro-Canada in 1991, and CN Rail in 1995. This was an era that had some remarkable similarities to the late nineteenth-early twentieth century period that is the focus of Baldwin's historical analysis, and these similarities made the lessons drawn from Canada's history of regulating natural monopolies that much more elucidating.

The period between 1870 and 1913 is often referred to as the "first era of globalization" (Estevadeordal, Frantz and Taylor 2003). The sharp decline in transport and information costs at this time, primarily due to rapid technological change in steam-driven ocean shipping and early electronic telecommunications (telegraph and telephones), triggered a boom in global trade volumes, transcontinental migration, and international investment flows. These global market forces put pressure on domestic industries in Canada, dramatically increasing foreign competition within domestic markets, opening foreign markets to Canadian natural resource intensive products, and differentially shifting both labour and capital supplies across local and provincial markets (Hamilton, Keay, and Lewis 2017).

As a result of these pressures, producers and governments had to innovate, intervene and adapt. Input prices were changing, incomes were rising, technological change was occurring at a dizzying pace, and consumers were quick to demand the new products and services that accompanied these changes, including household electrification, indoor plumbing fixtures, both commercial and residential climate control systems, and transport networks capable of facilitating urban sprawl. Delivery networks of increasing sophistication (and cost) grew with the rapid and fluid integration of markets for the goods and services that were on the technological frontier. In municipal, provincial, and national markets, natural monopolies formed in the industries that supplied the water, transport, telecommunication, and power for these products, and governments' regulatory efforts to limit and redistribute the resultant monopoly rents had to evolve to manage these structural changes.

Baldwin describes the impact of growing information asymmetries and transactions costs that resulted from the rapid changes that were occurring in global and domestic markets during the late nineteenth and early twentieth centuries. The need to regulate natural monopolies sprang up in multiple markets in a short span of time, and a diverse set of policy instruments were implemented to meet this need. The policy relevance and broader societal importance of Baldwin's study stems from the historical parallels that linked the changes that occurred in global markets, technology, and the Canadian economic environment during the late nineteenth and early twentieth centuries, to similar changes that were again becoming apparent during the late twentieth century when the Economic Council of Canada first published *Regulatory Failure and Renewal*.

It was during the late 1970s and early 1980s that computing speeds began their exponential rise, fibre optic and satellite communication networks were being built, and container shipping was being widely adopted for trans-oceanic freight. The result of these innovations was the beginning of what has to become another era of rapid and wide-spread technological change and globalization. Again, the need for regulatory intervention grew with these shifts in the economic environment. The efficiency and effectiveness of the policy tools that had first been developed to regulate Canada's natural monopolies one hundred years earlier,

xviii   Introduction to the New Edition

was called into question. Just as Baldwin described for Canada's national rail networks, municipal water works and transport systems, and electricity networks during the post-Confederation – pre-World War II period, globalization forces during the late twentieth century motivated the search for a new set of policy instruments to regulate markets that continued to be prone to the formation of natural monopolies.

Late twentieth-century globalization shifted the economic and technological environment in Canada, eroding the long-standing incentives for government opportunism, increasing the possibility of (often international) competition in many markets traditionally controlled by local natural monopolists, and changing the pattern of transactions costs. Into this transformative environment, Canada also began to see the effects of a century of common law legal precedent that cemented the constructionist approach and, although constitutional protection for private property was still absent, substantively constrained governments' ability to behave opportunistically (Metcalf 2015). Rather than the opportunism, expropriation, and public ownership that had been historically present in Canadian utilities, the 1980s and 1990s saw Canadian crown corporations broken up and sold off to private interests. The patterns in transactions costs had changed such that public ownership was no long necessary to internalize these costs. The hope was that the newly privatized companies could be effectively regulated by arms-length, quasi-judicial bodies, similar to the regulatory agencies that had been dominant in the US since the mid-1800s.

Baldwin motivates his study of policy choice in the regulation of natural monopolies by asking why public ownership was more common in Canada than in the United States during the late nineteenth and early twentieth centuries. He could just as well have asked why rapid globalization and technological change in the late 1800s triggered public ownership among Canadian natural monopolies, while similar forces in the late 1900s triggered a move away from public ownership, towards privatization and regulation by arms-length regulatory bodies.

In 1989, the insights Baldwin articulates in his study were applicable in both historical and contemporary contexts. Specifically, transactions costs associated with negotiation and regulation were still related to the threat of expropriation without compensation by the government. Where the incentive to expropriate is large and the legal constraints are weak, internalization of these costs through public ownership is more likely. This conclusion is not necessarily dependent on factors such as technology or industrial structure.

Baldwin reveals that in the US during the last half of the nineteenth century, the constitutional protection for private property in the fifth amendment constrained the threat of government opportunism, so arms-length regulatory agencies were a feasible and relatively effective policy option. In Canada at this time, because legal constraints were weaker and the incentive to expropriate was larger, uncertainty and information asymmetries were more prevalent, and the internalization of transactions costs through public ownership was much more common. By the late 1980s and early 1990s, common law precedent in Canada had evolved to such an extent that the legal constraints on expropriation and opportunism were comparable to those in the US, and it was therefore possible to effectively break up and privatize many of the crown corporations that had been formed during the earlier globalization period (Boardman and Vining 2012; Iaobucci and Trebilcock 2012).

During the late 1980s, the value of Baldwin's analysis of the historical regulation of Canada's natural monopolies in *Regulatory Failure and Renewal*, flowed from his identification of the fundamental forces that led to the adoption of public ownership as policy instrument during the first era of globalization. Recognizing and understanding these forces was key to any contemporary assessment of the efficacy and advisability of the privatization policies being pursued by governments at that time. Of course, the lessons that could be learned for modern policy analysis depend critically on what are, in some cases, complex and tangled historical details. As Baldwin's case studies make clear, policy choices varied widely across jurisdictions and industries, but it is exactly this historical heterogeneity that reveals the common features underlying these choices. These common features, and the theoretical structure that allows us to interpret them, are necessary to bring the historical lessons learned into a more modern policy making environment.

Rather than simply reiterating and summarizing Baldwin's analysis, I now turn to a review of his model and historical case studies. The review focuses on the heterogeneity in the historical evidence that he uses to isolate causal factors that are common across industries, right through the twentieth and into the twenty-first century.

Heterogeneity and Common Themes: Regulating Canada's Natural Monopolies

To allow for causal interpretations of the historical detail that Baldwin provides in the main body of *Regulatory Failure and Renewal*, he begins by establishing some theoretical structure for his analysis. In his 1975 work on Canada's airline industry, *The Regulatory Agency and the Public Corporation*, Baldwin uses Oliver Williamson's (1971, 1981) industrial organization models of firm formation to illustrate how transactions costs stemming from uncertainty over governments' ability and willingness to expropriate capital can be internalized through public ownership. Where the information asymmetry and uncertainty, and therefore transactions costs, associated with negotiations between firms and governments are unusually high, regulatory agencies may be unable to settle negotiations over prices and service standards. In this situation, the internalization of transactions costs through public ownership can become an attractive policy option.

The resource intensity of production in Canada, combined with the distribution of population across geographically dispersed, but densely populated urban centres, contributes to the formation of natural monopolies in national transport networks, such as railways or airlines. The presence of these monopolies introduces economic inefficiencies into unfettered markets. These inefficiencies motivate governments to regulate service standards and prices in an effort to restrain monopolists' efforts to capture rents from consumers. In his earlier work on Canadian airlines, Baldwin shows how Williamson's model can capture the process of internalizing transaction costs when information asymmetries arise. In the context of regulating natural monopolies, these asymmetries can grow large when governments have an incentive to behave opportunistically, and legal constraints on opportunism are weak. In *Regulatory Failure and Renewal*, Baldwin generalizes Williamson's theoretical approach, applying the key insights of the transactions cost perspective across a wide range of economic, technological, and historical environments. Baldwin uses the insights from the model to focus his historical analysis on the causal factors contributing to internalization, and the early tendency towards expropriation and public ownership in Canada.

The Canadian experience with the regulation of natural monopolies in utility industries during the late nineteenth and early twentieth centuries varied widely across provinces, cities, and time. To make sense of, and draw lessons from the range of policy instruments adopted during this period, Baldwin needs a more stable and uniform comparative context. The United States provides this context, and Baldwin quickly establishes his key themes when he reviews the history of US regulation of natural monopolies.

During the mid-nineteenth century in the US, municipalities recognized the need for substantial investments in expensive and complex delivery networks for technologically novel and rapidly evolving products and services. Demand for water, intra-urban transport, telecommunications, and electricity was expanding rapidly, and at least initially there was considerable competition among firms for the provision of these products and services. Governments signed franchise contracts with private firms to build and operate the required networks. Because the initial investments were long-lived and specific, they were largely irreversible. This meant that the terms of the franchise contracts tended to be long, prices were often specified at fixed rates over the life of the contract, and narrowly defined service standards specifying the quality, technological content, and geographic extent of the products and services delivered were usually articulated in painstaking detail.

Of course, the problem with franchise contracts that were structured with such detail was that they were inflexible. As demand grew and technological changes accelerated through the last half of the 1800s, the need to adjust the terms of these contracts became more acute. The problem with frequent renegotiation was that the initial cost of building the delivery networks increased entry costs to such an extent that natural monopolies formed. When governments sought to renegotiate, the incumbent private firms had a huge advantage because they owned the capital invested in the existing delivery network. The absence of competition constrained governments' ability to regulate monopoly rents with franchise contracts on an ongoing basis. Even in the US, where we might safely say there was a strong cultural distaste for the expropriation of private property, governments clearly had an incentive to behave opportunistically by seizing private firms' initial investments and operating utility networks as public enterprises. However, for the most part, this did not happen. Since the first era of globalization in the late nineteenth and early twentieth centuries, arms-length, quasi-judicial regulatory bodies have been the predominant policy tool used to limit and redistribute rents among US natural monopolies.

Baldwin provides a rich historical overview of US nineteenth-century property rights jurisprudence. He illustrates how US courts came to interpret the fifth amendment of the constitution to be a guarantee that any private capital expropriated by US governments would receive fair-return-on-fair-value. This meant that compensation would not be based on the contemporaneous, depreciated value of the capital, or even the replacement value, but compensation would have to cover the present value of the stream of lifetime returns on all expropriated capital. This is a high bar that effectively limits governments' ability to threaten expropriation, thereby reducing the uncertainty and transactions costs associated with negotiations between governments and natural monopolists. With the imposition of this legal constraint on government opportunism, internalization was not necessary, and relatively effective, low cost, arms-length regulatory agencies could be put in place. The US experience, therefore, provides Baldwin with a convenient benchmark for his analysis of the environments in which Canadian natural monopolies were regulated once franchise contracts became untenable.

Baldwin's first Canadian historical case study documents the federal government's regulation of the railway sector. Among the other utilities he considers, railways are most closely aligned with his earlier work on pubic ownership in the Canadian airline sector (Baldwin 1975). Again, the themes of heterogeneity in policy choice and opportunism are clearly defined. In the late nineteenth century there was a strong political and economic rationale for building and operating trans-continental rail lines entirely on Canadian territory that could link eastern and western markets. By the early 1900s, through both direct and indirect subsidization, including loan guarantees, land grants, construction material grants, and tax breaks, the federal government had successfully encouraged the construction of not one, but three rail lines connecting central Canada to British Columbia's Pacific coast. The Canadian Pacific Railway (CPR) was completed in 1885, the Canadian Northern (CN) began trans-continental operations in 1915, and the last western section of the Grand Trunk/National Trans-continental (GTR) was finished in 1914.

Recognizing the possibility of rent capture, the federal government regulated service standards and freight rates for all three lines. Canada's regulated rates were approximately equal to US rates until the late 1910s and early 1920s, when real freight rates in Canada dropped sharply. Baldwin describes how the federal government's Board of Railway Commissioners refused to allow rates to rise during the inflationary period following the end of World War I. This policy to maintain nominal rates at low levels, coupled with the government's insistence on maintaining service on some unprofitable routes, put the railways under severe financial pressure, particularly the companies that relied on debt financing to construct their lines.

Ex post the land grants and construction subsidies that made up most of the government support provided to the CPR were particularly generous, and as a result, aside from a few short intervals, that company has remained profitable and under private control (Emery and MacKenzie 1996). In contrast, Canadian Northern's construction subsidies were primarily loan guarantees, which meant that the liabilities on their balance sheets were dominated by long-term debt. When the government effectively cut real freight rates immediately after the war, Baldwin's analysis of CN's financial position shows that they could not pay their bond holders, and as a result, they quickly sank into bankruptcy. The federal government bought CN's assets at replacement cost and began to operate the line as a public enterprise. This take-over was essentially an expropriation due to necessity and, although the (predominantly Canadian) capital owners did receive some compensation, CN's balance sheets reveal that the buy-out was less than the "fair-return-on-fair-value" they would have received had the take-over occurred in the US.

The third trans-continental line was a joint venture between the largely British-owned Grand Trunk Railway and the federal government. Like Canadian Northern, the GTR's construction subsidies for the western section of the line were predominantly loan guarantees. These guarantees encouraged the company to raise its debt/equity ratio to levels that Baldwin shows to have been unsustainable when the regulator refused to allow nominal freight rates to rise with post-war inflation. By late 1919 the federal government was effectively expropriating the Grand Trunk investors' capital, and although compensation was offered, it was only equal to the current value of the initial investment, which was essentially zero because, in a brilliant illustration of the effects of moral hazard, government regulators would not allow freight rates to rise and would not take over the unprofitable routes that they were forcing the GTR to operate.

We can easily see why Baldwin started with such a careful and detailed historical analysis of the regulation of the early Canadian railway system. High entry costs established local natural monopoly conditions for all three Canadian trans-continental lines. Ostensibly to limit rent capture, the federal government set up a regulatory body – the Board of Railway Commissioners – that was neither arms-length, nor quasi-judicial. In the absence of legal constraints on expropriation, this body was clearly open to moral hazard and opportunism, and its policies quite quickly drove two of the lines into bankruptcy. Baldwin documents the extent to which the Canadian investors who controlled CN received some compensation, while the GTR's British investors saw their capital expropriated with virtually no compensation. The assets of CN and GTR were merged into the Canadian National Railway, and operated as a publicly owned crown corporation until privatization in 1995. In sharp contrast to railway regulation in the US, the Canadian federal government failed to establish an effective and independent regulatory body, which opened the door for opportunism, expropriation, and public ownership. The key themes that Baldwin wants to emphasize throughout his study are sharply defined in this case study of the Canadian railway network. He next turns his attention to three counter-examples – the establishment and operation of successful regulatory agencies in Nova Scotia, New Brunswick, and Alberta. These counter-examples show that the tendency towards public ownership was not ubiquitous in Canada during the first era of globalization.

The constructionist approach to private property rights protection that characterizes Canadian common law was slower to develop than US jurisprudence, but by the early twentieth century Canadian courts were seeking to limit expropriation to cases where it was explicitly allowed by legislation. The Canadian courts were even slower to move towards the US method for valuing expropriated capital.

Rather than the fair-return-on-fair-value standard that had been adopted in the US, Canadian courts remained open to compensation at what amounted to replacement value less depreciation. The common law precedents that evolved in Canada, therefore, set a relatively low bar for government compensation, and this significantly increased the risk of private capital losses due to expropriation. This risk, in turn, raised the transactions costs faced by natural monopolists and government regulators who were seeking to negotiate (and renegotiate) franchise contracts. As a result of these factors, and as Baldwin's historical case studies illustrate, regulatory bodies were relatively rare in Canada. However, it is revealing that they were not totally absent. In Nova Scotia, New Brunswick, and Alberta, arms-length, quasi-judicial public utility commissions (PUC) were established to regulate prices and service standards for natural monopolies in municipal utilities, including water, urban-transport, electricity, and gas.

The effective operation of these provincial regulatory bodies required the establishment of credible independence. By freeing the PUC decision-making processes from political control, the possibility of moral hazard and opportunism was reduced. This allowed negotiations over rates and service standards to occur free from potential opportunism, which decreased uncertainty, transactions costs, and the threat of expropriation. Evidence of the PUC's independence in these provinces comes from the adoption of what Baldwin calls "prudent investment standards" in the ongoing adjustment of municipal utility rates – allowing the natural monopolists to expect reasonable returns on their investments, even as economic and technological conditions changed. Baldwin's detailed analysis of the municipal utility rates, network coverage, and the investment returns earned by the private utility companies, reveals both the complexity of the economic and financial considerations involved, and the sophistication of these provinces' PUC regulatory bodies.

The two Maritime provinces, Nova Scotia and New Brunswick, were early adopters of independent public utility commissions, and Baldwin argues that the effectiveness of similar bodies in the New England states, particularly Massachusetts, provided a model that cities such as Halifax and St. John were able to emulate. In Alberta there is evidence that the provincial government was also able to make a credible commitment to maintain an independent regulatory body. Freedom from political influence has allowed the Alberta Board of Public Utilities Commissioners to effectively regulate utility rates and service standards since the early 1900s. Public ownership and expropriation of the utility networks was never seriously considered in any of these three provinces.

The regulatory environment in Toronto and Montreal during the late nineteenth and early twentieth centuries differed in some important ways from Halifax, St. John, and municipalities in Alberta. In terms of both the intensive and extensive margins of growth – the density and absolute size of the cities' population levels and macroeconomic activity – Toronto and Montreal were expanding at historically unprecedented rates, they had significant and heavily industrialized commercial markets, and neither city had an obvious, geographically proximate US regulatory model to copy. As a result, the policy tools that were adopted to manage the cities' natural monopolies differed across utilities and time, but arms-length regulatory agencies were slow to appear in both Toronto and Montreal.

The failure of the initial franchise contracts for water delivery, for example, led to public ownership and operation of municipal water and sanitation systems, rather than private ownership under the regulatory oversight of a PUC. Baldwin argues that in the case of water and sanitation, rather than government opportunism, these systems were brought under public control due to private market failures. The provision of water and sanitation has strong positive public health and fire suppression externalities. Private suppliers cannot force all those who benefit from the wide-spread provision of clean water and effective sanitation to pay for these services. Municipal governments, on the other hand, can use their tax powers to make all residents pay, thereby covering the cost of the systems' external benefits.

Like water and sanitation, the delivery of natural gas requires an extensive network of above and below ground piping. However, during the nineteenth and early twentieth centuries in Toronto and Montreal, the delivery network for gas did not raise entry costs to such an extent that strong natural monopolies formed; there were relatively few large institutional and industrial consumers of natural gas; rapid advances in electricity technologies meant that competition for power and lighting was strong; and gas did not have the same positive externalities as water and sanitation. As a result, Baldwin argues that in the case of gas, there were small numbers of suppliers and consumers, the opportunity for rent capture was weak, and the incentive for governments to behave opportunistically was low. For the natural gas utility companies, therefore, renegotiation of franchise contracts in response to economic and technological changes was possible. The original franchise contracts were more persistent, and even when they did fail, private internalization rather than public ownership was adopted. Baldwin uses the consumer cooperative that formed to internalize transactions costs in mid-nineteenth century Toronto as an example to illustrate this point.

Intra-urban transport systems in Toronto and Montreal – horse-drawn and eventually steam- and electricity-powered trams – were different again. Rapid technological change, relatively elastic demand, and the availability of close substitutes meant that frequent renegotiation of the original franchise contracts was needed, but the monopoly power held by the incumbents was never particularly strong. Baldwin's evidence on tram ticket prices shows how rate setting could be flexible, allowing for a reasonable return on the operators' initial investments without excessive rent capture. There was more tension associated with service standards because the municipal governments in Toronto and Montreal sought improvements in road maintenance and safety, and route extensions into newly built residential and commercial areas. Franchise contracts with private tram companies were repeatedly renegotiated and renewed through the late nineteenth century, and government control of the intra-urban systems in both Toronto and Montreal was not imposed until the size and complexity of the networks had risen to a level that limited the number of private competitors. Full public ownership and operation of the systems was not put in place until the eventual establishment of the Toronto Transit Commission (TTC) in 1921, and the Commission de Transport de Montréal (CTM) in 1951.

Baldwin's next example again reveals relatively persistent franchise contracting, except in British Columbia it was not the presence of private competitors and weak market power that limited transactions costs and facilitated public-private renegotiations. The British Columbia Electric Railway Company (BCER) relied on political influence and sophisticated and astute business strategies, to suppress competition, fend-off effective regulation, and avoid government opportunism. Baldwin documents how franchise contracts for intra-urban transport, and the generation, transmission, and distribution of electricity were repeatedly renewed and extended on favourable terms for the BCER until the introduction of a provincial PUC in the early 1920s. Even then, "fair and reasonable returns" for the private company were guaranteed in the legislation that established the regulatory commission.

The strong financial position of the BCER allowed the company to buy up potential competitors, and the firm's largely British investors effectively applied political pressure in the provincial legislature, which took the form of a constant and quite explicit threat to expose any opportunistic behaviour on behalf of the government in the London capital market. Given the capital intensity of BC's resource extractive industries, and the reliance on British bond markets to fund these industries, this threat was particularly ominous for the provincial and municipal governments at this time. This approach was so successful that there was no real threat of expropriation and public ownership in BC, and the contracting terms specifying utility rates and service standards for the lower mainland were never overly fastidious about limiting and redistributing monopoly rents. Among Baldwin's historical case studies, this example of persistent market power is depicted as one of just a few rare exceptions. In most other localities, either through opportunistic expropriation or arms-length regulation, rent capture appears to have been effectively limited and service standards were vigorously enforced. The BCER, therefore, serves to highlight both the heterogeneity in Canadian regulatory efforts, and the potentially confounding role strategic behaviour can play in the regulation of natural monopolies.

Although the BC Electric Railway Company was unusually successful in its efforts to influence government regulation, its strategy was not entirely unique. Baldwin documents a second example of a natural monopolist strategically engaging with government regulators, but this time regulation fell under federal jurisdiction. By the turn of the twentieth century, the Bell Telephone Company had recognized and effectively neutered the threat posed by municipal regulation. Bell invested heavily in the suppression of competition, connecting local markets with long distance lines to form a national network, and inflating its building and maintenance costs. This business strategy successfully strengthened the company's position as a natural monopoly by increasing entry costs, and Baldwin shows how this allowed Bell to put forward a convincing legal case supporting its role as a national network that should be subject to federal, rather than municipal or provincial regulation. As it turns out, Bell correctly believed that political influence could be more narrowly targeted at the federal level.

Bell, like the BCER in British Columbia, used its business acumen and financial resources to effectively limit and channel regulatory oversight. Baldwin documents the extent to which the federal government's Board of Railway Commissioners, who were assigned the task of regulating Bell, included individuals with close ties to Bell's executive board, and these individuals appear to have been working quite openly to ensure that federal government ownership of the network was never considered as a viable policy option. Municipal and provincial franchise contracts for telecommunication services were avoided when Bell successfully argued that its long distance lines linking Canada's dense, but dispersed municipal markets made it a national network, subject only to federal jurisdiction.

The contrast between the railway companies' experience with federal regulation and Bell's experience is stark, and although Baldwin emphasizes Bell's canny strategic behaviour in his assessment of the company's response to regulation, it is important to note that the technological and economic environment faced by Bell was also quite different. Dense urban markets could be connected with long distance lines running parallel to railway right-of-ways, and marginal operating costs were extremely low. This meant that Bell's building subsidies could be relatively low, and the absence of loan guarantees in these subsidies reduced Bell's debt/equity ratios to easily manageable levels. Bell also enjoyed dramatically rising residential and commercial demand for telephones at this time. All of these features of the telecommunications sector in Canada around the turn of the twentieth century were distinct from conditions in the railway sector, and they all contributed to Bell's success channeling and limiting federal regulatory actions. Baldwin's next case study illustrates how, despite their successful national strategy, Bell was not always successful in establishing its dominant monopoly position in all local markets across the country.

During the first years of the twentieth century the provincial government in Manitoba became dissatisfied with the rural service being offered by Bell. In 1904 the courts ruled that Bell was a national enterprise that fell under federal jurisdiction, and as Baldwin describes, this left the Manitoba legislature with no negotiating power to force service improvements outside of its cities. The provincial government turned to its taxation power, effectively expropriating Bell's assets in Manitoba through high tax rates. Although its natural monopoly outside of Manitoba remained intact, Bell's private ownership of all municipal networks in Canada was lost. In an interesting twist, the provincial government did not just rely on public ownership to limit and redistribute monopoly rents in the telecommunications industry – it also established an independent public utilities commission to oversee the construction subsidies, rates, and service standards for its own publicly operated telecommunications company.

The PUC in Manitoba not only regulated the publicly owned telephone company, but Baldwin also describes how privately owned intra-urban transport operators and private electricity generating, transmission, and distribution companies actively pursued the establishment of arms-length regulation by a provincial government body. In Manitoba (specifically Winnipeg) in the early 1900s, the publicly owned transportation and power companies were in competition with privately owned firms. The public enterprises received generous subsidies from the provincial government that allowed them to set low prices for residential and commercial consumers that drove private competition out of business. The private firms asked the government to establish a PUC to regulate prices. However, in this case price regulation was not intended to limit rent capture by imposing a ceiling on prices, but the Manitoba PUC put a floor on prices so that public and private enterprises could co-exist and compete in the Winnipeg tram and electricity markets. What is more broadly interesting about this historical quirk that Baldwin documents with wonderfully detailed information on the changing financial fortunes of the Winnipeg Electric Railway Company, is how it reveals the importance of independence among regulatory agencies. In Manitoba during the early years of the twentieth century we find public ownership in the utility sector competing with private capital, and all of the enterprises welcomed regulation by a provincial utilities commission. If the Manitoba PUC had not enjoyed considerable autonomy from the provincial and municipal governments, it would not have been able to simultaneously limit rent capture by the privately owned producers, and opportunistic pricing behaviour by the governments' publicly owned crown corporations.

The formation of Ontario Hydro, a publicly owned company that was established in the years immediately prior to World War I to generate, transmit, and distribute electricity, is a fascinating illustration of all of the key elements in Baldwin's explanation for the more frequent adoption of public ownership in Canada relative to the United States. The fast flowing water over Niagara Falls created nearly ideal conditions for the generation of hydro-electricity during the late nineteenth century. By 1900 there were multiple privately owned generating stations serving Canadian and US markets on both sides of the falls. The Canadian stations supplied power to residential and commercial users throughout southwestern Ontario, including Toronto. During this early pre-World War I period, franchise contracts were signed between Toronto (and other southern Ontario municipalities) and the privately owned power companies, often in conjunction with agreements to build and operate intra-urban transport systems that were among the earliest adopters of electricity as a source of motive power.

As Baldwin ably documents across historical contexts, inflationary pressure, technological change, and disagreements over service standards motivated the renegotiation of initial contracts. He shows how entry costs for the building of transport and electricity distribution networks grew rapidly through the late 1800s, which effectively limited meaningful competition in these renegotiations. Local natural monopolies formed, transactions costs rose, and the possibility of opportunistic behaviour on behalf of municipal and the provincial governments grew. All of the conditions for expropriation and public ownership that Baldwin has identified in his case studies were present, and again in southern Ontario we see US-style regulatory bodies passed over in favour of the formation of a public enterprise. In the second decade of the twentieth century, it was not municipalities that stepped in, but rather the provincial government. Initially, the province focused on transmission, purchasing electricity from private generating stations to supply government-owned long-distance transmission lines throughout southern Ontario. However, it was not long before generation facilities at Niagara Falls were built specifically for the provincial lines, and municipal distribution networks, particularly the network in Toronto that incorporated an extensive intra-urban transport system, shifted their contracts from private suppliers to the provincial power company.

The private power and transport companies' capital investments in Ontario were not quite as directly expropriated as had been the case for the Grand Trunk Railway or the local Bell network in Manitoba. However, the balance sheet figures Baldwin documents reveal how the building of heavily subsidized electricity generation, transmission, and distribution facilities allowed Ontario Hydro to price private competitors out of the market. This is another case of effective, but indirect expropriation – the legislative protection against the establishment of a publicly owned competitor was ignored, circumvented, and eventually removed. The key question that remains for Baldwin is why sweeping public ownership was adopted for the generation, transmission, and distribution of power in Ontario, when quite similar circumstances in many states in the US, as well as BC, Alberta, New Brunswick, and Nova Scotia, led to some combination of public-private competition and oversight by an arms-length regulatory body.

Baldwin seems unconvinced by Henry Nelles' (1975) idea that a taste for public ownership was unusually strong in Ontario at this time – represented by a "statist political tradition" and a particularly active and engaged populist movement among municipal stakeholders – or that "economic backwardness" somehow increased the incentives for public ownership. Instead, he points once more to the absence of a constitutional guarantee for private property. In Ontario the courts were unable to restrain government opportunism, which facilitated the break-down of the original franchise contracts, raised the risk of expropriation, increased transactions costs, and precluded the establishment of effective arms-length regulatory agencies. Baldwin's focus on the judiciary's inability to impose legal constraints on government actions provides a clean, and wholly convincing explanation for the differences in Canadian and US policy responses to the formation of natural monopolies. However, it does not help us explain why we do not see a historical equivalent to Ontario Hydro being formed in BC, Alberta, New Brunswick, or Nova Scotia.

To understand why provincial public ownership was adopted in the market for electricity in Ontario, but not other provinces, and more generally to explore the source of the policy heterogeneity within Canada that Baldwin's historical case studies reveal, we might want to consider reframing Nelles' argument. More specifically, rather than a story about "backwardness" in Ontario around the turn of the twentieth century, perhaps industrial success in the form of openness to global markets, technological transformation, and rapid industrial expansion, played a determinative role in the early regulation of the province's natural monopolies.

The cost of fuel represents a large share of total costs for many manufacturers, and the technological and structural changes that were occurring within the industrial sector at the end of the 1800s created conditions favourable to the adoption of electricity as a source of motive power, particularly in southern Ontario (Jaworski and Keay 2020; Wylie 1990). These forces could have raised the stakes considerably for industrial users of the electricity generation, transmission, and distribution system in the province at this time. The potential cost savings from replacing privately owned natural monopolies with publicly owned enterprises could have motivated industrial and commercial consumers to exert their growing political influence in an effort to promote expropriation. Being less industrial and less reliant on electricity-using industries, provincial governments outside of Ontario are unlikely to have felt the same pressure to pursue public ownership. This does not mean that the courts' inability to constrain government opportunism was not important – in the Canada-US comparative context it almost certainly was – but within Canada the heterogeneity in policy choices points to other factors, including differences in industrialists' willingness to apply pressure to adopt public ownership. Baldwin's historical narratives do not just document the myriad of policy responses across monopolists, municipalities, and provinces during the late nineteenth- and early twentieth-century period, they also reveal how differences in local economic environments affected the strength of the political pressures originating from the demand side of the country's utility markets.

A brief comment on utilities regulation in Quebec concludes this review of the historical evidence Baldwin presents in *Regulatory Failure and Renewal*. Given the size and importance of the industrial sector in Quebec, the easy access to local urban and international markets, and the availability of relatively cheap hydroelectric power, one might reasonably expect the policy options adopted in Quebec, and even more specifically in Montreal, to mirror those adopted in Toronto and, more generally, all of Ontario. However, we do not find a public enterprise similar to Ontario Hydro in Quebec until the formation of Hydro-Québec in 1944. In Montreal, in particular, there was little sustained pressure for public ownership of electricity distribution or intra-urban transport. The original franchise contracts were simply extended and renewed throughout the late nineteenth and early twentieth centuries.

This difference in policy choice is surprising because, similar to Ontario, industrial interests in Quebec must have been motivated by potential cost savings, which would have encouraged them to seek restraints on private natural monopolies in the market for electricity. Strangely, these interests do not appear to have successfully applied much political pressure on the provincial or municipal governments in pursuit of public ownership. Baldwin quite convincingly argues that an important explanation for the absence of effective political pressure in Quebec relative to Ontario was the unique "cultural environment" in Quebec at the time. Countering the influence of Quebec's largely anglophone, protestant, and urban industrial interests, the Catholic Church in Quebec still held considerable influence over government decision-making in the early twentieth century; religious and linguistic conflict was an ongoing policy distraction; and rural-Francophone politicians comprised a significant portion of both provincial and municipal legislative bodies. These factors diffused some of the political influence that industrial interests seeking to restrain monopoly rent capture by private power companies could have brought to bear, and none of these factors would have been appreciable in Ontario. In other words, the industrial interests in Quebec may have been closely aligned with those in Ontario in terms of their goals and strength, but they were not able to effectively exert their political influence to encourage provincial or municipal government opportunism. One might say that in Quebec in the late nineteenth and early twentieth centuries, the unique "cultural environment" played the same role as the fifth amendment in the US, or British investors in the BC capital market – reducing the threat of opportunism, thereby lowering uncertainty and transactions costs so that public-private contracting was possible, and public ownership was avoided.

Continued Relevance: Lessons Learned
for the Twenty-First Century

Transactions costs arise from uncertainty and the need for market participants to accumulate and process information that will allow them to manage and mitigate this uncertainty. In the late nineteenth and early twentieth centuries, rapid technological change, globalization, and shifting market structures generated pressure to renegotiate early franchise contracts between governments and natural monopolists operating in Canada's utility industries. In *Regulatory Failure and Renewal*, Baldwin reveals that the transactions costs associated with these renegotiations were often very high, in part because there was uncertainty stemming from the relatively weak constraints imposed on government opportunism by the Canadian judiciary. Internalization of these transactions costs through expropriation and public ownership became a common, but not ubiquitous policy response.

In a modern context, uncertainty and information asymmetry in negotiations between governments and private firms operating in industries prone to the formation of natural monopolies do not always originate from the same sources that Baldwin documents in the Canadian historical context. Environmental degradation and climate change, for example, have triggered domestic and international policy commitments that can impinge on the objectives and capabilities of governments and private actors (McKenzie 2002). Conflicts across jurisdictions over the division of power within the Canadian federal system are not new, but they have become more frequent, entrenched and costly to resolve with the rise of Quebec nationalism and western alienation over the past half century. And finally, the formalization and legal interpretation of section 35.1 of the 1982 Constitution Act, which "recognizes and affirms" the treaty rights of Indigenous peoples in Canada, is ongoing and deeply complex (Keay and Metcalf 2011). Unresolved questions about the nature of Indigenous land rights in Canada reach into virtually all aspects of government and private investors' decision-making. The historical sources of uncertainty documented by Baldwin are still present and costly, but over time they have been augmented in many negotiations between governments and private firms by asymmetries associated with commitments and constraints imposed by environmental, jurisdictional, and Indigenous rights.

The shifting source and composition of transactions costs in the regulation of natural monopolies through the early twenty-first century does not undermine the key insights articulated by Baldwin in *Regulatory Failure and Renewal*. In some ways, the modern policy-making environment makes these insights even more relevant because they focus our attention on the common, persistent themes that can be identified in the historical narrative. In the regulation of natural monopolies, transactions costs matter; governments' objectives and constraints matter; private firms' objectives, constraints, and strategies matter; and the legal system's ability to firmly and concretely protect private property rights matters. These themes were true during the period covered by Baldwin's historical analyses, they were true when *Regulatory Failure and Renewal* was first published in 1989, and they are still true in our early twenty-first century domestic and international policy-making context.

When we consider more recent regulatory approaches adopted in Canada, we see the same kind of heterogeneity that Baldwin describes in his historical case studies. Across jurisdictions there has been mounting pressure to revisit the traditional policy tools used to manage service standards and rent capture by natural monopolists. The responses to this pressure have included a mix of the status quo, such as the continued federal ownership of Canada's only inter-regional passenger rail service (Via Rail); new forays into public ownership, such as the federal government's acquisition of Trans Mountain Pipeline assets; privatization, as in the Ontario government's break up of Ontario Hydro; and renewed responsibilities allocated to arms-length regulatory bodies in industries as diverse as transportation, telecommunications, security exchanges, insurance, banking, and even cannabis. Just as Baldwin identified in his historical settings, changes in the source and distribution of transactions costs can be seen as important factors influencing instrument choice across all of these modern examples of government engagement with private investors in markets that are vulnerable to the formation of natural monopolies.

Of course, the regulation of natural monopolies has never been a uniquely Canadian problem. Complex and expensive delivery networks, high entry costs, and transactions costs arising from information asymmetries among governments and private sector firms, can be found around the world throughout history. During the first decades of the twenty-first century, state-owned enterprises remain common across a wide range of some of the wealthiest market-based economies around the globe, including important examples in Argentina, Finland, Sweden, and Italy. However, even in these countries where public ownership is a frequent and widely accepted regulatory response to the formation of natural monopolies, arms-length public utility commissions can also be found regulating both public and private monopolists in sub-national and municipal markets (Estrin and Pelletier 2018). Sometimes fierce debates about the feasibility and advisability of regulation and privatization in markets for water, power, telecommunications, and transportation – utilities that have traditionally been publicly owned – have sprung up in many developing economies, most notably those that have sought aid and policy advice from international bodies such as the World Bank and International Monetary Fund (Brune, Garrett, and Kogut 2004). Again, Baldwin's examination of policy choice in the Canadian context helps us to understand the presence of this heterogeneity and conflict across the broader, global regulatory environment.

Discussions, debate, and tension over the desirability of regulation, privatization, and public ownership among stake-holders in Canada and abroad often span ideological divides and institutional frameworks. Baldwin's study makes important contributions to these ongoing policy discussions because it provides a careful documentation of the forces that lead to the adoption of various forms of arms-length regulation, public ownership, and in some cases, long-lived public-private franchise contracting in Canada – an institutionally secure, wealthy, industrialized, but diverse economy. The forces Baldwin identifies, including opportunism, market power, technological and structural change, and legal restraints on government actions, may have shifted and evolved over time and across jurisdictions within Canada and abroad, but they have also proven to be remarkably persistent and widespread.

Since the publication of Baldwin's study, others have drawn on and extended his work, identifying and probing similar forces and patterns in both Canadian and international contexts. Benjamin Depoorter (2000), for example, documents examples of natural monopolies that span international markets, and he explores policy responses with particular attention paid to the efficacy of internalizing transactions costs. The relevance of the Canadian historical experience for this work stems from the presence of both public and private natural monopolists operating across municipal and provincial jurisdictions in Canada, and the varied allocation of jurisdictional responsibility for their regulation.

The long history of regulation in Canada that Baldwin documents provides authors such as Thomas Quinn (2002) with an extended comparative benchmark for other countries at similar stages of economic development and industrial complexity. Quinn specifically looks at the development of arms-length regulatory agencies in the US, and consequences stemming from the adoption of this particular policy tool as a response to the formation of a wide range of natural monopolies through the nineteenth century. Steven High (1997) also draws on Baldwin's historical analysis, but rather than using this analysis to establish an international comparative benchmark, his work has a domestic focus. High digs deeply into the regulation of utilities in a municipality not covered in Baldwin's case studies – Thunder Bay, Ontario. Not surprisingly, he is able to identify transactions cost patterns and political pressures in Thunder Bay that are similar to those Baldwin documents for other Canadian cities.

The common thread linking Baldwin's study to the ongoing march of academic and policy-oriented research is the search for underlying patterns amongst the heterogeneous regulatory responses adopted in the presence of natural monopolies. Baldwin uses a transactions cost model of firm formation, legal analysis, and a depth of historical detail to identify and document patterns in Canadian regulatory responses through the late nineteenth and early twentieth centuries. This effort continues to provide a foundation for others seeking similar patterns in other contexts, other eras, and other localities.

Heterogeneity in the tools used to regulate natural monopolies has not diminished since the late nineteenth and early twentieth centuries when Canada was first moving beyond franchise contracting, and the debates, tension, and political pressure involved in selecting among policy options continues unabated. Questions about privatization and public ownership still swirl around Canada's pipelines, telecommunication networks, and transport systems. In our pursuit of answers to these questions, Baldwin's work helps us to make sense of policy heterogeneity by encouraging us to look carefully at how transactions costs have shifted across time and space; how courts have constrained government opportunism and defined property rights; how local industrial, economic, and technological environments have interacted with political pressures; and how private and public stakeholders have strategically engaged with the policy-making process in pursuit of influence and control.

Bibliography

Baldwin, John R. 1975. *The Regulatory Agency and the Public Corporation.* Cambridge, MA: Ballinger.

Boardman, Anthony E., and Aidan R. Vining. 2012. "A Review and Assessment of Privatizations in Canada." *University of Calgary School of Public Policy: Research Papers* 5, no. 4: 1–31.

Braeutigam, Ronald R. 1989. "Optimal Policies for Natural Monopolies." In *Handbook of Industrial Organization*, vol. 2, edited by Richard Schmalensee and Robert Willig, 1289–1346. Amsterdam: North-Holland.

Brune, Nancy, Geoffrey Garrett, and Bruce Kogut. 2004. "The International Monetary Fund and the Global Spread of Privatization." *IMF Staff Papers* 51, no. 2: 195–219.

Depoorter, Benjamin. 2000. "Regulation of Natural Monopoly." In *Encyclopedia of Law and Economics*, vol. 3, edited by Boudewijn Bouckaert and Berrit De Geest, 498–532. Cheltenham UK: Edward Elgar.

Emery, J.C. Herbert, and Kenneth J. McKenzie. 1996. "Damned if you Do, Damned if you Don't: An Option Value Approach to Evaluation the Subsidy of the CPR Mainline." *Canadian Journal of Economics* 29, no. 2: 255–70.

Estevadeordal, Antoni, Brian Frantz, and Alan Taylor. 2003. "The Rise and Fall of World Trade, 1870–1939." *Quarterly Journal of Economics* 118, no. 2: 359–407.

Estrin, Saul, and Adeline Pelletier. 2018. "Privatization in Developing Countries: What are the Lessons of Recent Experience?" *World Bank Research Observer* 33, no. 1: 65–102.

Hamilton, Gillian, Ian Keay, and Frank Lewis. 2017. "Contributions to Canadian Economic History: The Last Thirty Years." *Canadian Journal of Economics* 50, no. 5: 1632–57.

High, Steven. 1997. "Planting the Municipal Ownership Idea in Port Arthur, 1875–1914." *Urban History Review* 26, no. 1: 3–17.

Iacobucci, Edward M., and Michael J. Trebilcock. 2012. "The Role of Crown Corporations in the Canadian Economy." *University of Calgary School of Public Policy: Research Papers* 5, no. 9: 1–41.

Jaworski, Taylor, and Ian Keay. 2020. "Openness to Trade and the Spread of Industrialization: Evidence from Canada during the First Era of Globalization." *NBER Working Paper No. 27716*. Boston, MA: National Bureau of Economic Research.

Keay, Ian, and Frank D. Lewis. 2019. "Cliometrics and the Study of Canadian Economic History." In *Handbook of Cliometrics*, vol. 2, edited by Claude Diebolt and Michael Haupert, 123–44. Berlin: Springer-Verlag.

Keay, Ian, and Cherie M. Metcalf. 2011. "Property Rights, Resource Access and Long Run Growth." *Journal of Empirical Legal Studies* 8, no. 4: 792–829.

Lewis, Frank D., and Mary MacKinnon. 1987. "Government Loan Guarantees and the Failure of the Canadian Northern Railway." *Journal of Economic History* 47, no. 1: 175–96.

McKenzie, Judith I. 2002. *Environmental Politics in Canada: Managing the Commons into the Twenty-First Century*. Toronto: Oxford University Press.

Metcalf, Cherie M. 2015. "The (Ir)Relevance of Constitutional Property Rights: Compensation for Takings in Canada and the US." *University of Toronto Law Journal* 65, no. 3: 143–85.

Nelles, Henry V. 1975. *The Politics of Development: Forests, Mines and Hydro-Electric Power in Ontario*. Toronto: Macmillan.

Quinn, Thomas. 2002. "Public Lands and Private Recreation Enterprise: Policy Issues from a Historical Perspective." *USFS General Technical Report, PNW-GTR-556*. Portland, OR: USDA Forest Service PNW Research Station.

Trebilcock, Michael, and Michael Rosenstock. 2015. "Infrastructure Public-Private Partnerships in the Developing World: Lessons from Recent Experience." *Journal of Development Studies* 51, no. 4: 335–54.

Williamson, Oliver E. 1971. "The Vertical Integration of Production: Market Failure Considerations." *American Economic Review* 61, no. 1: 112–23.

—. 1981. "The Modern Corporation: Origins, Evolution, Attributes." *Journal of Economic Literature* 19, no. 4: 537–70.

Wylie, Peter. 1990. "Indigenous Technological Development in Canada's Industrialization, 1900–1929." *Canadian Journal of Economics* 23, no. 4: 755–72.

Preface

This work commenced as an attempt to explain why Canada has chosen public enterprise as a regulatory instrument more often than has the United States. It is related to earlier work done on the airline industry (Baldwin, 1975) where I was interested more in the behavioural similarities of a public enterprise and a regulatory agency. Here the reason for choosing one rather than the other as an instrument of government policy is examined. The previous work explained observed behaviour using a model that postulated both entities pursued a multi-faceted objective function subject to certain constraints. This monograph adopts essentially the same format: that is, it attempts to explain why one regulatory instrument is chosen over another by examining the objectives of the state and the nature of constraints that restrain behaviour. The framework that is adopted is the burgeoning transactions-failure literature that has been used elsewhere to explain why certain arm's-length transactions are internalized within firms. In this case, its taxonomy is employed to understand the reason that the original franchise contract was replaced with the more complex contract associated with a regulatory tribunal.

Earlier related work (Baldwin, 1984) emphasized the effect of the difference between Canadian and American judicial constraints on the choice of public enterprise rather than regulation. It noted that where judicial constraints are inoperative, the state may act opportunistically to confiscate property, and transactions failure leads to internalization of the regulatory transaction through the use of public enterprise. When the state proves unable to negotiate fairly, public enterprise is the concomitant result. The earlier paper concentrated on examples of opportunistic behaviour on the part of the Canadian state. This monograph extends the earlier study to examine more broadly the evolution of the regulation of Canadian utilities.

The extension serves to answer the question posed by Demsetz (1968): Why do we regulate when a contract between consumers and producers would do the job? By examining the reasons that the original franchise contract between the state and utilities was abandoned, this study provides an understanding of why we regulate today via independent tribunal.

In addition, this monograph fills a void in the field of law and economics. It describes how the legal environment affected the type of solution chosen to resolve contractual transactions failures. It is also an exercise in business history, since it demonstrates how business policy attenuated some of the institutional problems that existed.

I would like to thank the Economic Council of Canada for its support of the project and, in particular, Ron Hirshhorn for his comments. I am also indebted to Dan Usher, Marvin McInnis, and Frank Lewis of the Queen's Economics Department, Dennis Magnusson of the Law School, and two anonymous referees for comments made on an earlier version. But most of all, I owe a debt of gratitude to Viv Nelles. His comments on the first version at a conference organized by the ECC goaded me into extending my analysis across the selection of industries described herein. Moreover, by allowing me access to his own manuscript on regulation (done jointly with Christopher Armstrong), he provided me with key source material.

Anyone working in the area of regulation in Canada quickly discovers the debt that is owed these two historians for their work in this area.

Finally, I would like to thank Juanita Hamilton for her unflagging diligence in typing this manuscript, Saskia Oltheten, Robert Fay and Tony Lempriere for research assistance, and my wife Adrianne for her editorial work.

John R. Baldwin
Department of Economics
Queen's University
Kingston, Ontario
March 1989

Foreword

This study was originally undertaken as a part of the Council's project on government enterprise. The Council report on this subject, *Minding the Public's Business*, came out at the end of 1986. The overall aim of this project has been to improve our understanding about federally and provincially owned and controlled entities which operate at arm's length from government and have important commercial functions. The project attempted in particular to answer two questions: What is the appropriate role of government enterprise as one of a number of instruments of public policy? And, second, how should the apparatus of control within government be structured so as to realize the full potential of this instrument?

The present study elaborates on, and extends, the work John Baldwin originally presented at a Symposium held by the Council in September 1984. The purpose of this research has been to explain why, in situations of natural monopoly, Canada has often resorted to public enterprise, as opposed to relying simply on regulation. Baldwin finds that the transactions-cost literature pioneered by Oliver Williamson provides important insights into this issue. Using that literature, this study examines the different constraints that have applied to governments in Canada and the United States; and it explores the connection between such constraints and the successful implementation of fairly made contracts between the state and private parties. It is where fair contracts cannot be successfully implemented that an alternative to regulation must be sought. To support his thesis, Baldwin examines a wide range of historical material. The result of this research is to provide us with some new insights into the general problem of instrument choice, and to challenge our traditional understanding of the origins of some important federal and provincial government enterprises.

John Baldwin has published numerous articles in the field of industrial organization. On the topic of regulation, he is best known for his 1975 study of the Canadian airline industry, *The Regulatory Agency and the Public Corporation*. John Baldwin is a professor of economics at Queen's University.

Judith Maxwell
Chairman

REGULATORY FAILURE AND RENEWAL

1 Introduction

Governments intervene to regulate markets in a number of different ways. Understanding the reasons for the choice of instrument is essential. Otherwise the debate on the need for regulatory agencies or for public corporations risks foundering on the seas of ideology. This monograph develops a framework to explain the choice of regulatory instrument and examines the evolution of regulation in Canada from the mid-1800s to the 1930s.

In order to understand the reasons for the choice of regulatory instrument, this study addresses several questions. Why do we regulate when a franchise contract between consumers and producers is an alternative? Was such an alternative ever tried? When it was tried, did it fail? Why did this alternative fail? What institutions were adopted in its stead? What were the prerequisites for the evolution of alternative institutions such as regulatory tribunals? Why did Canada lag behind the United States in choosing the independent regulatory tribunal? Why did Canada choose public enterprise more frequently than the United States? To what extent was the outcome of the state's attempts to choose an ideal regulatory instrument influenced by business strategy?

The first set of questions about the possibility of regulating by contract is of interest to those who have begun to question the need for regulation by independent tribunal – because of the rigidities that this institution is perceived to have introduced into the market system. There is little use in advocating the adoption of other institutions if they have already been tried and found wanting. The question about the reason why public enterprise was adopted is of interest to those who wish to reduce the number of these companies via privatization. The question about the rate of adoption of regulation goes to the heart of the issue of instrument choice and is related to the reason why public enterprise was adopted more frequently in Canada. Finally, the question of the effect of business strategy on the formation of institutions stresses the fact that institutions are shaped not only by the judicial but also by the political system and that the interaction between the two can be complex.

This study proceeds by pointing out that the earliest form of regulation was a contract between consumers and the monopolist. Regulation first took the form of a franchise contract. This instrument was tried and gradually abandoned in

the early part of this century. The study also examines the reasons for the abandonment of the original franchise contract. It points out that this type of contract was inherently flawed and was succeeded in the United States with regulatory tribunals. It argues that Canada chose to adopt regulatory tribunals only haltingly because the constitutional and judicial prerequisites for the success of this institution were missing. The Canadian constitution unlike the American did not guarantee private property. The regulatory tribunal was ideally suited for solving one of the key problems that led to the failure of the franchise contract that was the original form of regulation; but the suitability of the regulatory agency depended on there being constitutional constraints on the exercise of coercive power by the state in contract renegotiations that were part and parcel of the regulatory process. These constitutional constraints were weaker in Canada than in the United States. Therefore, regulation sometimes took a different form in Canada. In particular, when contract failure occurred with the early form of franchise contract, Canada turned frequently to public enterprise because of the inherent defects in the protection offered private capital in its constitutional environment. The adoption of public enterprise was associated not so much with rational choice but with contract failure – occasions when governments exercised the coercive power of the state and confiscated or threatened to confiscate the capital that had been invested in several of the early utilities.

Finally, the monograph demonstrates that the failures were mixed with successes. Not all political jurisdictions allowed the franchise contract to fail; and where it did, not all acted coercively. In some instances, regulatory agencies were adopted. Not all businesses acted passively; some devised strategies which served to deflect opportunistic political forces. All this meant that while the early franchise contracts possessed severe problems, a variety of "regulatory" solutions were eventually chosen.

The analysis in this study relies first on the field of industrial economics. It uses the transaction-failure analysis of Williamson (1975) to provide a framework for the study of the choice of regulatory instrument. This framework has been used to explain why different contractual relationships develop between firms, and between firms and their workers. The monograph applies this theory to the dealings between the state and the producers of utility services. This study is also an exercise in law and economics. It describes how the choice of regulatory instrument was determined by the legal environment; in particular, by the protection provided to private property as a result of constitutional or Common Law constraints. It also is a study in business policy. Institutions like products have substitutes. Transactions failures may be prevented through the choice of an appropriate contract or institution, but imperfections in the instrument chosen can be mitigated by a well chosen business strategy. This monograph, by examining how the providers of capital protected themselves from the opportunistic behaviour of the state, shows how even imperfect institutions can be partially offset by the appropriate business strategy. Finally, the monograph is an exercise in economic history. By examining a broad sweep of events from the mid-nineteenth century to the third decade of the twentieth century, it illustrates how varied is the response of society to a similar set of economic problems.

Before developing the foundation on which the investigations of the evolution of the regulatory instrument are built, it is useful to place this study in context. There are two strands of literature that are relevant. The first deals with traditional forms of regulation – that is, the use of the regulatory tribunal that is peculiarly, but not exclusively, an American phenomenon. The second is the literature on the use of public enterprise as a regulatory instrument.

Economic theories of regulation of natural monopolies can be divided into two groups. The conventional view is that regulation should be viewed as enhancing the public interest in a Paretian sense. At one time, it was based solely on the notion that regulation was required to protect consumers from monopolistic exploitation. It now also embraces sustainability theories that suggest multiproduct firms may need protection from entrants.[1] The conventional view has been challenged by those who argue that regulation is the result of a trade-off between public and private interests. This alternate theory treats the regulatory institution as a government agent that attempts to maximize a political objective function,[2] resulting in a price-production outcome that is generally somewhere between the monopolistic and competitive outcome. Implicit in this alternate theory is the notion that regulation favouring producers cannot be in the public interest.

The notion that there must be a loss to society when regulation benefits producers has received wide dissemination. Case studies of the performance of regulators in some industries, such as trucking and airlines, support the notion that regulators do favour regulated enterprises.[3] These are industries where economies of scale would appear to be so negligible as to call into question the necessity of regulation. Of greater significance are several studies that suggest even in the area of electrical utilities, where scale economies have been found, regulation does not aid consumers.[4] Notwithstanding these efforts, the profession has not yet so readily accepted the view that regulation is either ineffective or perverse in the utility sector.[5]

This study takes the view that regulation was invoked and evolved to serve the interests of both consumers and producers. Because it was a contract between the two, it was meant to serve the interests of both parties. Finding that it served the interests of the producer, therefore, should not be interpreted as support for those who have argued for the capture theory of regulation. Moreover, it is argued herein that a well functioning regulatory contract protects the interests of the natural monopolist from bankruptcy occasioned by the state – for otherwise there will be regulatory failure. It may still be that regulation did not serve to constrain the profits of the monopolist to any great extent, but that is a matter for another study. What does become evident from the following chapters is that any general conclusion about the ultimate efficacy of utility regulation is difficult to draw at this stage. There are two reasons for this. First, regulation in Canada took many forms in response to similar problems. Therefore, it is inappropriate in the Canadian case, as we shall see, to refer to regulation as one and only one phenomenon. An evaluation of regulation requires the study of different regulatory regimes in separate time periods. Second, the division of benefits between consumers and producers changed over the period of the regulatory contract as unforeseen events made the original terms increasingly inappropriate. In some cases, profits moved to levels that were not anticipated; in other cases, unanticipated inflation led to a decline in profits below the original levels. If a study focuses on a time period when the transition is taking place from one regulatory regime to another, such as occurred in the early part of the twentieth century, it would not be surprising to find one party improving its position relative to the other. The reason such a transition occurs is the original regulatory contract has been found wanting. One or other of the parties involved has found the division of benefits, envisaged ex ante, were not realized, and has asked for renegotiations. Finding an increase in the benefits one party to the regulatory contract, say the producers, receive as a result of the renegotiations does not permit us to draw conclusions about the long-run effects of regulation. The change in benefits that producers receive at the time of renegotiations may only restore them to their original position. A comprehensive study, therefore, of the effects of regulation cannot involve a cross-section of industries at a single point in time or the results are likely to be misleading.

The second literature that has a bearing on the work contained herein is that which deals with public enterprise. Economic analysis in the area of public enterprise has generally been directed at an evaluation of the "economic" efficiency of these firms (Borcherding, 1983). More recently, a literature has developed that attempts to analyse the reason for instrument choice – why public enterprise might be chosen even if it were less efficient than other governing instruments in terms of its use of resources (Trebilcock and Prichard, 1983).

Together these two strands in the literature can too readily degenerate into an uninteresting clash of ideology between those who emphasize "economic" efficiency and decry the use of public enterprise and those who argue that the very use of public enterprise demonstrates its superior ability to meet important public goals. The debate over the efficacy of public enterprise then shifts to the desirability of these public goals. Focusing the debate, however, at this level leaves a number of important issues unresolved. These are issues that must be addressed before debates on privatization and its desirability can be concluded in a satisfactory fashion.

The instrument-choice literature is ultimately the avenue by which our understanding of the evolution of different institutions will be improved. However, it is important not to turn it into a deterministic rationalization of the status quo. Elsewhere, it has been argued that the behaviour of regulatory agencies and public enterprise can be analysed using a model that postulates each of these agents is trying to maximize a multifaceted objective function, but is constrained by certain exogenous factors (Baldwin, 1975). Adoption of this approach is useful since it serves to emphasize that exhorting these institutions to change their behaviour may have little impact if the objective function and the relevant constraints faced by each remain the same. It is a change in the nature of the constraints that might affect behaviour, although these constraints may be beyond the policy-maker in some situations.

This monograph uses the same format to examine the reason for the choice of public enterprise, rather than regulation, as a means of controlling natural monopoly. While directed only at the question of the type of regulatory instrument chosen, it is meant to facilitate our understanding of the general process of the choice of a governing instrument.

Regulation and public enterprise as instruments of public policy differ substantially in terms of their characteristics. Regulation generally leaves private ownership intact and establishes an "independent" regulatory agency to mediate conflicts over matters such as the price level. The regulatory process leaves the organization of production in the private domain. While some would claim this has an efficiency advantage because production decisions are left in private hands, the regulatory process itself involves real costs. It can be long and involved compared to the potential for direct control inherent in public enterprise. Moreover, the handling of subsidies for specific services may be more easily audited when government enterprise is used. If public enterprise is adopted and given a monopoly, the franchise competition phenomenon, which is inherent in a regulated situation where there are several private parties competing for franchises, may be avoided or reduced. Many of these potential advantages of a public enterprise over regulation can be subsumed under the broad rubric of the avoidance of "contractual" difficulties.

It might be argued that Canada chose public enterprise in a number of areas because our desire is greater for specific objectives that are best met by public enterprise. If specific policy goals, such as those that require direct subsidies, are more important, then public enterprise may be chosen because it is the superior instrument in these circumstances. This is not the rationale adopted here to explain the use of public enterprise in Canada. The focus of this monograph is on contractual problems – but problems that, if not solved, preclude society from being able to choose between regulation and public enterprise. Regulation is a viable alternative to public enterprise only if the state is bound to a fair contract that regulators as agents are asked to negotiate. While contractual problems may develop because of the state's inability to monitor private activity with a regulatory agency, it is argued here that an equally important problem that has received inadequate attention lies in the behaviour that the state itself occasionally exhibits. Where the state controls the judicial and police apparatus, it has much greater potential for abrogating fairly made contracts than do private parties. Only when some constraints are imposed upon the state can the relative desirability of regulation, as opposed to public enterprise, be considered on the basis of monitoring costs and the ease by which government policy can be implemented. These constraints may originate in a Common Law tradition or in specific constitutional guarantees given to private property.

This monograph examines the effect that different constraints on the state's behaviour, emanating from different constitutions in Canada and the United States, have had on instrument choice. It is argued that, in Canada, public enterprise was chosen in a number of key instances because of the difference in the constraints placed on the political process during the search for the optimal institution to regulate natural monopolies.

The emphasis contained herein may appear somewhat different from that contained in the fledgling literature on instrument choice that treats the latter as a rational matching of institutions to objectives on the basis of effectiveness; but the methodological framework is not. It is argued that, as industries which are characterized as being natural monopolies have evolved, the state sought to find an institution that would act as the agent to draw up a contract between consumers and privately owned firms. In experimenting with alternate institutions, Canada and the United States initially diverged because of different constraints imposed upon the search process. These constraints, in turn, differed because the respective constitutional environments affecting government behaviour were dissimilar. Thus, in this monograph, the choice of governing instrument is set within the context of an objective function and a set of constraints that affect the way in which the public weal can be attained. The distinction between the approach adopted here and that found elsewhere lies in the importance assigned herein to the existence (or lack) of a constitutional constraint that can be exercised on the behaviour of the state when it attempts to abrogate fairly set contracts without due compensation.

The argument contained in the following sections can be succinctly summarized. Where the government cannot be bound to abide by fairly written contracts, the cost of its abrogating such contracts will be less. In certain situations, political pressures to abrogate contracts without compensation will be too great for even fair-minded politicians who are reasonably cognizant of the long-run consequences of their actions. When this occurs, the regulatory process is more likely to fail and the contractual problem will be "internalized" via the creation of public enterprise. These overriding political pressures will not arise in every situation. When they do, they may be resisted. But, over time, if constraints on the actions of the state do not emerge, the regulatory process will gradually be supplanted by the creation of public enterprise in those sectors where these contractual difficulties are greatest.

This argument should not be construed to mean that all franchise contract failures resulted in the creation of public enterprise. Nor does it mean that all political jurisdictions exploited the coercive power that they possessed. Some provinces adopted regulatory tribunals to resolve the contractual crises that developed when regulatory contracts required revisions. In other cases, new contracts were created in an attempt to overcome the deficiencies of the original contracts. Nor should the previous argument be interpreted to imply that the constitutional constraints that were weak at the outset in Canada remained so throughout the period. Decisions of the judicial system increasingly came to constrain the actions of the state and thereby created the needed conditions for regulation to work. The history that follows shows that the process by which Canada moved from one set of regulatory instruments (the franchise contract) to another (the regulatory tribunal) was slow and complex. It involved a learning process as politicians and businessmen sought to respond to the pressures requiring a change in the governing instrument.

The following chapters focus first on the theory of regulation of natural monopoly, then on the manner in which the judicial constraints imposed on the behaviour of the state set the preconditions for the emergence of the regulatory agency in the United States. Next, the constraints placed on the Canadian state's ability to confiscate property without compensation are examined. Following this, individual case studies of the evolution of the regulatory instrument in Canada are presented.

2 A Theory of Natural Monopoly Regulation

Economists have long wrestled with the issue of why society regulates. The straightforward answer that regulation is the instrument used to restrain the exploitation of monopolistic power has become less popular in recent years. Theories of regulation have turned to models of rent-seeking behaviour to explain the outcome of the regulatory process.

This chapter develops a theory of regulation. It does not make use of a political model of rent-seeking behaviour. It starts with the observation that regulation in its original form was a contract between the state and the industrialist. As all contracts are, it was meant to provide benefits to both parties. Over time, the nature of regulation changed. The original franchise contract could not adapt to the changes required of it and new instruments had to be chosen.

The framework that is developed in this chapter focuses on the reasons for this change. Regulation should not be regarded as suddenly emerging in the twentieth century or as taking only one form, that of the modern regulatory tribunal. Regulation existed from the very beginning of most utilities in the form of franchise contracts; it later took on other forms with the use of flexible, sliding-scale contracts. In the United States, the twentieth century saw the widespread adoption of the regulatory tribunal with a codified standard to control prices based on "fair return" on "fair value" of rate base. In Canada, the transition to regulatory tribunal was quite different. For one thing, it was much slower. Moreover, the fair-value standards did not receive the same widespread acceptance as they did in the United States. Finally, a different instrument was more widely used in Canada. Public enterprises or Crown corporations were adopted as the regulatory instrument in a number of key sectors such as railways at the federal level, electricity in Ontario, and telephones in the Prairie provinces.

This chapter provides a framework that will aid our understanding of the reasons for the choice of governing instrument in the case of regulation. It builds on the Williamson transactions-failure literature (1975) to make three points. First, changes in regulation have evolved in response to the inherent inability of the earlier forms of regulatory contracts to handle problems that arose from technical progress and other exogenous changes in the environment. Second, while regulation can be found in the presence of natural monopoly, the economy of scale

characteristics normally stressed are not the only critical factors determining the need for regulation. Regulation is the result of a transactions failure that relates not so much to economies of scale as to the characteristics of capital invested in the industry – characteristics that lead to a contracting problem that has resulted in the modern regulatory tribunal. Finally, it will be argued that regulation works primarily where the law guarantees private property the right to freedom from confiscation by public authorities. Where such guarantees do not exist, either under Common Law or as the result of protection under a constitution, the problems that give rise to the need for regulation will often lead the state to provide that service through state-run or public enterprise.

Natural Monopoly and the Need for a Regulatory Agent

Before the issue of optimal instrument choice is discussed, the reason for government intervention in natural monopoly markets needs to be developed. Standard expositions in this area are inadequate. They concentrate on the impossibility of competition because of a numbers problem; whereas the appropriate answer lies in the likelihood of contractual failure because of the peculiar nature of the transactions and the capital involved in natural monopoly markets. Once the nature of the contractual failure is recognized, the question of optimal instrument choice can be addressed.

The conventional reason given for government intervention in a natural monopoly situation is that regulation is required to protect consumers in situations where economies of scale lead to natural monopoly. This view has been expressed by two disparate groups. Those who find a rationale for political activity based on normative microeconomic theory have stressed that regulation should be associated with the presence of natural monopoly.[1] In contrast, rent-seeking theories have stressed regulation to be the result of the interaction of demand and supply for government activity. In the presence of natural monopolies, it is consumers who are making the request for protection from exploitation and who might be expected to benefit from regulation.

Neither of these arguments explaining the existence of natural monopoly regulation is adequate. Demsetz (1968) has noted that regulation per se is not needed in the case of natural monopoly. An *ex ante* contract between consumers and the monopoly producer could avoid the deadweight loss associated with monopolistic pricing. *Ex ante* contracts specify the terms in advance, and may or may not have clauses to handle both expected and unforeseen contingencies. Examples of such contracts can be cited – especially where the number of consumers is relatively small. For example, there are considerable economies in providing central collecting facilities at the well-head in the crude oil and natural gas industry. Producers invite bids from companies for such facilities and assess one another lump-sum fees to cover fixed costs and then charge a unit price to cover marginal costs. Independent state-run regulatory tribunals are not used to monitor these arrangements.

Regulation, where it does develop, might still be explained as the result of a transactions failure. It could be argued that in some cases the number of consumers who face natural monopolists – for example, the electrical utilities and telephone companies – is too large to overcome the organizational difficulties required to devise the required Demsetz-type contract.

This modification of the conventional view is not fully convincing. While large numbers of parties to one side of a contract – in this case, consumers – may make the contractual process more costly, it does not require regulation as it has developed in North America, where the state acts as agent for consumers. Private parties fulfil the agent's role elsewhere where there are large numbers of consumers. Department stores offer their services as an intermediary between consumers on one side and what are often a small number of producers in some product lines. Buying clubs, a type of department store, are another example of a private agent acting on behalf of a large number of consumers. In the case of an electrical generating plant that is subject to increasing returns to scale, local electric utility distributors often fulfil the function of an agent and are privately owned in many U.S. jurisdictions. They have several alternative sources of electricity available from which they purchase and act as the Demsetz-type contracting agent for local consumers. Thus, the large-numbers problem only gives rise to the need for an agent – not necessarily the public agent with the specific characteristics of North American regulatory agencies.

Notwithstanding the inadequacy of the large-numbers explanation of regulation, pursuit of Demsetz' argument does focus on the relevant issue: the problem of writing a contract between consumers and the natural monopoly.

While there are difficulties associated with organizing a large number of consumers, this is not the only reason for transactions failures. Concentrating on numbers per se ignores other important characteristics associated with what have become classified as natural monopolies. These characteristics have caused the *ex ante* franchise contract to be supplanted by a more complex type of contract administered by a regulatory agency. When the nature of these characteristics is recognized, a more complete understanding of the evolution of regulation emerges.

The Cause of Transactions Failures

The transactions-failure literature, pioneered by Williamson, specifies the characteristics that lead to problems when independent parties contract one with another on an arm's-length basis through market transactions. When such problems arise, it is argued, market failure develops and some method of internalizing the transactions generally emerges – via a more complex form of contract.

Williamson argues that in the face of uncertainty about future events and because of imperfect knowledge on the part of decision-makers, there will be a general need to revise the initial terms of most contracts. Man is sufficiently imperfect and time is too costly to provide for all contingencies in any transaction. As a result, recontracting will be required. Recontracting imposes costs that are greater where conditions facilitate what Williamson has termed "opportunism." Opportunism is the use of misrepresentation that could, but does not necessarily, involve dishonest behaviour.

Opportunistic behaviour is possible, and therefore most deleterious, where bargaining takes place in a small-numbers situation; that is, where so few alternative parties exist that the participants in the bargaining process will continue to bargain one with another even though opportunistic behaviour, if it emerges, will increase the costs of the recontracting process. In large-numbers bargaining situations, opportunism will be attenuated, since either party to the recontracting process may turn to others who have not exhibited the type of behaviour that leads to recontracting difficulties.

The small-numbers situation creates difficulties during recontracting even if opportunism does not arise. If there are few outside bidders, the adjudication of the fairness of the new contract becomes much more difficult. Where parties to the negotiation are unable to use market signals to evaluate the fairness of the new contractual terms, other mechanisms (some form of internalization) are likely to develop for this purpose.

It is important to note that even though the initial contract may have been forged in an environment characterized by large numbers, where neither party could gain by opportunistic behaviour, the recontracting process may take place in a small-numbers bargaining context. There are two characteristics of an industry that may turn a large-numbers into a small-numbers bargaining situation. These characteristics are asset specificity and asset longevity. Asset specificity occurs when the dedication of capital to a specific use results in the value of that capital in its next best use being considerably reduced below the original value. For example, commitment of an airplane to one route does not result in a low scrap value for that plane; capital equipment in this industry can readily be switched to another route. That is not the case for the electrical utility industry. Once capital has been committed to one use or one location, its value is minimal should it not continue in that use, because of the high costs of relocating the services of the capital used in the generation of electricity. If a seller of electrical utility services dedicates considerable assets to the provision of electrical service in a particular municipality, the nature of the fixed-capital equipment means that the producer effectively becomes a hostage to consumers during any recontracting process. Similarly, a commitment by a consumer may place him in the same exposed bargaining position.

The second characteristic that exacerbates the cost of opportunism in a small-numbers situation is asset longevity. If the use-specific or location-specific capital has a life that is short relative to the recontracting period, then opportunistic behaviour on the part of consumers will impose less of a cost on the owner of the facilities. In this case, while capital may be specific, it has no inherent captive value.

The transactions-failure framework has been used to explain why transactions take place, not through market or external relationships, but via internal or firm-like arrangements. When asset specificity and longevity create recontracting difficulties, a more complex contract will evolve to reduce the costs of adapting to uncertainty. One such complex contract involves internalization of the transaction in a firm. The transactions-failure literature has provided a rich set of implications for questions pertaining to the nature of a firm, the reason for various institutions in labour markets, and the extent to which vertical integration is a response to transactions failures.[2] The same literature serves an important role in explaining the reason for regulation in the presence of natural monopolies.

Transactions Failure and Regulation

The transactions-failure literature provides a useful framework for understanding the evolution of the regulatory contract in the utility sector. Originally, regulation took place via an *ex ante* franchise contract; but renegotiation problems caused this instrument to be supplanted. These problems emerged because the bargaining process changed from a large-numbers to a small-numbers situation and opportunism developed. In addition, the nature of capital employed meant that opportunism was relatively costly. Both factors, therefore, created an incentive to develop a superior agent to renegotiate the contract between consumers and producers.

The emerging utilities were characterized by capital with considerable asset specificity as well as asset longevity. A telephone or electrical distribution system with its poles and wires was not removable to another location without considerable cost should consumers engage in opportunistic behaviour after the equipment was installed. The central generating or switching equipment of electrical and telephone producers was therefore captive to opportunistic behaviour on the part of consumers, though perhaps less so today than at the turn of the century when regulation evolved in this industry. At that time, the costs of long-distance high-voltage transmission were sufficiently high that an electrical generating station would find it too costly to send power to jurisdictions other than the one in which it was located. Telephone switching systems too were originally only suitable for very localized service. Because of these characteristics, capital found itself particularly susceptible to opportunistic behaviour on the part of the state during renegotiation exercises.

Producers were not the only party to face potential capital losses from opportunistic behaviour in these industries. Consumers of energy – whether in the form of electricity or natural gas – made use-specific long-lived investments in appliances. As a consequence, opportunistic behaviour on the part of producers could threaten these assets. Similarly, once municipalities had come to rely on the service provided by the utility, they found themselves particularly vulnerable to any threat of termination of service. Utilities could and did threaten to cut off service that had come to be regarded as a necessity. For instance, the Toronto gas company turned off the street lights during one set of negotiations in the early 1800s, thereby threatening the public safety.

In the telephone industry, a different problem was faced by consumers. Contrary to the energy sector, consumers, until recently, have not made substantial investments in telephone equipment. Indeed, for most of this century, they could only rent their equipment from most Bell subsidiaries. Here the problem faced by consumers was related to the severity of the small-numbers problem. Telephone franchises were first awarded at the municipal level for short-distance voice transmission. Substantial first-mover advantages were conferred upon the first firm, Bell, to receive enough local telephone franchises to create an extensive long-distance network joining the local exchanges. Because of the commanding position in long-distance lines that the Bell system developed, consumers in individual jurisdictions were no longer able to contemplate switching producers – except at the local level. And if they did, long-distance service was threatened since local telephone companies that were not Bell franchises encountered considerable difficulties in linking into the Bell long-distance network.[3] Thus, once the telephone franchise was granted, local municipalities had little opportunity for recontracting with anyone else. When recontracting was required they were forced to accept Bell's terms or do without service. Finding this situation intolerable, consumers turned to the state to provide an agent that would provide them with greater bargaining power.

This is just one example of many where the Demsetzian *ex ante* franchise regulatory contract proved inadequate. Whereas there might have been several companies initially bidding for utility franchises, by the time the first franchises expired, this was often no longer the case. Whether because of economies of scale, first-mover advantages, or entry barriers, the initial large-numbers bargaining process tended to degenerate into a small-numbers game. That capital was both dedicated to a specific location and long-lived made it particularly susceptible to opportunistic behaviour. At the same time, cities no longer found themselves, in many situations, able to switch suppliers. They had become captive customers and no longer felt the bargaining process was equitable. A more complex regulatory instrument was required to deal with the transactions failure that occurred in these industries during contract renegotiations.

Two alternatives were available. When contractual failure develops between two intermediate stages in the production process, internalization via the merging of autonomous contractors into a single firm is one option. Its counterpart here, at the final stage of the production process, is a public enterprise where the consumer ultimately owns the production facilities. The other alternative is a more complex form of contract that provides for the arbitration of unforeseen contingencies or that attempts to specify in advance how the consequences of any change will be apportioned between consumers and the public utility. Alternatives to public enterprise will be sought if the costs of internal organization are particularly high or, conversely, if the benefits of decentralized decision-making are great enough to warrant extra effort being spent on the nature of the contract – in order to reduce some of the recontracting

problems. The latter, of course, is feasible where the nature of the events that will induce recontracting is understood, even though their occurrence remains unpredictable, and where the terms that must be renegotiated are relatively simple.

The regulatory agency can be regarded as the alternate institution to public enterprise that has evolved to negotiate the terms of a complex form of contract between consumers and producers. Regulatory agencies developed the same characteristics that the transactions literature lists as essential to the efficacy of internal organization (Williamson, 1975, ch. 2). Internal organization has to develop internal auditing systems. The regulatory agency has developed expert staff to detect misrepresentations by consumers or producers. Internal organizations must develop effective mediation procedures. The regulatory agency has developed elaborate rules for arbitration. Finally, internal organization must attenuate the ability of parties to appropriate gains from opportunistic behaviour. Here the prerequisite for successful operation has been imposed upon the process from outside – by judicial authorities. How this was done is the subject of the next chapter.

The modern regulatory tribunal then provides an arbitration process employing public semijudicial agencies. The decision-making process generally is accompanied by public hearings that give both sides an opportunity to present their cases. In these hearings, the veracity of arguments is subject to cross-examination by both parties. This aspect of the decision process is generally similar to the judicial process. Regulatory agencies differ from more formal judicial bodies in two respects that make their decision process somewhat more efficacious for the task required. First, they develop considerable expertise because of their limited areas of interest and the frequency with which the same issues arise – for example, the adequacy of earnings. Somewhat like internal organizations, they develop rules of thumb – such as acceptable rates of return – that considerably simplify the arbitration process. Second, these semijudicial agencies develop specialized information systems and expert staffs. As such, they more closely resemble internal organizations than the traditional arbitration procedure provided by the judicial system.

Regulators are both agents and arbiters. They are agents of the state who are called upon both to set the terms of the contract between consumers and producers and to adjudicate disputes that may arise. That the agent chosen is a public and not a private institution relates to the technical conditions that require the participation of public authorities. Almost all of the industries that have come to be classified as natural monopolies – electricity, natural gas, and telephones –

require dedicated rights of way and have come to use public property for the purpose. As a result, public authorities have naturally involved themselves in the specification of the terms and conditions of service from the outset.

The use of the political process as an agent to referee transactions between consumers and natural monopolies created a particularly difficult problem. Any organ of the state is, quite appropriately, susceptible to political pressure. Unfortunately, political pressure from consumers may develop to exploit producers. Opportunism, it must be re-called, is not just a problem arising from the deceitful use of information. It also includes false representations made by those who fervently believe in their own positions. The political process, associated as it is with some ideologies that are antagonistic to private property, is probably more susceptible to opportunistic behaviour than commercial negotiations.

The concept of opportunism that is central to the transactions-failure literature is not always precise. For what might be described by some as a hard bargain, well-struck could be interpreted by others as ill-gotten gains that arise from misrepresentation. There is generally no autonomous standard that can be used to adjudicate the fairness of the division of rewards. In the case that we are dealing with here, this problem is reduced, for there is a relatively well defined standard by which to judge opportunism associated with renegotiating a regulatory contract. Opportunism on the part of the state will be defined as expropriation without appro-priate recompense. The opportunity cost of foregone earnings is the standard used to decide upon appropriate recompense.

While regulatory agencies were given a semijudicial, independent status to reduce the impact of opportunistic influences emanating from the political systems, they were not isolated from all political pressure. Bounds had to be placed upon the agency's ability to act in an opportunistic fashion during the recontracting process. There must be a check or balance that permits the agency to resist the worst type of opportunistic behaviour emanating from the political process – the tendency to expropriate long-lived producer capital in the utility sector. Therefore, regulatory agencies have been constrained either under Common Law or through constitutional provisions that guarantee the sanctity of property.

Where such laws do not exist, where property rights are not enshrined in a constitution or protected by tradition, then the transactions literature would predict that the substitute institution that internalizes transactions in a naturally monopolistic industry would be adopted more frequently. A primary substitute for regulation is the public provision of goods and services. If consumers attempt to exploit private natural monopolies and if they fail to create a legal setting that prevents such exploitation, then exploitation can be avoided essentially by making consumers owners of the enterprise through nationalization. In this situation, attempts to exploit capital will be less successful because consumers, by doing so, can only exploit themselves.[4] As such, we should expect to find public enterprise being chosen more often in a jurisdiction like Canada where property rights have received less protection than in the United States.

Conclusion

The process of regulation in the case of natural monopoly can be seen to follow logically from the existence of scale economies and the need for consumers to contract with monopolists so as not to permit the exploitation of the former by the latter. The existence of a large number of consumers requires the use of an intermediary to act as agent to nego-tiate the contract. Because of asset specificity and asset longevity in the industries concerned, the recontracting process can be extremely costly when opportunistic behav-iour develops on the part of consumers. Since there is a particular tendency for the state, acting as agent, to engage in opportunistic behaviour if not constrained from doing so, the type of regulation chosen works only where opportunis-tic behaviour is constrained. If it is not so constrained, there will be less likelihood that the regulatory process will last, since a necessary condition for successful recontracting will not exist.

Subsequent chapters examine the evolution of regulation in a number of different industries and political jurisdictions. The transactions-failure literature provides the basic frame-work that is used to organize the investigation of the evolu-tion of regulation in the public utility sector in Canada. The case studies that follow serve two main purposes. On the one hand, they illustrate the relevance of the general theory. More importantly, they fill in the detail that the general framework lacks at this stage. The case studies permit an evaluation as to whether the problems that led to recon-tracting were widespread, how often opportunism affected the final result, to what extent businesses were other than passive participants and were able to deflect the forces that caused contractual failure, and to what extent their defensive strategies caused other problems.

The transactions-failure framework describes the general tendencies and broad-ranging problems that have to be resolved. While the case studies are meant to show the relevance of this framework, they do more than that. It is all very well to argue that franchise contracts were destined to be replaced by more complex forms of contracts and that the legal environment helped to shape the type of contract that emerged; but only a historical study can provide the type of detail on the human experience that shows how ingenious and varied were the solutions chosen to resolve a similar set of problems.

The case studies also provide an understanding of the relationship between business and government during the evolution of the regulatory contract. Businesses that were created with the original franchise contracts were not passive participants in the process. Their actions affected the nature of the problems that the state was called upon to resolve and the solutions chosen. When institutions are imperfect, as they were in Canada, a well devised business strategy may reduce some of the problems and give rise to others. The case studies illustrate the manner in which businesses protected themselves from opportunistic behaviour on the part of their partner, the state. They also demonstrate that these strategies had unforeseen consequences.

What the case studies do best is to emphasize that within the general framework outlined here, a number of different solutions were chosen for the problem of regulatory failure. The richness of human experience illustrated by the historical approach taken here then complements the methodological approach that stresses the importance of formulating laws that are general in their application. The common or general thread provided by the theory developed herein is the problem that had to be resolved. The case studies show that different political jurisdictions adopted different solutions to resolve similar problems. In some cases, business strategy served to avoid the contractual problem. In other circumstances, foresight and tolerance were in sufficient supply to prevent the problems from arising. In others, opportunistic behaviour led to contractual failure and the adoption of new institutional forms.

3 The Transition from Franchise Contract to Regulatory Tribunal in the United States

While regulatory agencies can be viewed as the institution that has been used to draft the terms of a complex form of contract needed to resolve a particular kind of transactions failure, they only emerged after a process of experimentation. In the United States, the emergence of the utility companies was accompanied by an evolution in the regulatory process as different agents and different types of contracts were tried in order to resolve the transactions-failure problem. The judiciary and the legislative branch of government initially were delegated the regulatory function, but eventually were rejected as agents capable of performing the required task. Municipalities also were given responsibility initially for setting the terms of contracts, but political opportunism caused this system to falter. Contracts of different durations, with different provisions for buyouts by municipalities of private utilities and with various clauses for automatic adjustments to avoid the need for explicit recontracting, were utilized before regulatory agencies were eventually adopted as the norm.

The modern regulatory system emerged when the American judiciary placed bounds on the policies that could be adopted by public regulatory agents. In doing so, it made use of constitutional clauses governing the sanctity of contract and the right of private property to be justly compensated should it be taken for public use. Once the courts interpreted this to mean that regulated capital deserved a nonconfiscatory level of income, they provided the constraint on the opportunistic exploitation of capital by the state that was necessary for the modern regulatory system to evolve.

The Emergence of the Utility Sector[1]

The growth of the privately owned utility sector in the United States was accompanied by an evolution in the regulatory process. Indeed, if the argument in the previous chapter is correct, the utilities would not have grown as quickly, nor remained outside of state control, if this evolution had not taken place. Without a well functioning regulatory institution, state ownership is likely to result from contractual failure.

The electrical generating sector evolved in the 1880s with the first central distribution station being constructed in New York City in 1882. Initially the distribution area of plants was limited; only the largest cities were served. Rapid growth in demand between 1902 and 1927, however, resulted in generating capacity doubling every five years.

Street railways also expanded in the 1880s – along with electric generation – because of their use of electricity as an energy source. By 1890, there were 789 street railway companies operating in the United States. By 1920, the industry reached its zenith and declined in importance thereafter (Barnes, 1942, p. 36).

The telephone industry began operations in the 1870s and expanded rapidly after 1900. Long-distance lines were built in the 1880s. By 1892, conversations between New York and Chicago were possible. After 1900, the introduction of copper wiring and the use of metallic circuits led to a dramatic expansion of the telephone system (Barnes, 1942, p. 38).

Two other utility industries, waterworks and gas companies, had their start much earlier in the 1800s. Technical advances that permitted a major expansion in the market for gas, however, did not occur until the 1880s. The discovery of the water gas process in 1873 substantially reduced costs and increased the demand for gas (Barnes, 1942, p. 26).

Table 3-1 summarizes the growth in four sectors: steam railroads, electricity, telephones, and street railways. Electric light and power, and telephones were both in their infancy prior to the turn of the century. Railroads and street railways developed the earliest and remained the largest sectors until the 1920s.

Of some significance is the fact that prior to the emergence of the well developed regulatory framework – which has been dated at around 1900 – the trend in established "natural monopolies" was toward state ownership. In the initial stages of the electrical industry, municipally owned plants predominated; but in terms of the percentage of customers served or current sold, the importance of municipal plants declined steadily from 1902 (Thompson and Smith, 1941, p. 601). By 1920, publicly owned utilities serviced no more than 15 per cent of all electrical customers, selling no more than 8 per cent of electrical energy generated. Table 3-2 shows the decline that took place in the relative

Table 3-1

The Growth of Net Value of Plant and Equipment for Regulated Industries in the United States, 1870-1930

	Steam railroads	Electric light and power	Telephones	Street railways
	Current million $			
1870	3,787	–	–	65
1875	4,844	–	–	91
1880	3,852	–	4	98
1885	5,390	3	26	133
1890	5,827	34	34	220
1895	6,194	96	59	430
1900	6,560	234	186	892
1905	7,483	474	385	1,444
1910	10,459	964	621	2,152
1915	12,687	1,595	738	2,286
1920	24,679	3,205	1,033	4,354
1925	23,270	4,606	1,526	3,355
1930	23,774	6,934	2,242	2,648

SOURCE   United States, Bureau of the Census, *The Statistical History of the United States from Colonial Times to the Present* (New York: Basic Books, 1976), p. 940.

Table 3-2

Private Versus Public Ownership in U.S. Electric Utilities, Installed Generating Capacity, 1902-25

	Total	Privately owned	Publicly owned
	000 kw		
1902	1,212	1,099	113
1907	2,709	2,500	209
1912	5,165	4,769	396
1917	8,994	8,412	582
1920	12,714	12,023	691
1925	21,472	20,045	1,427

SOURCE   United States, Bureau of the Census, *The Statistical History of the United States from Colonial Times to the Present* (New York: Basic Books, 1976), p. 825.

importance of public ownership in the generation of electrical power. The same trend occurred in the importance of public ownership of gas service. In 1914, over 11 per cent of the establishments manufacturing gas were municipally owned; by 1921, only 5 per cent were. In the case of electrical street railways, public ownership never was very important. In 1927, when the number of municipal street railways reached their maximum, there were 21 municipal systems in comparison with 942 commercial systems. The municipal systems operated less than 5 per cent of the track mileage and carried less than 5 per cent of the passengers (Barnes, 1942, pp. 816 and 819-20).

This same reliance upon private ownership did not occur in other countries. In Britain, electrical utilities and gas companies increasingly became state-owned. In Canada, a state-owned electric utility – Ontario Hydro – was created in 1906. By 1918, some one-half of the railway system in Canada had been acquired by the federal government and was thereafter run as a Crown corporation – the Canadian National Railways system. While central Canada was served throughout the period by a privately owned subsidiary of the American Telephone and Telegraph System (AT&T), the western Canadian provinces turned to state-owned telephone companies. The U.S. institutional framework managed to resolve the consumer-producer contractual problems in the utility sector in a very different way than in Canada and the United Kingdom.

The Early Evolution of the Regulatory System

Regulation as an institution evolved slowly in the United States. In the period prior to 1870, the first tentative steps taken to regulate the utility sector were unsuccessful. Judicial oversight was tried and discarded (Barnes, 1942, p. 170). English Common Law required industries with "public service" characteristics to render adequate service at reasonable prices. But this form of protection proved inadequate because the judiciary, as normally constituted, does not have the characteristics required for the role of regulatory agent. The courts are meant to be arbiters of the terms of contracts, not the originators of those contracts. They are not constituted to handle the type of ongoing supervision of a contract that is necessary. Their procedures are too costly and too time-consuming. Finally, because of their wide-ranging responsibilities, they lack the expertise that is necessary to resolve quickly and inexpensively the ongoing issues that the regulatory agent must renegotiate. Judicial protection, via the Common Law obligation to render adequate service at reasonable prices, therefore, proved inadequate.

Many of the same reasons led to the failure of the early attempts to regulate via legislative control. Legislatures were involved from the very outset insofar as they incorporated local utilities through special acts. These acts contained many of the clauses that formed the terms of the contract between the public and the utility – such as rates to be charged and service obligations. But this was a cumbersome process that did not allow for ready amendment of the terms of the franchise when renegotiation was required. Legislatures with their infrequent sessions and their other responsibilities could not give adequate consideration to changes in the terms of the act of incorporation as new conditions warranted. Just as important, direct legislative control was observed to lead to political corruption. Barnes noted:

> . . . it led to so much log-rolling and political corruption in an effort to serve special privileges and advantages from the legislature that it finally became customary for the legislatures to pass self-denying statutes forswearing the special incorporation of businesses (Barnes, 1942, p. 171).

This is the contract problem arising from opportunism. As argued earlier, where the opportunity for corruption is not constrained either voluntarily or via judicial controls, a public regulatory agent is likely to fail.

Between 1870 and 1900, two other forms of regulation evolved to handle the agent problem. In the 1870s, a number of mid-western American states created railway regulatory commissions under the prodding of the Granger movement. While the Interstate Commerce Commission emerged at the federal level in 1887, it did not provide the definitive model for the regulatory process, probably because it was called upon not so much to protect the consumer from exploitation as to moderate the extent of interfirm rivalry within the railway industry (MacAvoy, 1965). At the same time, a system of municipal regulation of electrical, telephone, and street railway utilities evolved. Because these utilities required use of the public streets, municipalities came to exert control over the issuance of franchises as a result of their power to police the public streets.

Both of these institutional forms offered improvements over previous attempts to solve the agency problem. Specializing in regulatory matters, the state railway commission began to develop expertise in rate matters. The municipal franchise brought the negotiation of the terms of the utility contract closer to those directly affected. Instead of state legislatures, municipal councils acquired the right to specify the terms of a contract for what were at this time essentially municipal utilities. Even so, considerable adaptation with these institutions was required before society managed to create the agent needed for the regulatory function. First, experimentation was required as to the type of contract that would best suit the conditions inherent in the industries concerned. Second, the legal system had to constrain the opportunism that can develop in small-numbers bargaining situations where the political process is involved. Without this constraint, the regulatory commission could not be relied upon to offer an effective alternative to the other internalization option – that of state ownership.

Regulation as a Contract

Regulation has evolved to handle the complex contracting problem between consumers and producers where transactions failures are likely to develop. The early history of attempts to use the municipal franchise to regulate the utility sector demonstrates the difficulty in writing a contract that can handle unforeseen events.

The earliest municipal franchise very much resembled a simple Demsetz-type contract between producers and consumers. In return for the privilege of a franchise (not necessarily exclusive), the utility entered a contract with the municipality that often specified both maximum rates and service standards.[2] For instance, it was not uncommon for gas company franchises to specify the candle-power of the gas. Franchises for street railways granted in the 1880s sometimes specified that horses were to be the motive force. The terms of the contract also generally covered the remuneration to be received by the municipality. In the case of California, franchises were sold to the highest bidder. New York and Chicago at one time charged a fee of 3 to 5 per cent of gross receipts. In the case of street railways, some cities received a portion of company revenues in excess of a given percentage return. In addition to cash payments, various forms of revenue in kind were demanded. Street railways were asked to provide service to city employees, street paving, and street cleaning; telephone and water companies to provide free service to certain public buildings; and electric companies to provide free street lighting.[3]

The early franchise contracts were not sufficiently flexible to handle transactions problems brought about by the need to renegotiate. Changes in technology that were not foreseen by the public authorities often rendered the maximum rates or the service standards meaningless and gave rise to public demands for a renegotiation. It was not only consumers that demanded renegotiation. When inflation increased costs, utilities found themselves without sufficient revenues to supply the contracted service.[4]

The difficulty involved in devising arm's-length contracts that adequately handled the uncertainties arising from technological change was faced not only by the regulatory process but also by the industry (Barnes, 1942, pp. 38-39). Originally, the American Telephone and Telegraph System licensed individual companies to operate local franchises and leased equipment to these franchises. As of 1877, the parent organization had about 185 such contracts covering most of the territory it served. Each franchise was for a relatively short period (five years) and provided for purchase of the franchise's assets at the end of the period. However, the problems that arose in coordinating activity between arm's-length parties during a period of rapid technological change led to a gradual shift towards the internalization of transactions. Permanent contracts were granted and the parent company took a minority interest in the local franchise. But even this change proved short-lived because of conflicts that arose, and gradually the parent organization acquired majority control of the various operating companies.

The same problems associated with recontracting arose in dealings between the state and the private utilities. The institutional framework prevailing at the time proved unable to deal with the renegotiations in an efficacious manner. Opportunism on the part of political authorities led to scandals for which the utilities were often blamed.[5] Assignment of the blame for the behaviour that was evidenced is not at issue here. It is sufficient to note the general perception that the political process could not handle the renegotiation. One observer wrote:

> ... taking the utility question out of local politics is likely to result in higher standards of conduct on the part of municipal and utility officials, for when utilities were charged with political corruption, it was usually forced upon them by a necessity of negotiating franchise renewals (Barnes, 1942, p. 221).

It has been argued that for a political body to function as a regulatory agent, its tendencies towards opportunism must first be restrained. The judicial system in the United States eventually came to define a set of bounds upon the behaviour of regulatory agencies that accomplished this.

The first problem the courts had to resolve was the extent to which a franchise was a contract and what conditions would govern renegotiations that might arise. Early court rulings defined a franchise as a contract between the state and a private party and subject to that section of the U.S. Constitution barring state laws "impairing the obligation of contracts."[6] By doing so, the courts made the franchise subject to judicial review should the legislative or executive branch impair the obligations imbedded in the contracts. This prevented franchises from being arbitrarily or capriciously revoked by municipal or state agencies.

That a franchise was interpreted as a contract did not prevent recontracting via the regulatory process. The courts also ruled that franchises might be contracts, but that the state could not by such contracts void the basic police powers of the state. It was this power to police in the interests of the health and safety of its citizens that was used in the first place to justify regulation. Franchises that voided these powers were ruled to be illegal. Franchises that alienated these basic rights were those that were inordinately long (a perpetual contract) or ones where some unreasonable privilege, such as freedom from price regulation, was granted. In the end, the Supreme Court came to recognize franchises as valid contracts if the state constitution specifically gave to the public body awarding the franchise the power to make rate contracts, and if the length of time during which the power of rate making was suspended was reasonable. As a result, states that included provisions in their constitutions restricting the extent and the terms of locally granted franchises could provide a means by which municipalities could enter into a contract whose terms were renegotiable. Many states did so and focused on the length of contract to be permitted – typically stipulating an upper limit (Thompson and Smith, 1941, pp. 160 and 165). But the process of more fully defining the limits possessed by municipalities was time-consuming, and thus the new institutional framework that allowed recontracting was slow to emerge.

Flexible Regulatory Contracts

Ensuring that recontracting could take place was only the first problem that had to be resolved. Avoiding contractual failure when the time for recontracting arose was equally important. To resolve this, different types of flexible regulatory contracts were tried. Each attempted to specify in advance the manner by which prices would change in response to future events. Each was found wanting.

As the need for flexible contracts became evident, two aspects of the franchise contract received special attention. These were the length of the contract and the remuneration due the provider of the service should the contract be cancelled. It was the latter aspect that was eventually constrained by the legal system; but the length of term was not. Here the political process experimented with short, long, and indeterminate-length contracts. Short contracts were those of less than 10 years; longer contracts had durations of 25 to 50 years; the indeterminate contract had no specific termination date, though it could contain provisions for termination.[7] If it did not, the indeterminate contract was really a perpetual franchise.

The shorter the length of the contract, the greater was the flexibility for the public; but this was countered by greater uncertainty for investors, especially where asset life was longer than the contract period. Early recognition was given to the uncertainty problem and its effect both on the cost of capital and on the tendency for a company to adopt a less than optimal maintenance strategy close to the expiry date of the franchise.

Except in the case of indeterminate-length franchises, specification of the terms by which the state could acquire the utility's property was essential for a franchise to function well. These clauses provided the utility with some protection from opportunistic behaviour on the part of the state at expiration. At the same time, they allowed the state the flexibility it needed to take into account changing circumstances. The franchise that specified that a buyout must occur, in the event of a termination of franchise, as well as the terms of the buyout, offered the greatest protection for the utility's investors. Otherwise, considerable uncertainty still remained for the private investor, since the state might authorize or start a competing new service at the termination of the franchise. A state-owned utility, which received subsidies from the public purse, could drive a private utility bankrupt and cause as much capital loss as direct expropriation without compensation.

Experiments were not restricted to the choice of different contract lives and buyout clauses. Attempts were made to devise contracts that reduced the need for recontracting. Several alternate forms of flexible contracts were tried. Each of these forms included provisions that allowed automatic changes in the contract, thus seeking to avoid the opportunism associated with recontracting. Each failed because the terms and conditions under which change was permitted could not be specified precisely enough to avoid recontracting.

Two variants were tried: the sliding-scale[8] and the service-at-cost contract. The sliding-scale contract stipulated how rates were to be adjusted as the profit earned by capital varied from a prespecified level. With each unit reduction in the rates charged to the customer, the utility was allowed to earn a higher rate of return; for each unit increase in the price of service, the allowed rate of return was reduced. This meant that prices would vary as costs changed; yet, there was still an incentive for increased efficiency since the company could capture part of any cost reduction.

The sliding-scale contract proved unable, however, to resolve the recontracting problem. First, it failed to handle major technological change or inflation. Since changes in costs served to change the rate of return, there came a time when rates reached such a high or low level that recontracting was required – recontracting which had not been envisaged in the original contract. Technological advance that reduced costs tended to increase profits to unacceptable levels, while inflation reduced the profit rate until it was below the opportunity cost of capital. Second, with the focus of the contract on prices and rates of return, room for opportunistic behaviour developed with respect to costs. Unless costs were supervised, and, in particular, unless depreciation reserves were carefully monitored, opportunistic behaviour on the part of the firm could contravene the intent of the arrangement.

An example of just such a problem can be found in the operation of the sliding-scale contract in the Boston gas industry. A holding company was accused of diverting profits to itself by charging excessively high prices for its coal, oil, and gas, and of subverting the purpose of the sliding-scale contract (Bussing, 1968, p. 84). A regulated rate of return monopolist has the incentive to inflate the price of an input if the profits on that input accrue to the owners of the monopoly (Dayan, 1972). The latter can be arranged if a holding company owns both the utility and the suppliers of the utility.

While the sliding-scale contract in Boston was terminated in 1926, an examination of the circumstances surrounding the cancellation suggests that contractual failure occurred not just because of public outcry that the holding company had "subverted" the underlying purpose of the scale. Rather, technological change rendered the original contract obsolete. Massachusetts wanted to use gas not just for its then current use involving illumination, but also for heating. In its latter capacity, gas would have provided a competitor for coal. The distribution company refused to be bound by the original contract because of the substantial changes in investment that would have been required (Bussing, 1968, pp. 81-82 and 84). This episode then shows the problem in writing a flexible contract, both because of the continuing potential for opportunistic behaviour, and because technological change was sufficiently rapid that the sliding-scale contract did not obviate the need for recontracting.

The second form of flexible contract, the service-at-cost franchise, was similar to the sliding-scale arrangement in that it also provided for automatic adjustments in rates. It differed because of its focus on costs rather than on the profits being earned as the trigger mechanism for change. The service-at-cost contract tended to develop during the decade between 1910 and 1920 when costs escalated dramatically because of inflation and when utilities requested more flexible adjustment mechanisms.[9]

These contracts also failed to provide the type of automatic control that abrogated the need for detailed auditing. Since costs depended upon levels of service, the various minutiae associated with appropriate standards of service had to be monitored. Thus, the service-at-cost contract still left ample opportunities for dispute. Another problem with this contract was that by focusing on costs, incentives for efficiency were reduced. Finally, while undue profits were prevented, provisions for losses due to technological change were not, and thus the contract threatened to prevent capital from earning on average its opportunity cost.

In the end, the flexible contract route proved unable to overcome the need for recontracting and the resulting potential for contract failure. Solutions to this problem had to be found elsewhere. The major difficulty alluded to earlier had to do with the length of contract chosen. And here the uncertainty that gave rise to difficulties essentially related to the opportunism that the state could engage in if the contract was not renewed. If the producer could not be certain of being adequately compensated for capital invested, the

length of the contract became an important determinant of costs. Fortunately, however, the judicial system eventually solved this difficulty by preventing the expropriation of capital. When this occurred, the franchise, in practice, became indeterminate. A system of ongoing regulation, often at the state level, was adopted. The modern regulatory tribunal had the power to revise the terms of the contract as the occasion warranted rather than at the fixed intervals that were initially stipulated. Observers of the regulatory process have referred to the post-1900 period as the era of the public service commission. Until then, regulatory commissions had either been advisory or had tended to cluster primarily in the railway industry. But before this could occur, before the regulatory agent could be relied upon to function impartially, the legal system had to define the bounds that would govern regulatory behaviour with respect to the compensation allowed capital.

Property Rights and the Role of the Judiciary

The leeway to be allowed the state when it intervened in the market system as a regulatory agent was determined in the courts in two separate stages. The first major challenge to regulation occurred when the U.S. legal system was asked to decide whether regulation was in the public interest – whether the legislative branch could invoke its general police power to regulate industry. In responding to this challenge, legal decisions focused on defining the circumstances that determined whether a business could be "affected with a public interest" and thus regulated. One taxonomy of public interest industries defined this group to include those industries such as railways that were granted privileges, those industries such as inns and gristmills to which Common Law duties adhered, and a third group that provided important services – all of which without regulation would charge monopolistic prices.[10]

Some observers concluded that this classification scheme was so broad that state legislatures could do as they saw fit, unless specifically constrained by state constitutions.[11] While cases before 1920 regarding railways,[12] grain elevators,[13] and insurance[14] all saw government regulatory powers confirmed, there were later instances where restrictions were placed on government intervention. In the 1920s, regulation in the case of theatre ticket brokers,[15] employment agencies,[16] and icemaking[17] was rejected because these industries were ruled not to be "affected with a public interest." However, the apparent constraint imposed by the courts in these decisions was substantially relaxed with the Nebbia case in the 1930s.[18] Here the Supreme Court ruled that a New York milk control board, which had the power to fix minimum wholesale and retail prices for fluid milk, was in the public interest. Since this industry fitted none of the well established categories that had been used to rationalize previous Supreme Court decisions, this ruling was widely interpreted to have extended the regulatory power of the state.[19] Whatever the case, while some constraints were imposed upon the state by these rulings, they did not severely limit the scope of the regulation in this early period.[20]

More important were the courts' rulings that defined which actions of regulatory bodies would not be tolerated during the renegotiation process. Two clauses in the U.S. Constitution guarantee property rights. The fifth amendment states: "no person shall . . . be deprived of life, liberty, or property without due process of law; nor shall private property be taken for public use, without just compensation." While this amendment bound the federal government, a similar amendment (the fourteenth), passed in 1868, applied to state governments. Between 1870 and 1890, these clauses were applied by the courts in such a way as to provide the legal constraints on political opportunism necessary for regulation to evolve.

The legal interpretations necessary for the successful evolution of regulation were relatively slow in emerging. Even in the Munn v. Illinois case in 1876, which has been widely quoted as providing a watershed with regard to the state's ability to use the police powers to regulate, the Supreme Court was unwilling to review the workings of the regulatory process and ruled that as long as the legislature had set a maximum price, the courts should not review what was reasonable. In an 1873 ruling,[21] the courts rejected the contention that property rights were affected by the regulation of butchers and as an *obiter dictum* observed that the fourteenth amendment was aimed at protecting the rights of negroes, and an exceptionally strong case would have to be made if this amendment was to be applied elsewhere (Barnes, 1942, p. 198). This position was to change. In the 1880s, the Supreme Court indicated that it was likely to consider the reasonableness of rate regulation. In 1886, as *obiter*, the Supreme Court observed that the power to regulate, which it had approved, was not a power to confiscate without just compensation and without due process.[22] In 1894, the Supreme Court assumed the right of judicial review of the decisions of regulators by setting aside a regulatory commission order on the grounds that the rate fixed was too low to afford a reasonable rate of return.[23]

This evolution in the protection offered regulated utilities resulted from two changes in the judiciary's interpretation of the terms of the property rights clauses of the Constitution. First, the due process clause had attached to it "a substantive as well as a procedural meaning" (Barnes, 1942, p. 2). By doing so, the judiciary shifted from consideration of the procedures followed to the substance of the rights protected (Thompson and Smith, 1941, p. 145). This is what Commons has referred to as the issue of "due purpose" (Commons, 1932, ch. 9). As a result, rights were interpreted to involve both the property expropriated as well as the method of expropriation.

Second, the judiciary came to attach a broader meaning to rights than mere ownership. As long as only ownership and not the fruits of ownership were considered to be the essential rights deserving of protection, it could ignore the actions of regulatory boards that affected only the income from ownership and not the title to the physical assets. The regulatory cases considered in the 1870s, in such cases as Munn v. Illinois, did not infringe upon the title to property, and therefore regulation was sustained. By the 1880s, the U.S. Supreme Court came to attach rights not just to ownership but also to the freedom to enjoy income from ownership of property.[24] By doing so, the judiciary broadened its concept of property rights and thus accepted the authority to rule on the extent to which the seeking of an "advantageous price" was a liberty that was being unduly affected by the regulatory process. It was the way in which it interpreted regulatory infringements on such a right that provided the foundation for the evolution of regulation in the twentieth century.

With the acceptance of a review role with respect to property rights, the U.S. Supreme Court then enunciated the principles to be used to evaluate whether capital was being duly remunerated. In Smyth v. Ames (1898)[25] the Supreme Court first described in some detail the principles that were to govern its decisions.[26] The regulated company, it ruled, was entitled to a "fair return upon the value of that which it employs for the public convenience" (Barnes, 1942, p. 373).

In ruling on the fair rate of return,[27] the Supreme Court established four basic points.[28] First, as early as 1894,[29] it recognized the right of a utility to earn a rate of return sufficient to attract new capital. Second, it recognized the rate should be tailored to the needs of the specific business.[30] In particular, it ruled that the rate should reflect the risk of the business. Third, it ruled that the rate should not reflect that earned in "highly profitable enterprises or speculative enterprises."[31] Fourth, it stipulated that the appropriate rate could vary – that it was not to be based on historical conditions, but that it had to be based on present, and even future, business conditions.[32]

In this way, the legal system provided a set of flexible guidelines for regulatory commissions. These guidelines meant that no one rate could be defined for all circum-stances and, therefore, allowed commissions to vary rates over time as inflation and business conditions affected nominal rates. In the 1920s, the Supreme Court was ob-served to increase the general rate it allowed from some 6 to about 8 per cent. By the 1930s, this was reduced to around 6 per cent (Thompson and Smith, 1941, pp. 355-59). While regulatory commissions were therefore constrained from engaging in opportunistic behaviour that confiscated prop-erty, the legal system did not act so as to obviate the necessity of efficiency. Inefficient management could be penalized (Barnes, 1942, p. 525); more importantly, the judiciary ruled that the inability of a company to obtain customers because of competition did not justify increased prices.[33]

It was in its interpretation of the fair value of the rate base that the Supreme Court faced more contentious issues. Here its rulings evolved in a sensible fashion. In the first cases brought before it, consumers argued that fair value of the rate base should not be equated to the capitalization of a company because of stock-watering schemes. They also argued that it should not be taken as reported construction costs, because construction companies were said to have funneled large un-productive expenditures into the hands of promoters.[34] Consumers argued for a concept more akin to the econo-mist's concept of opportunity cost – the reproduction cost of the capital or the present market value of the property. While the U.S. Supreme Court refused to specify a formula in detail, its decisions favoured the present market value of property – at least in the earlier period – if only because it rejected the utilities' arguments that the base should be their original expenditures or their capitalization (Barnes, 1942, p. 378).

Between 1900 and 1920, the Supreme Court continued to stress the economically meaningful concept, and increas-ingly focused on reproduction costs rather than original cost. In 1909,[35] it noted that rising prices should be considered in determining present value. The difference between histori-cal or original costs became even more important between 1914 and 1929 as the price level increased dramatically. In 1922, it affirmed that present prices should be used for reproduction costs,[36] and in 1926,[37] it went so far as to argue that expected future prices had to be considered. These decisions set reproduction costs as the basis on which regulatory commissions functioned over much of this period (Thompson and Smith, 1941, pp. 292-95). One scholar has noted that the majority of commissions adhered to these fair-value standards and were "deferential to the precedents es-tablished by the federal courts" (Barnes, 1942, p. 504).

Throughout this period, the Supreme Court refused to be bound by a specific formula, thereby providing itself with the flexibility required for changing circumstances. Just as rising prices prior to 1929 required a modification of its initial rule, declining prices in the 1930s required another modification. The Supreme Court shifted to an "end-result" criterion. In a landmark decision,[38] the Supreme Court rejected a lower court's decision that used a slavish devotion to the reproduction concept to argue that rates were confis-catory. It ruled that the ability of the company in question to pay reasonable dividends and to operate successfully had not been impaired, and thus rates were not confiscatory. Other decisions at this time also rejected reproduction costs based on extrapolating historical costs using price indexes. These decisions freed regulatory commissions from rigidly fol-lowing a formula determining reproduction costs. With the Hope Decision of 1944,[39] the Supreme Court stressed that regulatory commissions had more responsibility in deter-mining the rate base than previously, although the Court still had the right to review the reasonableness of the resulting decisions (Phillips, 1965, pp. 227 and 230). In effect, the Supreme Court recognized that the reproduction cost for-mula, which it had initially used, was becoming difficult to apply as price levels fluctuated and technology changed. While it may have been possible to use a simple reproduction cost formula early in the century when utilities were rela-tively young, this was impractical and too imprecise a method by the 1930s.

There is a second reason that the Supreme Court changed its emphasis in the 1930s leaving regulatory commissions with more responsibility for assessing the rate base. Its very success in providing the framework for responsible regula-tory commissions meant it could rely more on the commis-sions' judgments as to the appropriate rate base. One ob-server has noted that the shift, which was observed in the 1930s, occurred after a series of vigorous dissents by a minority on the Supreme Court. This minority disagreed that reproduction costs provided an appropriate rate base stan-dard and argued for a prudent investment standard (Phillips, 1965, pp. 224-29).

The prudent investment standard establishes the rate base as that amount prudently invested in a company. It was not a new concept. Massachusetts had long followed a related practice.[40] The Massachusetts experience had been rela-tively successful since, when utilities were originally formed in this state, there had been relatively little stock-watering and subsequent capital issues had received close scrutiny of the regulatory authorities (Barnes, 1942, pp. 506-14). As such, the prudent investment base satisfied the Supreme Court's interpretation of a fair rate base.

This would not have been the case everywhere at the turn of the twentieth century. At that time, the legal constraints necessary to constrain opportunism were only being put in place. These decisions ushered in the age of the modern regulatory commission. The period after 1900 was characterized by a shift from the municipal franchise to the state regulatory commission. In the case of electrical utilities, only one state (Massachusetts) had a state commission before 1907; but some 27 states enacted public utility laws between 1907 and 1914.[41]

Wisconsin and New York led the way with the passage of regulatory statutes in 1907 that were widely emulated. The Wisconsin legislation converted existing franchises to "indeterminate" permits, thereby resolving the length of contract problem. While buyouts were permissible, the state commission was given the power to set the purchase price – being constrained by then as to what fair value was by previous Supreme Court's rulings (Jarrell, 1978, pp. 270-71). Wisconsin gave the state commission control not only over rates but also over the rate base, since capitalization and the issuance of securities also fell within the purview of the state commission. With the Supreme Court rulings regarding fair return on fair value already established, the state commissions could be expected to perform their agency task with relative efficiency.

Thus, the Supreme Court's regulatory restrictions on actions that might expropriate capital had by 1930 led to the widespread adoption of a system that was making the type of decisions required to ascertain a prudent value rate base. Original cost determinations had been made and subsequent investments at least scrutinized if not always explicitly approved. Therefore, the task of determining the rate base required less judicial interference than previously. In this situation, it is not surprising that the judicial system showed common sense in leaving the detailed scrutiny of the rate base to what by 1930 had become a mature regulatory commission system.

Conclusion

The evolution of regulation in the United States from a franchise contract to an independent tribunal may be ascribed to two factors. The first was the existence of a constitution with an entrenched property-rights clause. The second was the existence of an independent judiciary entrusted with evaluating the legality of both the executive and legislative branches' actions in light of constitutionally protected rights.

The absence of these conditions in Canada meant that the evolution of regulation followed a different route. In Canada, regulation also was implemented originally via *ex ante* franchise contracts. In Canada, the same pressures arose for renegotiations, and the same problems developed during recontracting. The difference between the two countries lay in the degree of constraint that the judicial system imposed on the political and regulatory process. Because the judiciary was considerably weaker in Canada, opportunism by the state could not be constrained in the same fashion. The independent regulatory tribunal, therefore, was less suited to act as agent and tended to be chosen less frequently. In addition, opportunism by the state led to an alternate institutional form being chosen by default. Public enterprise was adopted when the state expropriated private capital during renegotiations over regulatory contracts. Subsequent chapters focus on the reason why one or other of these agents emerged in different Canadian jurisdictions.

4 Public Enterprise in the Canadian Railway Industry

There is a striking dissimilarity between Canada and the United States with respect to the methods chosen to regulate industry. Canada, in contrast to the United States, has adopted public enterprise more often. The railway, electric utility, telephone, and airline sectors all have Crown corporations either at the federal or the provincial level – often with a regulatory commission imposed as well. In Chapter 2, it was argued that the choice of public enterprise as a government regulatory instrument may often be associated with contractual transactions failure. This chapter examines the extent to which this was true of the nationalization of Canadian railways that occurred during World War I.

The idea that Canadian "National" policy and railway policy are part and parcel of the same nation-building experience has been deeply imbedded in the Canadian psyche. An economist then treads warily when he argues that the process was fundamentally flawed, and that nationalization was not so much the result of the Canadian dream but rather an example of a recurrent Canadian problem with its regulatory system. The railway system is only one of several regulated industries where Canadian governments have intervened to abrogate contracts and confiscate property during renegotiation of the original regulatory contract.

Nationalization is likely to result, it was argued in the second chapter, when a particularly difficult set of contracts – those between the state and private enterprise – cannot be written. Transactions failure in general arises when the presence of uncertainty, bounded rationality, opportunism, and confiscation of investments means arm's-length transactions cannot be relied upon. Nationalization, in particular, occurs when private property cannot be protected from exploitation by the state, since the internalization solution to transactions failure in this case necessarily involves the linking of the consumer and the enterprise through state ownership rather than through any other contractual form.

Nationalization need not involve expropriation. But when part of the capital of the public enterprise can be acquired for less than its value, myopic politicians will have a greater incentive to take over the enterprise, especially when other pressures seem to increase the importance of national goals. It should be noted that venality is not a prerequisite to nationalization; highly laudable national or provincial goals may be present. The Canadian government's desire to unify the country via its railway system is well known. The argument presented here is that where changed circumstances require contract renegotiation, in some instances opportunism will arise and arm's-length transactions will fail. When the state is involved, as it is with the regulatory process, opportunism may be cloaked in political ideals – ideals which are salutary when taken by themselves, but which may lead to an opportunism that precludes anything other than public enterprise. Thus nationalization will be correlated with expropriation and contractual failure, though the former need not always accompany the latter if Common Law or tradition constrains the state's ability to confiscate.

The Canadian government was involved in two different but related contractual exercises with its railways. Contracts were used to stimulate the construction of the railway lines. In addition, both implicit and explicit contracts associated with a regulatory system emerged to control freight rates. Each of the problems that has been posited to produce transactions failure is found in the historical literature that describes the evolution of the relationship between state and private enterprise prior to the nationalization of the Canadian railways.

Uncertainty led to less than perfect specification of contingencies and to substantial renegotiations of the terms of contracts. Imperfect foresight in the specification of construction contracts led to regulatory difficulties at a later stage. During the actual construction process and later as regulation developed, monitoring costs were large and the enforcement of contractual terms, a continuous problem. Although these were problems that also existed in the United States, the two countries differed in terms of the evolution of their respective regulatory processes. In Canada, no constraint was placed upon the regulatory agency to prevent confiscation. The pressures of World War I led the regulatory agency to restrain price increases to less than the inflation rate, which contributed to the eventual bankruptcy of two of the Canadian transcontinental railway systems and their ultimate nationalization. Moreover, during the nationalization process, the state responded to political pressure and confiscated property of the British-owned Grand Trunk – a railway which had been particularly unpopular with the public.[1]

The Conventional View

Canadian history has long stressed the evolution of National policy around three themes: tariffs, immigration, and a unifying railway system. Nationalization of a substantial sector of the railway system at the end of World War I, therefore, is readily accepted as the culmination of one of the three policies. The historian of the government-owned railway system has characterized the result as a mistake brought on by circumstances beyond the control of those who engineered it. Referring to the government of the time, he writes:

> ... they had been nagged and badgered into public ownership by circumstances beyond their control, and they had only adopted such a programme as a makeshift solution to which there seemed to be no alternative (Stevens, 1962, p. 509).

Even more influential in shaping a generation of students is the explanation given by the Easterbrook and Aitken economic history text:

> At the time when the Canadian National Railways system was formed, the principle of government ownership had few supporters in Canada. Nationalization was undertaken not on grounds of principle but as a pragmatic necessity, to prevent the bankruptcy of enterprises in which many private individuals had invested their savings, the dissolution of transportation systems of great national importance, and the possibility of serious damage to Canada's credit in foreign capital markets (Easterbrook and Aitken, 1963, p. 443).

These explanations are either incomplete or misleading. First, bankruptcy without nationalization would not have dissolved the transportation systems; it would have led to their reorganization. Rails, bridges, and ballast do not disappear when reorganization takes place. Second, it is difficult to argue that Canada's credit reputation required nationalization. Almost all the capital of the Grand Trunk Pacific was guaranteed by the Canadian government and was therefore not in jeopardy; a similar situation existed in the case of the Canadian Northern.[2] Private bankruptcy would not, therefore, have led to much loss of private investments. Moreover, the outcry of the British financial community that accompanied the perceived confiscation of the assets of several shareholder classes of the Grand Trunk during the nationalization process hardly protected Canada's reputation in the United Kingdom.[3]

Traditional accounts of the nationalization process fail to delineate the contractual problems that caused government policy to fail. Treating government officials as being badgered into an unwanted nationalization or as acting prag-matically ignores the basic reason for failure. Moreover, it risks leaving us with a faulty explanation – that Canadians somehow have a taste for public enterprise or that Canadian governments have a greater sense of national responsibility in the case of a failing enterprise.

The Contractual Process and Transactions Failure

The history of government involvement in the Canadian railway industry is replete with contractual difficulties of two types. The first involved contracts between governments and railways for construction purposes. The second involved regulation of the railways and affected the ability of the railways to fulfil the terms of the first. Because of imperfect foresight, contractual difficulties that arose in the first case impinged on the second and contributed to the regulatory failure that occurred. But just as important, the contractual process foundered on the moral hazard problem, in that the ability of the private sector to fulfil the terms of the construction contracts came to depend upon the government's control of the regulatory process – a control that was exercised to the detriment of private capital's ability to fulfil its contractual obligations under the construction contracts.

The Canadian government involved itself with the construction of three major transcontinental systems. With Confederation came the government-constructed and operated Intercolonial Railway that by 1876 linked the Maritimes and Quebec. At the same time, the Canadian Pacific (CPR) was begun under private auspices, but with government support, and completed between Montreal and Vancouver in 1885. A third line, the Canadian Northern, was constructed between 1896 and 1915 on a piecemeal basis with intermittent government support. The fourth, the National Transcontinental, was a partnership between the Canadian government and a well established central Canadian railway – the Grand Trunk. Under the terms of the contract, the Grand Trunk built the western section – the Grand Trunk Pacific was finished in 1914 – while the Canadian government constructed the eastern section. The latter was to be rented by the Grand Trunk at 3 per cent of capital costs and operated as one system with the Grand Trunk Pacific. Started in 1905, the National Transcontinental was also finished during World War I.

The federal government encouraged the three major transcontinental railways by subsidizing construction. This was done with contracts that specified the subsidy, usually per mile, and often gave control over the location and other aspects such as grade to the government. Control over the route was specified so as to attenuate the opportunistic behaviour that resulted when early contractors unnecessarily extended lines to increase receipts (Glazebrook, 1964, p. 12). Equally important was the government's national policy goal of ensuring an all-Canadian route[4] – one that did not use U.S. territory. This meant that support was made conditional on the location being entirely within Canada.

The nature of the contract with regards to both the form and the amount of subsidy adopted by the government changed in an important way over time. In the case of the CPR, the government used cash subsidies and land grants extensively during the 1870s. The Canadian Northern was able to complete a transcontinental line with a piecemeal construction and purchase program, through cash subsidies from federal, provincial, and municipal governments, land grants,[5] and the sale of bonds, some of which were guaranteed by the Dominion government. With the National Transcontinental agreement in 1903 between the Canadian government and the Grand Trunk, only bond guarantees were used to provide government support (Glazebrook, 1964, pp. 137 and 145). Cash subsidies and land grants were conspicuous by their absence.

This inequality of government support had a serious effect on the ability of the separate lines to weather financial adversity. For example, as of 1917, some $260 million of the $582 million issued capital of the CPR consisted of ordinary shares. Issued capital made up only 69 per cent of net railway property investment of some $841 million (Canadian Pacific Railway Company, 1949, p. 27). This sound financial position was made possible by the generous terms of the subsidies granted to the CPR. Mercer has calculated that land, cash, and railway subsidies together totalled 56 per cent of investment in present value terms – the most generous subsidy received by all land-grant railways in North America (Mercer, 1972, p. 293). In contrast to the CPR, the Canadian Northern was much more heavily debt-laden. As of 1916, it had some $428 million in outstanding debt, and no infusions of equity (Fournier, 1935, p. 43). It had received only $38 million in cash subsidies and some $17 million from the sale of land grants. Together these subsidies made up about 10 per cent of invested capital. The Grand Trunk Pacific was left in the worst position. All of its $216 million capital stock had been funded as debt (Fournier, 1935, p. 43); no cash subsidies or land grants supplemented this source of capital.

The varying debt-equity ratios of the Canadian railways created substantial difficulties for the newly emerging regulatory process. Rates that covered the costs of the new transcontinental systems would leave the CPR with large "profits." Public opinion, especially in the West, was hostile to the CPR.[6] In 1888 the extent of the antipathy led the government to revoke the monopoly protection clause in its original contract with the CPR – in return for which the CPR received relatively minor compensation (Glazebrook, 1964, p. 115). The intensity of public antipathy to the CPR had also led to the political pressure that encouraged the expansion of a second and third transcontinental system. Thus a rate structure that appeared to favour the CPR was unacceptable. On the other hand, differential rates that reflected the variations of capital subsidies were equally unacceptable in light of the intense pressure that was placed upon the regulatory commission to equalize rates for different western points.[7]

There was considerable lack of foresight exhibited by those who crafted the original contracts to build the transcontinental railways. However, the widespread existence of uncertainty and the bounded rationality of contracting agents mean all contingencies cannot be specified in advance. It is the manner in which recontracting takes place when required that sheds light on the reasons for transactions failure. As it became clear that capital grants alone were not sufficient in certain areas, either because of the intrinsic lack of traffic or because of government regulatory policy, alternate forms of contractual arrangements were possible.

One alternative for the government would have been to pay operating subsidies to privately owned carriers for lines that were unprofitable. In 1892 the CPR offered to operate the government-run Intercolonial in return for a federal subsidy equivalent to the deficit then in existence. But this offer came to naught. The difficulties of monitoring an ongoing agreement such as this were potentially too great; the difficulties of enforcing a construction agreement had already proven onerous. The arbitration proceedings to value the Grand Trunk, which were held in 1920, proved how easy it was for a private party to manipulate its books.[8] And no government, sensitive to public opinion, was going to agree to a fixed subsidy that did not reflect true losses. To discover what those losses might be, required an ongoing evaluation of the operations of the private parties that proved impossible given the informational difficulties involved in such monitoring.

Moral Hazard and Regulatory Failure

Of the various flaws in the contractual process, perhaps the most fatal was that associated with moral hazard. Moral hazard problems arise when parties to a contract can, by their behaviour, change the division of benefits from those originally agreed upon. The usual examples are insurance problems where the insured party may not take the appropriate loss-reducing actions or cost-plus contracts that may undermine incentives for cost efficiency. The particular problem that arose in the railway industry stemmed from the government's ability, via the regulatory process, to affect the degree to which the privately owned railways might fulfil their part of the construction contract – to build and operate the railway without continuous recourse to the public purse.

Canada, in contrast to the United States, placed no restrictions upon the regulatory process. Prior to 1886, regulation of rates was limited to the stipulation of maxima in charters. In 1886, the Railway Committee of the Privy Council, a subcommittee of the Cabinet, was entrusted with the control of rates. It was not until 1903 that the Board of Railway Commissioners was established as an independent railway tribunal similar to the American Interstate Commerce Commission.[9] But the Canadian regulatory board was not constrained to the same extent by the judicial system to make certain that capital was not confiscated. Indeed, it rejected the argument that rates should be based on fair value standards similar to those adopted in the United States (Currie, 1946, pp. 148-49).

Several attempts, in particular by the CPR, have been made to introduce the U.S. fairness standard to Canada. All have been rejected. In 1935, the CPR appealed a regulatory rate decision to the Canadian Supreme Court arguing that the Board's decision, in rejecting the rate base and fair-rate-of-return concept, denied it just and reasonable tolls. It argued that under British Common Law no one can be deprived of property without explicit statute. Moreover, it argued, a regulatory authority acts improperly if, without authority of a statute, it does not allow a carrier a fair return on fair value. The Supreme Court refused to hear the case, however, thereby sanctioning existing regulatory practice. As late as 1951, the CPR argued before the Royal Commission on Transportation that the "fair-value-on-rate-base" criterion should be written into legislation. It received an unsympathetic response (Currie, 1959, p. 135).

The Canadian regulatory board has generally concerned itself not so much with the adequacy of the rate level as with the structure of rates.[10] When it did consider the general rate level, it tended to adopt as a standard the revenue needs of the CPR, which was the low-cost transcontinental line.[11] The use of this standard and the events of World War I precipitated a regulatory crisis.

Regulatory failure came to a head in World War I. Concern over war-profiteering and the large operating surplus of the CPR made it increasingly difficult for the regulatory agency to grant rate increases for the industry in general. This was a particularly difficult time for both the Canadian Northern and the National Transcontinental

because they were in the process of completing their lines. It was a time when operating deficits might have been expected to have occurred as new lines were constructed. The regulatory agency exacerbated the financial problem faced by these two newly constructed railways because it failed to grant price increases that were commensurate with mounting costs. Indeed, at the outset of the war the agency actually reduced Prairie rates by some 7.5 per cent and British Columbia rates by 25 per cent.[12] During the subsequent four years, the Prime Minister (Borden) made it clear to the regulatory agency that rail rates were to be kept down (Currie, 1957, p. 478). Rate increases were therefore extremely slow in being granted. Table 4-1 shows the course of both Canadian and U.S. freight rates during this time. The nominal rate per ton-mile was actually lower in 1917 than it was at the outbreak of the war – even though the wholesale price index stood at 179 relative to 1913. Real rates fell from 78 cents per ton-mile in 1913 to less than 39 cents per ton-mile by 1917 for the CPR.

In response to a request for a rate increase made in early 1917, the regulatory commission finally granted a 15-percent increase in March of 1918. The constraint that the unequal construction subsidies imposed upon the regulatory board is evidenced by the fact that this increase was accompanied by the imposition of an excess war-profits tax on the CPR that then removed most of the benefits of the rate increase from the financially healthy CPR – a compromise that was possible only in wartime. But labour settlements in the rail industry rendered this increase inadequate for the other railways. The McAdoo award granted to railway labour in the United States increased rail wages substantially, and this inevitably spilled over into Canada.[13] Average compensation of Canadian railway employees was 64 per cent higher in 1919 than in 1917. Other rail costs also escalated dramatically. Freight fuel costs increased by over 55 per cent during the same period (Fournier, 1935, p. 88). But nominal freight rates increased by only about 40 per cent (Table 4-1).

The result was a dramatic decline in profitability and ultimately the bankruptcy of the railways that had been financed almost solely from debt. The ratio of net earnings to gross revenues for Canadian and American railways is presented in Table 4-2. For the CPR this ratio was halved between 1917 and 1920, but still remained positive. For all other Canadian railways taken together, it became negative by 1921. In the United States, it had fallen to levels in 1920 that meant debt could not be serviced.

The difference, however, was that the American government temporarily took over its railway network in order to compensate shareholders. This safeguarded the rights of the

Table 4-1

A Comparison of Real and Nominal Revenue per Railway Ton-Mile, Canada and United States, 1890-1922

	Nominal				Real (1913 = 100)	
	All Canadian	CPR	United States		CPR	United States
			Cents/ton-mile (Cdn.)			
1890		84	94		104	117
1891		91	90		113	113
1892		84	90		112	120
1893		87	88		115	115
1894		87	86		123	125
1895		80	84		115	120
1896		75	81		112	122
1897		78	80		115	120
1898		76	75		107	108
1899		74	72		102	96
1900		79	73		106	91
1901		75	75		98	95
1902		75	76		94	90
1903		74	76		91	89
1904		77	78		94	91
1905		77	77		91	89
1906		74	75		87	85
1907	82	78	76		85	81
1908	72	75	75		82	83
1909	73	76	76		82	78
1910	74	78	75		83	74
1911	78	82	74		84	80
1912	76	77	73		75	74
1913	76	78	72		78	72
1914	74	75	72		73	74
1915	75	77	72		70	72
1916	65	64	71		49	58
1917	69	70	72		39	43
1918	74	85	85	86*	43	45
1919	96	100	97	101*	48	49
1920	100	104	105	118*	43	47
1921	107	120	128	143*	70	92
1922	120	100	118	120*	66	85

* Corrected for exchange rate differential using Canada-U.S. annual exchange rates found in *Historical Statistics of Canada*, p. 276.

NOTE   Real rates are the nominal rates deflated by the wholesale price index found in the Canadian Pacific Railway Company, 1949 Submission.

SOURCE   Canadian Pacific Railway Company, *Submission to the Royal Commission on Transportation*, Appendix to Part I (Montreal, Quebec, 1949), pp. 5-7; and M. C. Urquhart and K. A. H. Buckley, *Historical Statistics of Canada*, 1st ed. (Cambridge: Cambridge University Press, 1965), pp. 276 and 539.

railway shareholders. The U.S. government did the same for the telephone industry. In Canada, however, two of the transcontinental railways ended up by being driven into bankruptcy and subsequently nationalized. The Canadian Northern's fate was sealed as of mid-1917 when the government passed a bill to acquire most of the stock remaining in private hands. The Grand Trunk and the Grand Trunk Pacific were forced into receivership by the Canadian government in 1919 and the take-over began in 1920 (Stevens, 1962, pp. 483 and 512). As was argued in the first section of

Table 4-2

A Comparison of the Ratio of Net[1] to Total Railway Earnings, Canada and United States, 1907-25

	Canada Steam Railway Total	CPR	Other Canadian[2]	United States[3]
	Per cent			
1907	29.3	36.4	22.6	32.5
1908	27.3	31.8	22.5	29.9
1909	27.9	30.1	25.8	33.3
1910	30.8	34.6	26.9	33.1
1911	30.6	34.8	26.0	30.7
1912	31.3	35.1	27.0	30.0
1913	29.1	32.9	25.1	30.0
1914	26.4	31.8	21.1	27.1
1915	26.1	33.7	19.7	29.4
1916	31.1	37.2	25.5	34.4
1917	28.3	34.1	23.1	29.4
1918	17.0	25.8	9.8	18.3
1919	10.7	19.9	3.9	14.3
1920	2.8	16.2	–7.8	5.6
1921	7.7	19.3	–0.7	17.1
1922	10.6	20.5	3.5	20.5
1923	13.5	19.6	9.3	22.5
1924	14.2	20.8	9.8	23.4
1925	18.3	23.0	15.1	25.9

1   Net is defined as total revenues less operating expenses. In Canada, total revenue is taken as gross revenues, and in the United States as operating revenues.
2   "Other Canadian" was calculated by deducting the CPR figures contained in the 1949 Submission from the railway statistics for the entire industry contained in *Historical Statistics of Canada*.
3   For the period 1907-16, the fiscal year ended June 30; for post-1916, the year ended December 31.
SOURCE   Columns 1, 2 and 3 are from the *Canada Yearbook*, various years; column 4, from the United States, Bureau of the Census, *Historical Statistics of the United States*, Part II, pp. 736-37.

this chapter, when the regulatory process is used in an opportunistic way, a utility can only continue to function if the public is called upon to provide the capital. This was the end result in Canada of a failure to overcome the potential for transactions failure in the regulatory process.

The Demise of the Grand Trunk

The demise of the Grand Trunk in 1919 was the result of a government that was unable or unwilling to recognize the impact of its own regulatory regime on the ability of the railway to fulfil its contractual obligations. In 1921, the government appointee on the Arbitration Board that was established to rule on the value of the equity shares of the Grand Trunk proclaimed:

> It is quite clear that, whether the war had occurred or not, it would have been utterly impossible for the Grand Trunk to carry the burden of its liability in respect of guarantees upon Grand Trunk Pacific Securities.[14]

The evidence quoted by the government appointee does not support that position, for between 1910 and 1917, the average yearly surplus available (after adjusting the Grand Trunk's books to reflect true profits) was some $5 million.[15] The Grand Trunk's absolute liabilities for payment of interest under the guarantees that it had incurred to build the Grand Trunk Pacific were, however, only $2,594,080.[16] There was a second guarantee of $1,395,170 annually, conditional upon there being enough surplus to pay dividends on the guaranteed stock. The annual prewar profits of the Grand Trunk would have covered both payments.

The railway nominee on the Arbitration Board, former U.S. President Taft, actively disputed the government's claim and attempted to rebut it with a counter-factual exercise.[17] Arguing that the profitability of the Grand Trunk in 1920 was unduly depressed by unusual circumstances related to inflation at the end of World War I, he projected revenues to 1926 using historical growth rates. He then used the historical average ratio of surplus to operating revenues (based on actual figures for the period 1910-16) to predict the future surplus available for payment of liabilities. His conclusion was that this surplus would have been more than adequate to meet both the Grand Trunk Pacific's interest liabilities and increased capital requirements for operating the Grand Trunk itself.

In order to assess the relative merits of the two positions, a more detailed assessment of the Grand Trunk's performance is required. This railway, which was formed in 1852, had become a major trunk carrier by the mid-1880s.[18] Its route stretched from Chicago to Toronto, via both Sarnia and Windsor, to Montreal and then to Portland, Maine. In Ontario, there were major branch lines, one of which linked Windsor to Niagara Falls and thence to railways that made their way to New York City. In Quebec, a branch line linked Montreal to Quebec City.

In the period after 1894, the railway reached its maturity and became increasingly profitable (see Table 4-3). Relatively little mileage was added between 1894 and 1913, but passenger and freight traffic grew almost continuously until World War I. So too did net revenues and surplus available for equity (columns 5 and 7). Dividends on various equity

Table 4-3

Grand Trunk Railway Freight Traffic and Revenue, 1894-1919[1]

	Mileage operated	Passengers	Tons freight	Gross revenue	Net revenue[2]	Fixed charges[3]	Surplus for equity[4]
		000	000	000 £	£	£	£
1894	3,506	5,901	8,115	3,649,957	1,024,481	1,122,111	–97,630
1895	3,506	5,838	8,394	3,637,055	1,204,175	1,141,487	62,688
1896	3,506	5,608	8,787	3,787,285	1,287,079	1,150,998	136,081
1897	3,506	6,590	9,186	3,969,642	1,574,631	1,174,859	399,772
1898	3,506	6,843	9,194	4,012,314	1,548,932	1,154,327	364,605
1899	3,506	6,632	10,301	4,407,016	1,724,367	1,189,891	534,476
1900	3,535	6,937	10,484	4,558,910	1,690,701	1,200,863	483,566
1901	3,535	7,652	11,080	4,857,600	1,736,651	1,227,717	508,934
1902	3,558	8,214	11,824	5,189,080	1,811,659	1,221,358	590,301
1903	3,562	9,100	13,484	5,916,548	1,891,170	1,223,897	667,274
1904	3,536	9,256	12,971	5,689,130	1,787,232	1,225,711	561,521
1905	3,536	10,059	14,143	6,018,001	1,951,232	1,230,130	724,882
1906	3,536	10,663	15,917	6,606,528	2,059,458	1,226,130	833,328
1907	3,536	11,227	17,392	7,144,506	2,080,068	1,224,343	855,725
1908	3,536	10,818	15,310	6,302,034	1,999,984	1,222,333	761,804
1909	3,536	11,029	16,773	6,499,371	1,781,103	1,231,236	542,923
1910	3,536	11,088	17,722	7,021,535	2,031,971*	1,270,400	761,571*
1911	3,545	11,985	19,312	7,696,957	2,235,277*	1,318,271	917,006*
1912	3,545	13,631	21,348	8,447,087	2,321,843*	1,348,254	973,589*
1913	3,546	12,400	23,219	9,620,176	2,275,313*	1,584,111	691,202*
1914	4,015	12,781	21,474	8,596,768	2,172,813*	1,747,240	425,573*
1915	4,015	12,082	20,697	8,292,688	3,151,573*	1,885,397	1,266,176*
1916	4,008	13,133	22,711	9,819,740	4,396,013*	1,858,713	2,537,300*
1917	4,008	12,133	25,272	10,725,483	2,776,915*	2,003,365	773,280*
1918	3,615	10,019	24,905	12,655,225	1,229,994*	1,931,188	–701,194*
1919	3,612	11,621	23,293	14,125,533	562,001*	1,954,509	–1,392,508*

1 Most figures reflect the calendar year. The reader is advised that some statistical reviews published data for a year ending June 30. Fixed charges for the years 1909 and 1910 were extrapolated from the June fiscal year results for 1908-13 found in Moody's, *Analyses of Investments, Steam Railroads.*
2 Net revenue is Gross operating revenue minus Operating expenses plus Other net revenue.
3 Fixed charges are interest plus lease costs.
4 Figures in Column 7, 1910-19, which are accompanied by asterisks, were revised from published figures according to data in Grand Trunk Arbitration Award, 12 George V, 1922, Sessional Papers no. 20. The changes were then also reflected in changes in net revenue in column 5 (marked by asterisks) – gross revenues and fixed charges were assumed not to have been affected by the revisions.
SOURCE   Henry E. Wallace, *The Manual of Statistics, Stock Exchange Handbook* (New York: Henry E. Wallace, various years) for 1894 to 1900; Poor's Publishing Company, *Manual of Railroads and Corporation Securities* (New York: Poor's Publishing Company, various years) for 1900-14; and Moody's Investors' Service, *Analyses of Investments, Steam Railroads* (New York: Moody's Investors' Service, various years) for 1915-19.

issues, the 4 per cent guaranteed and the first two preference stocks, were steadily paid from 1898 to World War I. Payments to equity doubled between 1899 and 1912 (see Table 4-4).

In the 1890s, the Grand Trunk's dominant position in central Canada was reduced as the CPR extended its network east to solidify its own transcontinental system. With the

gradual development of the Canadian Northern as a western competitor, the CPR faced the possibility that the Canadian Northern would link with the Grand Trunk and that eastern originating traffic would be interlined to its competitor.

The Grand Trunk fought what it regarded as an incursion to its natural market by trying to get constraints imposed in central Canada upon the CPR.[19] When it lost this battle, it

Table 4-4

Dividends Paid by the Grand Trunk Railway, 1898-1913

	4% guaranteed	Yield	First preference	Yield	Second preference	Yield	Third preference	Yield	Total
	£	%	£	%	£	%	£	%	£
1898	104,396	2.0	102,505	3.0	–	–	–	–	206,901
1899	208,792	4.0	170,842	5.0	82,225	3.25	–	–	461,859
1900	208,792	4.0	170,842	5.0	75,852	3.00	–	–	455,486
1901	208,792	4.0	170,842	5.0	101,135	4.00	–	–	480,769
1902	208,792	4.0	170,842	5.0	126,420	5.00	71,646	1.0	577,700
1903	208,792	4.0	170,842	5.0	126,420	5.00	143,293	2.0	649,347
1904	255,532	4.0	170,842	5.0	126,420	5.00	–	–	552,794
1905	275,359	4.0	170,842	5.0	126,420	5.00	143,293	2.0	715,914
1906	312,412	4.0	170,842	5.0	126,420	5.00	214,939	3.0	824,613
1907	336,771	4.0	170,842	5.0	126,420	5.00	214,939	3.0	848,972
1908	382,422	4.0	170,842	5.0	63,210	2.50	–	–	616,474
1909	393,600	4.0	170,842	5.0	126,420	5.00	–	–	690,862
1910	402,775	4.0	170,842	5.0	126,420	5.00	35,823	0.5	735,860
1911	427,430	4.0	170,842	5.0	126,420	5.00	107,470	1.3	832,162
1912	483,112	4.0	170,842	5.0	126,420	5.00	179,116	2.5	959,490
1913	496,823	3.5	170,842	5.0	126,420	5.00	179,116	2.5	973,201

NOTE   Percentage yield was calculated on par value.
SOURCE   Poor's Publishing Company, *Manual of Railroads and Corporation Securities* (New York: Poor's Publishing Company, various years).

turned to build its own western subsidiary. The Grand Trunk Pacific was created in 1903 for this purpose. The federal government provided guarantees of principal and interest, and took on the building of an eastern extension (the National Transcontinental) which was to link with the Grand Trunk Pacific in Manitoba and thus provide a second transcontinental system.

The first construction phase concentrated on the relatively flat Prairie system. By 1909, the line stretched from Manitoba through to a point 130 miles west of Edmonton. By 1912, trains were running from Winnipeg through to Port Colborne, Ontario. In late 1913, the mountain section was completed and the first transcontinental train over the system reached Prince Rupert from central Canada in April 1914.

Financial difficulties developed at an early stage. The Grand Trunk Pacific's operating income from 1913 to 1917 was positive but less than its debt charges. The deficit after these charges was $2.7, $4.1, $5.5, $5.3 and $5.7 million from 1913 to 1917 inclusive; for an accumulated deficit of $23.3 million.

The deficit incurred on the government-constructed eastern section of the new transcontinental line was just as

bad. In its first year of operations, it posted a loss after debt charges of close to $6 million (Stevens, 1962, p. 465). The construction costs of this segment had trebled over original estimates, and the 1904 contract that required the Grand Trunk Pacific to pay an annual rent of 3 per cent of the construction costs and run the system would have bankrupted the Grand Trunk. Thus, from 1912 onward, whenever the government asked the Grand Trunk to take over the National Transcontinental, it refused. Up to 1915, it could legitimately do so under the terms of the 1904 contract, because the system was not finished. But each time the Grand Trunk rejected government overtures to take over the line, it indicated that even if the line had been completed, it would have been unable to support the debt payments that would be required.

Problems with the 1904 contract had developed at an early date. Since the government was in charge of construction, the legitimacy of all construction costs concerned the Grand Trunk's management. The original estimates would have resulted in an annual lease cost of about $1.5 million; but by 1917, the construction cost of the National Transcontinental had risen to over $170 million, which would have required an annual payment of over $5,160,000, an amount that was beyond the capabilities of the Grand Trunk. While unexpected costs were partially responsible for the higher than predicted construction expenditures, at least 25 per cent was found by a Royal Commission to have been "waste" (Stevens, 1962, pp. 170, 209-21 and 465).

There were other conflicts that arose over the 1904 contract. The Ontario government sponsored a branch from the main Transcontinental line at Superior Junction to Port Arthur/Fort William. The Grand Trunk proceeded rapidly with the branch because it opened the possibility of linking the western Grand Trunk Pacific system to its Ontario network via lake freighters before the difficult eastern section being built through the Canadian Shield was finished. Although the eastern section to Port Arthur was completed in 1908, the government delayed completion of its own section from Superior Junction to Winnipeg (Stevens, 1962, p. 221). The Grand Trunk Pacific could not enter Winnipeg from the lakehead until 1911. The Royal Commission that examined the National Transcontinental's construction costs also investigated the reason for the delay. Stevens summarized its findings: "It could not be conclusively proved that such a delay was deliberate, but there was more circumstantial evidence to this effect than has hanged many a man" (Stevens, 1962, p. 220).

From 1912 onward, discussions were held between the Grand Trunk and the government as to the ultimate disposition of the Grand Trunk Pacific and the National Transcontinental. The size of the National Transcontinental's debt burden reduced the options that were feasible. In 1912, the Grand Trunk refused the government's request to take over the National Transcontinental, ostensibly because the system was not finished. Private discussions were held with the Prime Minister at which time the Grand Trunk indicated the financial impossibility of the request. The Prime Minister offered informally to take over the Grand Trunk Pacific and pay back the advances made by the Grand Trunk (Currie, 1957, p. 438). But the Grand Trunk rejected the offer since it would thereby be cut off from western traffic. In 1915, the government once more asked the Grand Trunk to take possession of the National Transcontinental. When apprised of the financial impossibility of the take-over, the government offered this time to advance the interest that could not be paid. But the interest would simply have been added to the debt outstanding, and it was now clear that the profits of the National Transcontinental were not going to cover those interest costs. In late December, the Grand Trunk offered to turn over controlling interest of the Grand Trunk Pacific, in return for the repayment of advances it had made to this company. But this was rejected by the government (Stevens, 1962, pp. 460 and 467).

By 1916, the government was running the National Transcontinental. It was also the *de facto* owner of the Canadian Northern, which by this time was totally reliant on government funds to prevent foreclosure (Stevens, 1962, pp. 110-15). Faced with a mounting railway problem, the Drayton-Acworth Royal Commission was constituted to look for a solution. The Drayton-Acworth Report recommended that both the Canadian Northern, the Grand Trunk Pacific, and the Grand Trunk be acquired by the government. The problems of the Grand Trunk, it was concluded, came neither from regulatory problems nor overbuilding, but from foreign ownership:

> The Grand Trunk Company's Board of Directors is 3,000 miles away. We cannot think that the state of affairs which our investigation as discussed could have arisen had the Board been on the spot. We are forced to the conclusion that the control of an important Canadian company should be in Canada, but this cannot be secured as long as the Grand Trunk Railway is owned by shareholders in England. We have come to the conclusion, therefore, that the control not only of the Grand Trunk Pacific Company but also of the Grand Trunk Railway Company of Canada should be surrendered into the hands of the people of Canada (Stevens, 1962, p. 474).

In 1917, the Canadian government introduced a bill to nationalize the Canadian Northern. Arbitration procedures were invoked that carefully inventoried the physical assets of the Canadian Northern on a reproduction cost basis. In the end, the assets were declared greater than the liabilities and the equity holders received a consideration of some $10 million.

The Grand Trunk was not accorded equal treatment. In 1918, the government offered an annuity, eventually rising to about $3.6 million to be divided amongst the shareholders. Since this would only meet payments on the 4 per cent guaranteed stock and the first preference stock (Stevens, 1962, p. 490), the Grand Trunk opened negotiations over the terms of the annuity. These failed. In 1919, the Grand Trunk Pacific was placed in receivership by the government. The government then refused to consider any annuity. It guaranteed the interest on Grand Trunk debentures and the 4 per cent guaranteed stock and sent the matter of additional compensation to an arbitration panel. That panel met in 1921, refused to consider the replacement value of the Grand Trunk, and concentrated only on its then state of profitability. It ruled that, given the Grand Trunk's profitability at the time, the remaining equity had no value. Thus, the Grand Trunk did not get its advances back, did not receive replacement value considerations, and had all preference and common stock reduced to zero in value.

In the end, the failure of its western subsidiary led to the collapse of the Grand Trunk. Much was made at the time of the causes. Clearly little sympathy was extended to the company, partially because it was seen as an arrogant absentee owner. As time has passed, the image proffered by the 1916 Drayton-Acworth Royal Commission has solidified; the Grand Trunk management, located thousands of miles away, was swept away by unrealistic visions of western growth. In the course of this excitement, they mortgaged their own future. The failure of the western venture inevitably meant the Grand Trunk would collapse as it did.

While there is undoubtedly a kernel of truth in this characterization of events, it does not do justice to the management of the Grand Trunk. In particular, a closer examination of the Grand Trunk's position does not point to fiscal irresponsibility. It suggests the regulatory regime was the primary cause of failure – not the pursuit of a western venture that was doomed to failure. Indeed, without the failure of the regulatory regime, there is good reason to argue that the Grand Trunk should have been able to cover the guarantees it made to the Grand Trunk Pacific without itself failing.

The Grand Trunk, by 1900, possessed a mature railway system. Freight and passenger traffic were expanding steadily and operating profits permitted not only fixed charges to be covered but also dividends to be paid contin-

Table 4-5

Select Statistics, Grand Trunk Railway, 1894-1919

	Freight revenue per ton	Passenger and express revenue/ passenger	Freight revenue per ton-mile	Revenue ton-miles per mile road	Average revenue train load	Average length of haul per ton
	£	£	¢[1]	000	Tons	Miles
1894	0.285	0.192				
1895	0.275	0.192				
1896	0.283	0.194				
1897	0.288	0.165				
1898	0.291	0.150				
1899	0.281	0.178				
1900	0.284	0.177				
1901	0.280	0.181				
1902	0.284	0.176				
1903	0.287	0.178				
1904	0.275	0.182	0.70	695	244	190
1905	0.269	0.204	0.70	749	249	187
1906	0.264	0.212	0.69	860	264	191
1907	0.266	0.211	0.67	944	290	192
1908	0.255	0.177	0.68	773	275	179
1909	0.245	0.171	0.68	848	278	179
1910	0.251	0.181	0.67	884	297	176
1911	0.253	0.182	0.66	1,082	298	178
1912	0.253	0.173	0.69	1,080	314	179
1913	0.264	0.218	0.69	1,155	323	176
1914	0.253	0.187	0.68	968	339	181
1915	0.260	0.175	0.70	934	358	181
1916	0.281	0.186	0.67	1,156	340	204
1917	0.291	0.191	0.76	1,173	424	186
1918	0.371	0.233	0.90	1,391	485	202
1919	0.426	0.267	1.05	1,268	462	197

1   The conversions in Moody's from £ to $ are made at the rate of $4.86 to 1£.

SOURCE   Columns 1 and 2 from Table 4-3; columns 4 and 6 from Moody's Investors' Service, *Analysis of Railroad Investments* (New York: Moody's Investors' Service, various years), and Poor's Publishing Company, *Manual of Railroads and Corporations Securities* (New York: Poor's Publishing Company, various years); columns 3 and 5 from Moody's, *Analysis of Railroad Investments*, various years.

uously on the guaranteed 4 per cent and both first and second preference stock from 1899 to 1912. The third preference stock received intermittent payments ranging from 1 to 3 per cent (see Table 4-4).

With the maturing of the Grand Trunk system by 1900, profits grew steadily as density of traffic increased. Table 4-5 contains revenue per ton (column 1) and per passenger (column 2) statistics that show a slow decline from 1894 to about 1909, then a gradual increase to 1917. Freight revenue per ton-mile (column 3) exhibits the same general tendency. Whereas average length of haul (column 6) was relatively constant, density of traffic increased. Both the number of revenue ton-miles per mile of road operated (column 4) and the average revenue train load (column 5) trended upwards prior to 1914.

As a result of increasing traffic density and relatively stable revenues per ton carried, revenues per train-mile increased gradually over the period, as Table 4-6 (column 1) demonstrates. Increased traffic density also led to higher operating costs (column 2). The result was that net earnings per train-mile remained about the same level from 1903 to 1913. During this time, net earnings averaged 0.474 cents per train-mile and fixed expenses 0.347 cents per train-mile. During the first three years of the war (1914-16), net earnings and fixed expenses both increased to average 0.640 and 0.476 cents per train-mile, respectively. However, starting in 1917, the ratio of operating expenses to operating revenues increased. They had averaged 71 per cent between 1903-13, and 69 per cent between 1914-16. In 1918, the ratio moved to 92 per cent; in 1919, to 99 per cent.[20] Net revenues fell below the fixed charges per mile in 1918 and 1919. The

Table 4-6

Revenues, Expenses, Net Earnings and Fixed Charges per Mile of Road for the Grand Trunk Railway, 1903-19

	Revenues per train-mile	Operating expenses per train-mile	Operating expenses to revenues	Net earnings per train-mile	Fixed charges per train-mile
	$	$	%	$	$
Years ending:					
1903 June 30	1.43	1.00	0.70	0.43	0.33
1904	1.50	1.07	0.71	0.43	0.34
1905	1.50	1.04	0.69	0.46	0.33
1906	1.60	1.12	0.70	0.48	0.34
1907	1.67	1.18	0.71	0.49	0.32
1908	1.61	1.14	0.71	0.47	0.32
1909	1.61	1.13	0.70	0.48	0.35
1910	1.71	1.25	0.73	0.46	0.36
1911	1.78	1.25	0.70	0.53	0.38
1912	1.86	1.32	0.71	0.54	0.38
1913 December 31	1.95	1.51	0.77	0.44	0.37
1914	1.90	1.51	0.80	0.39	0.44
1915	1.96	1.37	0.70	0.59	0.48
1916	2.17	1.23	0.57	0.94	0.51
1917	2.60	2.00	0.77	0.60	0.53
1918	3.53	3.26	0.92	0.27	0.63
1919	3.85	3.80	0.99	0.05	0.61

NOTE   The figures taken from Moody's are expressed in U.S. dollars and are apparently derived from the £ values given in the Grank Trunk annual reports. The currency conversion was US$4.86 per £ throughout the period. Net earnings does not include other income. The surplus figures derived from Moody's for the 1910-19 period were corrected. See fn. 3, Table 4-3. These changes were then made to net revenue and operating expenses, but not gross revenue or fixed charges.

SOURCE   Columns 1, 2, 4 and 5 were taken from Moody's Investors' Service, *Analyses of Investments*, *Steam Railroads* (New York: Moody's Investors' Service, various years). Operating expenses and Net earnings in columns 2, 3 and 4 were taken from Moody's as well, but adjusted from information in Canada, House of Commons, *Sessional Papers*, no. 20, vol. LVIII, no. 6, 1922, *Grand Trunk Arbitration Award*, pp. 171 and 201.

rapid inflation experienced during the period 1917-19 and the failure of the regulatory system to increase freight rates in step with inflation (Table 4-1) was the immediate cause of the bankruptcy of the line by the end of the period.

While the regulatory regime may have forced the Grand Trunk into bankruptcy, the railway may still have acted irresponsibly in taking on guarantees for the Grand Trunk Pacific that it could not reasonably have expected to cover. In order to evaluate whether this was the case, we have to compare the guarantee, for which the Grand Trunk made itself responsible, to the surplus that might have been expected to have been generated by the operations of the Grand Trunk. Table 4-7 presents the fixed charges and the surplus after fixed charges per mile of road operated. Fixed charges were relatively constant per mile between 1900 and 1910. During much of the earlier period, improvements were financed out of operating revenues as a charge to maintenance. But as the mountain section of the Grand Trunk Pacific was built, the Grand Trunk's fixed charges increased as it advanced funds to its own subsidiary. Tables 4-8 and 4-9 show the change in the Grand Trunk's capital structure over this period. Despite the increase in debt, the surplus per mile available for the guarantee continued to increase over the period. It averaged £158 ($766) per mile between 1899 and 1903, £211 ($1,027) between 1905 and 1909, and £287 ($1,378) between 1910 and 1916. The average over the entire period (1900-16) was £226 ($1,097) per mile per year. The absolute guarantee for which the Grand Trunk was responsible was £117 ($571) per mile (1914 mileage); the conditional guarantee was £71 ($347) per mile. The absolute guarantee was covered from the beginning; both could have been met whether the 1905-09, or the 1910-16 experience is used.[21]

Table 4-7

Fixed Charges and Operating Surplus of the Grand Trunk Railway, 1894-1919

	Fixed charges as a percentage of net revenue	Fixed charges per mile	Operating surplus minus fixed charges per mile
	%	£	£
1894	110	320	neg.
1895	95	326	18
1896	89	328	39
1897	75	335	114
1898	75	329	113
1899	69	339	152
1900	71	340	139
1901	71	347	144
1902	67	343	166
1903	65	343	187
1904	69	346	159
1905	63	347	205
1906	60	348	234
1907	59	346	242
1908	61	346	220
1909	69	348	156
1910	63	359	215
1911	59	372	259
1912	58	380	275
1913	70	447	195
1914	80	435	106
1915	60	470	315
1916	42	464	641
1917	72	500	192
1918	157	534	neg.
1919	348	541	neg.

SOURCE   See Table 4-3.

Table 4-8

Capital Stock of the Grand Trunk Railway, 1894-1915

	Debt	Equity	Surplus	Total liabilities
		£		
1894	21,296,413	40,813,834		66,476,647
1904	24,389,826	42,223,355	436,466	73,046,659
1910	25,842,912	46,134,058	398,517	78,671,798
1915	43,368,106	49,573,492	327,507	102,526,045

NOTE   Debt and equity results are for December 31. Surplus is mid-year. Debt consists of debenture stock and loan capital for the years 1894, 1904, and 1910. In 1915, secured gold notes and equipment trust notes were also added.
SOURCE   Poor's Publishing Company, *Manual of the Railroads of the United States* (New York: Poor's Publishing Company, various years).

Table 4-9

Changes in Capital Stock Issued by the Grand Trunk Railway, 1894-1915

	Debt[1]		Equity and surplus		Total[2]	
	£	%	£	%	£	%
1894-1904	3,093,413	62.6	1,845,987	37.3	4,938,995	100
1904-10	1,453,086	27.3	3,872,754	72.7	5,325,840	100
1910-15	17,525,194	83.9	3,368,424	16.1	20,893,618	100
1894-1915	22,071,693	70.8	9,087,165	29.2	31,158,858	100

1 For a definition of debt, see Table 4-8.
2 This is the total of debt and equity changes.
SOURCE Poor's Publishing Company, *Manual of the Railroads of the United States* (New York: Poor's Publishing Company, various years).

In summary, two methods both show the Grand Trunk, in the absence of the aberrant 1917-19 years, should have been able to cover its liabilities. Whether we use Taft's method of projecting revenues to 1926, or examine pre-1917 historical experience, the same conclusion is reached.

Confiscation During the Expropriation Process

Considerable controversy has developed around the differential treatment accorded the two transcontinental systems. The Canadian Northern shareholders had their property evaluated on a reproduction cost basis; the Grand Trunk did not. One observer diplomatically described the difference: the Canadian government "treated a Canadian-owned railway generously; it was niggardly in its dealing with the Grand Trunk which was owned in Britain and whose shareholders had little political influence with the Dominion" (Currie, 1957, p. 479).

The difference in treatment has been ascribed to political "expediency" (Stevens, 1962, p. 499). In 1915 Borden indicated, in a letter to the Canadian High Commissioner in London, that the government's concern for the Canadian Northern arose "not so much by reason of the fate of the Canadian Northern itself as on account of our concern for the stability and reputation of a large financial institution" (Currie, 1957, p. 479). The Bank of Commerce held a large block of Canadian Northern stock and was in financial difficulty.

The stock of the Grand Trunk by way of contrast was held in England. The government in its actions and its

words left the impression that it deliberately squeezed the Grand Trunk because it was needed as the core for a government-owned system. While introducing the legislation to take over the Grand Trunk, the Minister of Railways emphasized the necessity of obtaining the Grand Trunk for good eastern terminals if the government railway was to compete with the CPR (Currie, 1957, p. 457). Similarly, the Prime Minister (Arthur Meighen), with what the official biographer of the Canadian National described as a "logical mind outrunning his sense of political discretion," informed a Canadian audience that:

> If we had not acquired that company, may I ask – was the Canadian National Railway to be called upon to duplicate the succession of feeding systems now spread through Ontario and Quebec? . . . will anyone argue or suggest that there is any possibility in the known world of making a system of railways a success which has only one fathering system in Western Canada and which has to support two trunk lines protruding eastward for thousands of lonely miles. Consequently the only proper thing to do, *by whatever method* – the essential thing to do – is to bring the Grand Trunk system of the East into corporate connection with the Canadian Northern of the West, uniting them by the two trunk lines that pass between (Stevens, 1962, p. 499).

Notwithstanding the sentiments revealed by these comments, it is true that in the period from 1912 onwards, the Canadian government offered on numerous occasions to remunerate Grand Trunk shareholders (Currie, 1957, pp. 438-41). Ultimately the lack of compensation can be ascribed to an Arbitration Board that ruled the stock had no value.[22] The arguments of the majority on this Board clearly demonstrate the failure of the regulatory system to safeguard the interests of capital. The Grand Trunk argued that U.S. precedent established fair value as reproduction value. The

Arbitration Board that had adjudicated the Canadian Northern case only two years before had valued the railway on this basis (Stevens, 1962, pp. 486-87). The Grand Trunk Arbitration Board rejected the reproduction cost standard after hearing the government argument that, since the railway regulatory agency (the Board of Railway Commissioners) did not recognize reproduction costs, the earnings upon which value of the company should depend were unlikely to be related to this rate base concept. What this argument ignored was the fact that the U.S. judiciary had ruled this to be the relevant concept not only for rate-making but also for purchase in the event of termination of the franchise. Moreover, the government argument shows that the ultimate failure of the process lay not so much in the expropriation proceedings but in the regulatory agency itself.

Even on the basis used by the Commission, it would appear that the nationalization of the Grand Trunk involved confiscation of property. The actual earnings of the Grand Trunk were understated just prior to nationalization in an attempt to get the government to aid the Grand Trunk Pacific. If these manipulations are taken into account, net earnings were positive and sufficient to cover even the Grand Trunk's obligations to the Grand Trunk Pacific. Therefore, prior to the disastrous decline in real railway rates in 1917-18, the stock of the railway cannot be said to have been worthless. To use the 1920 operating results, as the government arbitrators did, to infer a lack of future profits ignores the distortions occasioned by regulation. From 1918 onward, the Canadian authorities kept Canadian rates at levels which Table 4-1 shows were below U.S. rates; whereas up to this time, railway rates were generally similar.

The American regulatory system, as indicated, was constrained from expropriating capital. After the railways were handed back to private owners following the war, the U.S. regulatory commission had to recognize the cost of capital by increasing railway charges. This did not happen at the same rate in Canada. At the time of arbitration, the Grand Trunk argued that, if regulation in Canada was bound by the same guidelines followed in the United States, it would be operating with a surplus available for distribution to shareholders (Glazebrook, 1964, p. 173). The confiscating effect of regulation was confirmed in the following year when the chairman of the newly formed government railway, the Canadian National, claimed:

> If the Canadian National Railways in 1921 had had the benefit of the same freight and passenger rates as prevailed in the United States, it would have enabled the National Railways to have paid their operating charges and to have a net of $5,500,000 instead of a deficit of $15,900,000 (Stevens, 1962, p. 521).

The government still could have operated the most unprofitable sections itself without nationalizing the entire system. In 1912, the Grand Trunk suggested that the government henceforth operate the eastern division of the National Transcontinental. The government refused to entertain the idea, partially because of its goals to have a unified system under government control (Stevens, 1962, p. 460); however, a second reason behind its refusal illustrates a different rationale for the connection between the choice of public enterprise as a policy instrument and the likelihood that confiscation will be involved. The government made it clear that it required the profitable section of the railway to make the entire system viable – or that it intended to cross-subsidize the sections which for reasons of national unity it had built itself.

In the opening chapter, it was suggested that public enterprise would be chosen when regulation is not constrained from exploiting privately provided capital. Even a society that generally respects property rights will occasionally succumb to pressures of ideology or to events which put extraordinary pressure on men and their normal ideals. The pressures of World War I led Canadian politicians to act with less regard for fairness than was the norm until that time. When the state is threatened, it may make demands upon individual liberty that are subsequently regretted. Consequently, these pressures led to a nationalization that was accompanied by a confiscation of property.

The original interpretation of the nationalization process and its association with confiscation still permits the inference that confiscation is often unintended and perhaps secondary to other goals. In contrast, the cross-subsidization motive does not. If a government acquires part of a system with the intent to use the profits derived therefrom to subsidize another purpose, confiscation is more likely. Should the state compensate the owners of capital for the income stream foregone, no cross-subsidization is possible. Only if the government nationalizes a competitive sector with the intent of moving earnings higher will there be no confiscation – for then it is the state's actions that create the supra-normal earnings, and it can hardly be characterized as expropriating what it creates. The latter characterization would seem to be inappropriate in the Canadian railway industry – especially in light of post-nationalization railway rate levels.

Conclusion

Nationalization cannot be ascribed to one motive. It emerges from a complex set of forces that determine the outcome of the political process. Yet, if the theory postulated here is correct, it may often be accompanied by a form of expropriation or confiscation which is the instrument of last choice in a state that prefers to rely upon private ownership of the means of production. It emerges when regulation fails as an efficient intermediator between the public and private sectors. The Canadian railway example shows how that failure can develop.

Pushed by the political pressures of war, faced with railways of different strengths (partially the result of previous government policy), unconstrained by judicial rulings like their counterparts in the United States, the Canadian regulators forced real rail rates to record low levels and reduced net earnings of some rail lines to zero. The Canadian government, reacting to political pressures as well as to a xenophobic dislike of one of the two railways that went bankrupt at the time, acted in what at best can be called a discriminatory fashion. Whether these results were beyond the control of those in charge is not the issue. It is clear that, in the end, capital had to rely on the goodwill of the state for protection from confiscation. Reliance on such goodwill, without the protection afforded by a written constitution that guaranteed the right to private property, proved inadequate in the case of the Canadian railway system.

5 Judicial Constraints in Canada and the Evolution of the Regulatory Process

The formation of the Canadian National Railways (CNR) illustrates one type of contractual failure that can occur during the regulatory process if the state is not prevented from exercising its powers to confiscate property. Nonetheless, there were other industries where contractual renegotiations were difficult, but where the state did not nationalize the utility. That this was the case does not diminish the importance of constraining the state so that it is prevented from acting in an opportunistic fashion during such renegotiations. Nor should it prevent questioning why nationalization was not more widespread. This chapter addresses this question.

If the reason was simply that the state showed little tendency to act in an opportunistic fashion, then the type of transactions failure described in the last chapter may be relatively unimportant. On the other hand, fortuitous circumstances may have constrained the operation of opportunistic behaviour on the part of the state. If this was the case, the right to have due process and the right to private property are still critical to the smooth functioning of the regulatory process. Finally, the outcome could have been the result of a strategy adopted by the industry to counter or to deflect the type of opportunistic behaviour of the state that leads to transactions failure. In the latter case, a study of events provides those who are interested in the nexus of government and business relationships with an outline of how a well defined business strategy can deflect the confiscatory power of the state. It also may serve to suggest the extent to which state powers, exercised in a less venal fashion (through traditional regulation), can equally be thwarted.

Each of these explanations is relevant to the history of the evolution of regulation in Canada. In some instances, the state was leery of expropriation and either avoided transactions failure during renegotiations or chose, for the renegotiation process, an alternate institution that essentially committed it to avoid the use of its confiscatory powers. In other cases, unforeseen events permitted the adoption of a business strategy that either forestalled or prevented opportunistic behaviour on the part of the state.

Understanding the relative importance of these alternate explanations of the way in which state-business relations developed requires separate case studies of events in different provinces. Regulation did evolve in Canada as the re-

contracting problem arose. But its form tended to differ substantially across the country – if only because the Canadian constitution gave to the provinces control over property at the local level, and most utilities were local in nature. Judicial rulings at the provincial level on the legality of regulatory activity created a diffuse set of precedents with less authority for the process as a whole than the U.S. Supreme Court's rulings that provided a single consistent set of guidelines for all of the United States.

In this and the following chapters, the variety of forces that led to contractual failure is described. In some cases, it was the opportunistic behaviour of the state. In other cases, it was the disappearance of the large-numbers situation which is a prerequisite for successful recontracting. Because of technological considerations or a consolidation strategy by a dominant firm that eliminated rivals, one company emerged as the sole party with which the public had to contract. Where the public no longer perceived that it had an alternative to the incumbent during recontracting exercises, it sought a new vehicle for regulation. In still other cases, the crisis developed when, either through a quirk of fate or by deliberate strategy, utilities managed to escape local regulation. Finally, in a few cases, the contracting process broke down because of the complexity of the service (usually a type of cross-subsidization) required by the state in return for the franchise it was granting.

Before these case studies can be examined in depth, the influence of the Canadian judicial system on the evolutionary process needs to be discussed. As was stressed in Chapter 3, constitutional provisions protecting private property and judicial decisions based thereon were critical for the evolution of the modern regulatory tribunal in the United States. While the judiciary played a less dominant role in Canada than in the United States, it nevertheless did eventually come to exert some restraint on the actions of the state.

The Role of the Judiciary in Canada

The creation of the Canadian National Railways system illustrates the latitude that the Canadian Parliament possesses. When the legislature wishes to confiscate, it can do so, although its powers in this area are not unlimited. The political system cannot generally ignore the moral standards of society that decry theft.

In Canada, these mores have evolved with the aid of a judicial system that managed to place restrictions on the ability of Parliament to confiscate private property. The judiciary did so by forcing the legislature to be specific about its desire to confiscate. As such, it raised the costs of confiscation by forcing the legislative branch to take full responsibility for its actions. In these circumstances, an electorate can more readily monitor the actions of its elected officials. As such, it is in a better position to enforce the same standards for public action as are applicable in the private domain.

Common Law and Confiscation

In the first instance, the Canadian judiciary relied on precedents from British Common Law to constrain the legislature during acts of expropriation. The legislature was conceded to have the ability to expropriate without compensation. As one judgment noted, "The prohibition 'thou shalt not steal' has no legal force upon the sovereign body and there would be no necessity for compensation to be given. We have no restriction upon the power of the legislature as is found in some states."[1]

Nevertheless, the Canadian judiciary did embrace British Common Law precedent that regarded the compulsory taking of property without compensation as exorbitant and to be used with due consideration. British law had insisted that expropriation must be based upon statute and that all such statutes would be strictly construed; that is, no powers would be read into an act of the legislature that were not explicitly stated – especially when it came to matters that affected private property. As a result, the judiciary adopted what has come to be known as the rule of strict construction: the right to private property cannot be removed unless it is clearly stated in a statute. Expropriation without compensation was such an interference with the right to property; therefore, Common Law tradition developed that government could confiscate only by specifically voiding the right to private property via statute (Challies, 1963, pp. 1-11, 13 and 77 ff.).

The Evolution of Rulings on
Regulation and Confiscation

The strict constructionist rule meant that, unless specifically authorized to take property without compensation, an agency created via statute by the state to negotiate or arbitrate a contract with utilities could be constrained by the judiciary from acting in an opportunistic fashion. By choosing the regulatory agency, government was essentially able to bind itself (though not permanently) to an arbitration process that was subject to the checks and balances inherent in judicial review. As such, regulatory agencies should not be regarded as instruments that were captured by the powerful interests they came to regulate – at least not with regards to the protection they offered private property. As long as the enabling legislation that created them did not specifically grant the power to take property without confiscation, their actions were constrained and their decisions were subject to judicial review. The degree of the constraint depended upon the actions that the judiciary perceived as confiscatory. Subject then to this caveat, the very choice of the instrument affected the outcome – at least when it came to the protection the regulatory process potentially offered to private property.

The judiciary's role, however, did not end with the creation of the regulatory agency. Rulings were still required to define the type of regulatory conduct that would be construed as confiscatory. Several types of decisions served eventually to give some protection to Canadian utilities.

The clearest set of judgments to emerge dealt with the terms that were to govern public take-overs. Franchises in Ontario allowed for termination and public purchase after a set period. Indeed, the *Ontario Municipal Act* and the *Ontario Railways Act* required a termination date, thereby preventing municipalities from voiding their right to renegotiation by granting perpetual franchises. The terms of the franchises, defined by a legislative act in most cases, generally allowed for arbitration of the purchase price. Clauses in municipal charters were also included in British Columbia, Manitoba, Ontario, and Quebec which required municipalities wishing to start their own utility, where a private utility already existed, to buy out the private party at an arbitrated price. Since none of these clauses gave public authorities the right to confiscate property without compensation, actions taken thereunder were subject to judicial review. Thus, the judiciary was given the opportunity to place constraints on the public taking of private property without adequate compensation.

It is a characteristic of the law that practice and judicial rulings are interrelated in such a way that it is sometimes difficult to point to a particular ruling that establishes a definitive precedent. While the Smyth v. Ames (1898) ruling is widely held to have provided a key turning point in U.S. regulatory history, it is more difficult to find a similar Canadian case – especially as it pertains to expropriation of a utility. While various expropriation laws provided the Canadian state with the power to take property, initially they were primarily directed to the taking of land in connection with public works and later for the construction of railways. The era of nationalization or municipalization of gas, electric companies, and municipal railways did not come until the turn of the century.

Nevertheless, municipalization of waterworks in several Canadian cities did occur prior to 1900. In both Toronto and Winnipeg, agreement for the public purchase of the utility was voluntarily reached between the municipality and a private company that would have had some value as a precedent. In Toronto the value placed on the works was essentially replacement value less depreciation plus an amount for goodwill because of unexpired franchises.[2]

The other precedents that Canadian courts would have had before them were early decisions on nationalization of utilities in the United Kingdom. McKay (1976) relates that the move to the municipalization of tramways was led by Edinburgh in 1894. In this case, the House of Lords ruled that reproduction cost less depreciation was the appropriate price to pay for the expropriated company.[3] This ruling was confirmed in other cases.[4]

In keeping with these decisions, the Canadian courts too ruled that the value of businesses being expropriated should be set equal to reproduction cost less depreciation, as early as 1904[5] – only six years after the U.S. Supreme Court's Smyth v. Ames decision. The use of reproduction cost was confirmed during the tumultuous first two decades of the twentieth century as various Ontario municipal governments moved to expropriate local street railway and power companies. In 1916, the courts ruled that public authorities could not value a utility as scrap no matter what plans they had for it.[6] In the Peterborough case, the Supreme Court of Ontario ruled that the amount paid should be what it would "reasonably and properly cost to produce a property of its character." Reproduction cost was confirmed as the standard when Toronto acquired the Toronto Railway Company in the early 1920s.[7] The Judicial Committee of the Privy Council in 1924 ruled that a fair method of valuing the railway was reproduction cost less depreciation (including obsolescence). This decision also stated that current (1922) prices had to be used to evaluate the property even though substantial inflation had just occurred, since, as of 1922, "prices had . . . become fairly stabilized." Even so, the decision noted that actual cost or market value might also be of assistance to arbitrators during take-over proceedings (Challies, 1963, pp. 171 and 175).

By the 1920s, these decisions provided a standard against which the actions of governments could be judged. In the British tradition, they served to influence the moral im-

perative under which the executive functions. The latter, with specifically worded statutes passed by the legislature, could still confiscate property. The Canadian railway case provides one such example. But as the number of decisions mounted as to what involved public theft in the utility sector, so too did the constraints that bound public behaviour.

Other judicial rulings served to place additional constraints on the expropriation process. Where only part of a property fell within the jurisdiction of a government, expropriation of that part, it was ruled, required payment that took into account the overall earning power of the expropriated portion in relation to the total concern. The courts ruled that the value of such a property could exceed its market value if it had been a separate entity – when the value to the owner was greater in light of the purpose to which the property was being used (Challies, 1963, p. 99). This meant that where part of a property was taken, compensation was to be arrived at by establishing the value of the entire property before and the value of the remaining property after expropriation, and then by subtracting the second from the first.[8] Thus, if the property to be expropriated was generating revenues that accrued to the system as a whole (a portion of a street railway), these revenues would have to be considered and more than just the replacement value of the assets of the particular entity being expropriated would have to be paid as compensation. This effectively increased the cost of expropriation in those circumstances where a municipality wanted to take over only part of a going concern. It also offered the perspicacious industrialist a strategy that could be used to increase the cost of a public buyout – the strategy being an agglomeration of franchises across several municipalities.

The judiciary also protected private property in some situations by recognizing the need to compensate for "going value." Going value, according to Challies, is "an expression of the added value of the plant as a whole over the sum of the values of its component parts which is attached to it because it is an active and successful operation and earning a return." Its use, however, seems to have been associated with the notion that a plant could have value above its reproduction cost because of an unexpired franchise. In three English decisions, going value was explicitly related to an unexpired franchise during the expropriation of water and gas utilities (Challies, 1963, pp. 192 and 194-95). This too offered additional protection. If a long-term franchise could be obtained, the costs of expropriation would be all that much higher.

Of course, in recognition of the paramountcy of Parliament, a statute could expressly rule out such compensation. In the case of Toronto's expropriation of the horsedrawn tramway in the early 1890s, the courts ruled no franchise value should be awarded because the franchise had been terminated with the take-over, as was specified in the original franchise contract.[9] In a case involving the Town of Berlin,[10] the Canadian courts ruled that no "going value" compensation was required because section 41 of the *Ontario Street Railways Act* prevented a city council from granting a franchise of more than 20 years and the franchise had expired. Implicitly then, going value would be higher where there was a perpetual franchise. Indeed, the English decisions recognizing going value involved capitalization of net earnings of the unexpired portion of a franchise (Challies, 1963, p. 188). Thus, in situations where utility owners could link the threatened portion of their utility system to other parts of a system that possessed a perpetual or longer-lived franchise, or where a perpetual franchise was obtained, the cost of expropriation would be increased because compensation would have to include more than just payment for reproduction cost.

The Evolution of Regulation via Independent Tribunal

If regulation was to provide an alternative to public enterprise, constraints had to be placed upon both the compensation required, if renegotiations broke down and take-over occurred, and also upon the decisions taken by the regulatory tribunal. Property can be expropriated, not only by physically transferring the ownership of assets, but also by interfering with the earnings stream from those assets. It was the U.S. Supreme Court's recognition of the latter problem that eventually led it to formulate the guidelines that allowed the modern regulatory agency to develop.

Even though Canada did not have the due process clauses of the U.S. Constitution, it did adopt the precedent of British Common Law with regards to property rights. The Canadian judiciary, by its adoption of the strict constructionist rule, placed bounds upon administrative actions. It thereby created the foundation for the emergence of the regulatory tribunal that was to be responsible for renegotiating utility contracts – an agent that was superior to the special bills committees of the provincial legislatures that up to about 1910 had most of the authority in the area.

Legislative committees (sometimes a railway committee, at other times the private bills committee), while not always directly involved at the outset in the negotiation of the franchises between the utility and a municipality, were responsible for approval of city charters and the incorporation bills of the utilities that specified the terms of the franchise agreements that were reached. These committees suffered several shortcomings: they had no particular expertise in utility matters; they were subject to the complaint that corruption tainted the validity of the contract; and finally, with the backing of a legislature which in Canada could confiscate without compensation, they could act in an opportunistic fashion and cause the bargaining process to break down.

Regulatory agencies offered potential solutions to all three problems. First, specialization in utility matters alone promised to improve the expertise that could be brought to bear on such difficult problems as debt-equity ratios, depreciation allowances, and the allowable rate of return – all problems that were becoming an increasing worry to the various authorities who were renegotiating franchise contracts with utilities at the turn of the century. Second, enabling legislation could specify conflict-of-interest guidelines to reduce the possibility of corruption. This was done by establishing the agencies as quasi-judicial entities – with appointments coming from the judiciary. It was also accomplished by stipulations such as those found in the Nova Scotia legislation[11] to the effect that commissioners could not be in the employ, own stock, or "be in any way interested" in the utilities under their jurisdiction.

The final and perhaps most important characteristic for the success of regulatory agencies was that with the appropriate judicial constraints they could be bound not to exercise the confiscatory power possessed by the legislature. In light of the strict constructionist view taken by the courts of legislation that affected property rights, regulatory agencies would not have been able to act with as much power as could the state – unless it was specifically provided for in the enabling legislation. But far from doing so, the state left no doubt that such power was not being bestowed. In creating the early regulatory boards, the enabling acts invariably referred to the responsibility of the agency to set a "just and reasonable" price. The regulatory agency, therefore, can be viewed as an instrument by which the state restricted its power of confiscation and transferred the difficult task of contract renegotiation to an institution of its own making that did not suffer the inherent defect of being too powerful.

The judicial system had a second indirect influence on the success of these agencies. Judicial decisions on the method of valuing property during expropriations provided a guide for regulatory behaviour. While eventually the reproduction cost standard was modified to a prudent investment standard to take into account changing circumstances, it provided an initial guideline for the regulatory agencies in Nova Scotia, New Brunswick, and Manitoba where the agencies most closely came to resemble the independent regulatory tribunals found in the United States and where such a standard had been adopted as the result of U.S. Supreme Court rulings.

This does not mean that the Canadian regulatory process in this early period was subject to the same constraints as existed in the United States. While the constructionist interpretation could restrict the latitude possessed by the agency, there was no clear-cut application of this doctrine to an agency's decision that created a widely quoted precedent as there was in the United States. The reason for this is that the constructionist doctrine appears to have been applied mainly to situations where title to physical assets was transferred. Regulatory situations where the income stream associated with ownership was affected did not receive the same attention in Canada as they did in the United States, perhaps because the Canadian judiciary took longer to recognize that abuse by the state of the latter also fell within its field of responsibility.

One manifestation of this judicial oversight is the lack of clear-cut precedent as to type of rate base that had to be used – or even whether a rate base need be used at all. The United States standard was confirmed as appropriate when used in New Brunswick rulings, but this decision noted other methods could also be applied. At the federal level, both for rail and telephones, they clearly were. Indeed, when the CPR tried to get the Canadian Supreme Court to consider whether failure to use the fair-return-on-fair-value standard violated the Common Law, the Canadian Supreme Court would not hear the case.

There was a second reason why the type of safeguards against opportunism in the use of regulatory agencies were not as absolute in Canada as in the United States. What the legislature gave could be taken away. Several examples of this can be found. Various utilities requested assurances from the state, before they committed capital, that the cities they served could not act opportunistically by creating their own subsidized competitors. Clauses were therefore put in city charters requiring them to buy the private utilities if they proceeded with municipally owned utilities. In some cases, the cities were able to have the legislature amend their charters at a later date and remove these buyout clauses.

The fate of the Grand Trunk also illustrates the uncertainty of the protection given private capital in Canada. While regulatory policy contributed in large part to this company's downfall, pursuit of legal remedies was academic once the expropriation legislation was passed because it had paramountcy.

Despite these shortcomings, regulatory boards did emerge in Canada at much the same time as they did in the United States. The advantages they possessed in terms of specialization of function, relative freedom from corruption, and the ability to continuously monitor the regulatory contract were sufficient to outweigh their disadvantage under a system of British Common Law that did not guarantee property rights. On the other hand, the latter situation may explain why regulatory boards were not extensively adopted in Canada.

At the federal level, the Board of Railway Commissioners was created in 1903 and given the additional jurisdiction over telephones in 1906 (Wright, 1963). Public utilities boards also emerged at the provincial level: in 1906 in Ontario, in 1909 in Quebec and Nova Scotia, in 1910 in New Brunswick, in 1912 in Manitoba, and in 1915 in Alberta. In the latter four jurisdictions, these boards came to develop rules somewhat akin to those used in the United States that tended to protect the long-lived capital that, once invested, was so susceptible to confiscation by irascible politicians.

The regulatory boards, which were adopted in Canada, differed in their authority. The Ontario Board was excluded from any influence in the electrical field, and found itself primarily overseeing rural telephone companies. In Quebec, full authority to set rates did not occur until 1935. Until then, the Quebec commission was essentially a court of last resort – to be used if a municipality and a utility could not reach agreement regarding a franchise contract. In Manitoba, the regulatory commission was chosen as much to oversee publicly owned companies as to negotiate a contract between the state and the privately owned utilities.

Because of the differences that emerged in instrument choice across the country, separate chapters are reserved for an examination of the nature of the regulatory environment that emerged in Ontario, Quebec, and Manitoba. Nova Scotia, New Brunswick, and Alberta, however, resembled one another in their development of an independent tribunal that played an important role in renegotiating regulatory contracts at the beginning of the century. In each case, the regulatory tribunal served to regularize the recontracting process, to change it from one characterized by intermittent crisis-laden confrontations to one that provided for ongoing adjustment of the terms of the contract between the state and the privately owned utility.

Nova Scotia

Nova Scotia adopted and developed the modern form of regulatory tribunal before all other provinces. Nova Scotia history in this area illustrates the success of this instrument during difficult renegotiations of the type that led to contractual failure at the national level in the railway industry.

Prior to 1900, separate companies were responsible for gas, lighting, and tramway service in Halifax. By 1902, however, the Halifax Electric Tramway Company Limited controlled the railway and all the electric lighting and gas in the city.[12] Its charter, granted in 1895,[13] gave the Halifax Electric Tramway Company the right to purchase the franchise of the existing Halifax Street Railway Company,[14] and the Nova Scotia Power Company.[15] These predecessors had been given the right to serve Halifax with electricity and to electrify the tramway system. But so little progress was made with electrification that the legislature turned to Boston interests in 1895 to complete the task. With the 1895 charter, the new company obtained the right to remove the property of its two predecessors and provision was made in the act to pay these companies the "then" value of the equipment so removed with no allowance for "past or future" profits. On the condition that the electrification terms were met and construction was completed within a given two-year time period, the new company received an exclusive franchise for transit in Halifax for a period of 21 years. A payment of 4 per cent of gross tramway revenues plus a $1,000 licence fee were to be remitted to the city. Tramway rates were set at 5 cents per single fare.

Until 1903, regulation of utilities in Nova Scotia was accomplished by franchise contract, with the terms often being directly included in the company's charter. While these terms might be negotiated at the municipal level, the charter required an act of the legislature and therefore left the senior government as an arbitrator. Regulatory powers, however, were enshrined in legislation separate from the company charters shortly after the turn of the century.

Nova Scotia not only looked to Boston interests to electrify its tramway system, but also adopted an interventionist regulatory approach that was more akin to that being followed in Massachusetts than that being pursued elsewhere in Canada. As early as 1903, Nova Scotia required telephone tolls to be filed with the government, and gave the Governor-in-Council the right to "alter, reduce, or modify" these rates.[16] In 1907, Nova Scotia required the prices of electric light and energy to be filed and gave the Governor-in-Council the right to disallow increases in these rates.[17] In 1909, a regulatory board, the Public Utility Commissioners (PUC), was given control over telephones, heat, light, water, and power. The PUC was entrusted with the task of ensuring that prices were "reasonable and just." It could order modifications in rates "as the justice of the case may require" and specify "on such terms and subject to such conditions as are just that the public utility furnish reasonably adequate service."[18] Amendments in 1912 gave the PUC the right to determine "the fair value of the property of any public utility."[19] It was also given the power of approval of new capital issues at the same time.

Following the 1912 amendments, the Nova Scotia Board immediately announced that it would begin to value the rate base of the utilities.[20] In 1914, it began a comprehensive audit of the capital base of the Maritime Telegraph and Telephone Company stating that it would look at the "existing value," what has come to be known as the reproduction cost standard. This company had been reorganized in 1910, taking over the assets of the Nova Scotia Telephone Company. The latter had been originally organized in 1886 to hold Bell Telephone's Nova Scotia properties. Because records of the preceding company were not complete, the PUC had to conduct a complete evaluation by inventorying all property and equipment of the Maritime Telegraph and Telephone Company, a task which was completed by January 1917. In its 1918 decision, the Board used the reproduction cost less depreciation to set the capital base.[21]

A year earlier, in 1917, the Nova Scotia legislature specified that the rate of return to which a public utility was entitled would be set at 8 per cent of the "value of its property, assets, and undertakings."[22] Any excess above this would be split between the company and the provincial treasurer in a ratio of 1 to 3. By 1923, this apportionment had been revised to allow for an equal division of the surplus. Moreover, the 8-per-cent rate was defined to include the depreciation allowance.[23]

Together, the definition of the rate base and the specification of the rate of return provided utilities with a precisely defined environment under which they could be expected to operate. The regulatory tribunal was a new institution and might have been expected to devise its rules somewhat slowly. Having U.S. decisions as precedents clearly facilitated its task.[24]

This new (at least for Canada) form of regulatory instrument served to diffuse a contractual crisis that developed in the relations between Halifax and the electrical and transit utility that served the city. The way in which this was done shows the efficacy of the independent tribunal, when operating under strict fair-value-on-fair-return guidelines. The crisis that faced the regulatory system resulted from a take-over of the Halifax Electric Tramway Company by a Montreal-based syndicate. Electric power and tramways companies tended to be owned by the same company because the transit operations guaranteed a large base load for the power system and thus substantially reduced the risk of early power developments. These early power developments were still risky undertakings, at least when it came to penetrating domestic households. Manufactured gas and kerosene offered competition for purposes of both cooking and illumination. Manufactured gas was also less expensive than electricity when the latter was generated by thermal power.

In other major Canadian cities, the development of new lower cost electric energy from hydro-power emerged during the first decade of the twentieth century. In Vancouver, the British Columbia Electric Railway was closely connected with the development of hydro-electricity through the Vancouver Power Company, which began producing hydro-electric power by 1904. In Manitoba, the Winnipeg Electric Railway Company was a joint partner with Ogilvie flour mill backers in the Winnipeg General Power Company. Power from the latter was flowing into Winnipeg by 1906. In Montreal, a syndicate headed by E. A. Robert joined the Montreal Street Railway Company around 1910 with a smaller power company – the Canadian Light and Power Company – thereby allowing the latter to expand into the Montreal market that was otherwise tightly controlled by Montreal Light, Heat and Power. Here hydro-power had already begun to serve Montreal by the late 1890s. In Ontario, the privately owned firm that produced hydro-electric power at Niagara Falls was linked to both the Toronto Electric Light Company and the Toronto Street Railway Company.

In contrast, no hydro-power had been developed to serve the Halifax area by the beginning of World War I. Table 5-1 compares the monthly bills for different kilowatt-hour classes for Vancouver, Winnipeg, Toronto, Montreal, and Halifax as of 1913. Halifax rates were higher than those of the other major cities being served by hydro-power.

Recognizing the potential advantages of hydro-electric power development, two groups obtained Nova Scotia charters to develop such power. In 1909, the Nova Scotia Power and Pulp Company, led by E. A. Robert, who was at the same time in the process of merging the Montreal Tramways Company with a power company he controlled, obtained the right to the Gaspereau site, 55 miles from Halifax.[25] In 1910, the Nova Scotia Hydraulic Company was chartered to develop power on the Mersey River.[26] In order to guarantee a base load for hydro-development, both groups began acquiring stock in the Halifax Electric Tramway Company. Initially, neither group was able to obtain sufficient stock for control.[27]

The management of the tramway company fought a rearguard effort to prevent take-over by seeking allies from the politicians in Halifax. In 1912, the street railway negotiated a new franchise contract with the city for another 21-year term. In return for the franchise extension, the company agreed to maintain its payment of 4 per cent of gross tramway revenues to the city, to make an additional payment of 2 per cent of lighting and gas receipts, and to restrict dividends to 8 per cent. The new contract, however, had to be approved by the Railway and Municipal Committee of the legislature. Those who were trying to gain control of the Halifax company opposed the new contract. The Committee responded by forwarding a bill to the legislature that gave the Governor-in-Council the right to approve the new contract,

Table 5-1

A Comparison of Monthly Electrical Bills in Vancouver, Winnipeg, Toronto, Montreal, and Halifax, by Consumption Class, 1913

	Vancouver	Winnipeg	Toronto	Montreal	Halifax
			Dollars		
Consumption class :					
15 kwh	1.44	0.50	0.76	1.11	1.58
20 kwh	1.89	0.60	1.04	1.43	2.10
40 kwh	3.64	1.20	1.66	2.71	4.20
60 kwh		1.80	2.20	3.99	6.30

SOURCE Canada, Dominion Bureau of Statistics, Public Utilities Branch, *Index Numbers of Rates for Electricity for Residence Lighting and Tables of Monthly Bills for Domestic Service* (Ottawa: Department of Industry, Trade and Commerce, 1931).

but forbade the creation of a new company for one year, thereby thwarting an immediate take-over and amalgamation by either of the two suitors.[28]

The new contract was not proclaimed, and in 1913 the old board of directors of the Halifax Electric Tramway Company was dismissed and the new board, now under control of the Montreal-led group, returned to the legislature for the right to incorporate a new company that would contain the Halifax Electric Tramway Company and have the right to develop power at the Gaspereau site. Halifax, now extremely concerned that it would have no regulatory control, asked the legislature for the right to acquire the street railway. Both requests were rejected. The legislature was then asked by the Halifax Electric Tramway Company for a new charter that would enable it to increase its capitalization to develop the Gaspereau site. Once more, the request was rejected. Finally, the company received an amendment in its charter to increase capitalization from $1.5 million to $2 million.[29]

In the midst of this conflict, the PUC was called upon to rule on the application of the company to issue new stock to bring the capitalization up to $2 million.[30] Opponents of the new management were concerned with the potential padding of the rate base that stock-watering might accomplish and the concomitant increase in utility rates that would follow.

The Board had already indicated in its 1913 annual report that it was carefully beginning to evaluate the cost of property of different public utilities and would examine the disposition of stock issues in the future. As such, it offered protection for the foes of the new stock issue who argued that such stock amounted to watering and would lead to higher dividend requirements and higher utility rates at a later date. If capital value for rate purposes did not include capital that was issued but not invested in plant and equipment, then the recapitalization of the company that was being sought would not have deleterious effects upon consumers.

When the PUC came to dealing with the Halifax tramway's request to issue new stock, it examined evidence on the value of capital invested in the company and found that the "then" value of plant and equipment was already greater than the permitted capitalization. Although the city objected to the issuance of stock at par of $100 when the market value was about $160, the Commissioners simply noted that it was not their concern how profits were distributed, since this did not affect the calculation of the rate base. Although the new capitalization would be $2 million, book value of plant and equipment was at least $2.8 million, and reproduction cost

less depreciation was undoubtedly higher (the city itself had been willing to pay about $3 million the previous year in its request for municipalization). The PUC therefore approved the new issue, subject to its being used to retire existing debt of an equal amount.

The PUC's actions gave it credibility as a competent arbitrator. Its reputation was utilized almost immediately by the legislature, for, in 1914, the new owners of the tramways applied for a charter for the Nova Scotia Tramways and Power Company that would permit the acquisition of the street railway and two potential hydro sites. Capitalization of $20 million (versus the previous $2 million) and freedom from PUC regulation were both sought. Opposition from Halifax developed immediately. Stock-watering and freedom from regulation were the two focal points around which opposition organized. While a bill was passed incorporating a new company,[31] it was made subject to PUC control. This meant that the issuance of new stock would be scrutinized. Protection was also granted to the city of Halifax. The charter specified that both tramway fares and electric rates could not be increased. The 4 per cent gross revenue tax was to be continued, with a guarantee that the aggregate yearly amount paid to Halifax not be less than that turned over in 1913. Moreover, the company agreed to pay 2 per cent of gross receipts on electrical energy and gas used for lighting and power in the city. In effect, this franchise was almost the same as that agreed to by the old management of the company and the city in 1912 – the major difference lying in the failure to specify an 8-per-cent constraint on profits. But the actions of the PUC and the 1917 legislative act limiting net earnings to 8 per cent brought about the latter.

After the creation of the new company, Nova Scotia Light and Power applied in 1915 to the Board to issue $12.5 million in equity and debt to effect the take-over. The Board deliberated for a year, and in early 1916 announced that it would allow only $5,550,000 to be issued.[32] The Board broke down its allowance as:

1	Value of tramway	$3,450,000
	less bonded debt	600,000
		2,850,000
2	Value of Gaspereau lands	300,000
3	Debt	600,000
4	Investment required for	
	development of Gaspereau power site	1,500,000
5	Working capital	300,000
	Total	$5,550,000

The value of the tramway was based on reproduction costs less depreciation.

The PUC therefore prevented stock from being issued for inflated values of the tramway. Moreover, its adoption of a useful capital concept in defining rate base meant that, in setting rates, it would not recognize the portion of capital issued that did not lead to power generation. As such, it ensured that stock-watering would have no impact on rates. Indeed, in subsequent years, the Board authorized expenditure of those funds raised but not used for the development of hydro-power, therefore keeping careful track of increments in capital stock actually used.[33]

The PUC was called upon to settle one other contentious rate issue connected with this company. In 1922, following the rapid inflationary period of the late war period, the Commission undertook to re-evaluate the rate base it was using. Arguing that the rapid inflation made reproduction costs no longer fair, it adopted a prudent investment standard. The new rate base was to be the original reproduction cost, determined in 1915, plus subsequent investment. Essentially the Commission argued that price levels had become so volatile that it had become unreasonable to set rates based on reproduction costs – especially when the rate base would be allowed to stand for a decade or so. By 1924, the Board was also using an 8-per-cent return on separately defined capitalization in each segment of the company's business to define required revenues therein.

The take-over and subsequent recapitalization of the Halifax Electric Tramway Company elicited substantial criticism at the time. As the contest for control of the Halifax company developed, the stock had been bid up from $97 per share in 1908 to $160 by 1914. Charges that higher stock prices would lead to higher interest and dividend payments were behind much of the public criticism. The actions of the PUC served to diffuse this criticism. Nevertheless, there is a residue of sentiment that, despite the protection offered by the PUC, Haligonians were bested. Armstrong and Nelles (1976) use the phrase "tweaked." In reality, it was the Nova Scotian regulatory system that won the contest. Much of the watered stock that was issued failed to see any return for the next decade.

The feeling that Nova Scotia was bested during the take-over process undoubtedly relates to the profits made by the promoters of the new hydro-scheme. Payment of inordinately high prices for the Halifax Electric Tramway Company was seen as one method by which the capital base might be padded. Table 5-2 contains financial statistics pertaining to the Halifax Electric Tramway Company that allow an evaluation of the extent to which the movement in stock prices was "speculative" and not based on underlying real trends. While the stock price moved up some 60 per cent from 1908 until the take-over in 1914 (column 1), the value

of capital when evaluated, using the market price of equity, did not reach excessive levels relative to either the value of initial capital subscribed plus surplus (column 4), or to the book value of property (column 5). Essentially the take-over battle simply moved equity prices from a value that was discounted relative to book value up to the latter level.

There was another reason that equity prices should have been expected to trend upwards over the period. Column 3 of Table 5-2 contains a measure of profitability – net earnings to capital subscribed plus surplus. The average return was 6.9 per cent between 1901 and 1905. It had increased to an average of 9.2 per cent between 1909 and 1913. It is natural therefore to find the price of the stock to have increased over this period.

Table 5-3 presents the return to total capital subscribed, and equity (columns 1 and 3; 2 and 4, respectively). In each case the return is calculated first by using capital subscribed (columns 1 and 3), and then using the market value of equity (columns 2 and 4). If the market value of equity was simply reflecting higher earnings and if risk was relatively constant, rates of return using market value of equity (columns 2 and 4) should be relatively constant – reflecting the required rate demanded by the market. The equity return based on market value is relatively constant from 1906 onward.[34] This suggests the increase in the market price of equity from 1908 to 1913 primarily reflected the increasing profits that were being generated by the company over this period and were not being generated by "speculative activity" of the acquiring firm.

The Board's decision that the rate base must be related to the reproduction cost of property and not to market value of stock reduced the incentive to inflate the latter. Nevertheless, it might be argued by critics that the regulatory system was overly generous in awarding the 8 per cent on capital (though this was the rate voluntarily agreed upon by Halifax and the management of the Halifax Electric Tramway Company in 1912). This does not appear to be the case. If this issue is examined from a cost-of-capital view, using the average equity yield produced by the market of 10.03 per cent (column 4) and debt costs of 5 per cent,[35] and the actual mean equity-debt ratio of 2.33 for the period 1911-15, capital costs were 8.52 per cent, somewhat more than the 8 per cent eventually granted. On both grounds then, we can reject the contention that regulation in Nova Scotia was excessively lenient.

Nor does the subsequent history of Nova Scotia Tramways and Power Company Limited suggest it was able to exploit the regulatory system to its own benefit. Table 5-4 depicts the financial history (gross and net earnings, interest

Table 5-2

Financial Statistics for the Halifax Electric Tramway Company Limited, 1901-14

	Average stock price[1]	Dividends	Net earnings[2]/ capital[3] plus surplus	Value of equity[4] plus debt/capital subscribed plus surplus	Value of equity plus debt/property account[5]
	Dollars	Per cent	Per cent	Per cent	Per cent
1901	95.3	5.0	7.7	95.8	97.3
1902	106.7	5.0	6.2	101.0	108.1
1903	97.1	5.0	6.1	93.4	95.9
1904	93.5	5.0	7.9	88.2	87.9
1905	105.0	6.0	6.5	94.1	93.7
1906	103.6	6.0	7.8	90.7	87.8
1907	97.4	6.0	7.8	85.1	81.3
1908	99.7	6.0	8.1	84.5	83.2
1909	114.3	6.3	8.5	90.2	91.2
1910	124.9	7.0	9.2	93.3	98.3
1911	145.8	8.0	9.4	101.6	109.9
1912	154.9	8.0	9.4	102.4	106.6
1913	158.4	8.0	9.6	100.8	104.3
1914	160.0 168[6]	8.0	9.2	97.2 101.8[7]	103.5 107.5[7]

1 Average of monthly high and low quotation taken from W. R. Houston, *Annual Financial Review*, W. Griggs (Toronto: various years).
2 Net earnings is gross revenue less operating expenses and taxes, various years.
3 Capital is the actual monies received by the firm.
4 Value of equity is calculated using average yearly stock price; debt is the value subscribed.
5 The property account is the book value of plant and equipment.
6 Price at which the Nova Scotia Tramways and Power Company acquired its shares from the syndicates that had purchased them (Armstrong and Nelles, 1976), p. 114.
7 Uses price quoted in note 6 above to value equity.
SOURCE   Houston, *Annual Financial Review* (Toronto: various years).

payments, and dividends) of this company and its predecessor. It is apparent that, except for the first three years of the operation of the new company (1917-19), no dividends were paid – and then only on the preference shares. Indeed, by 1928, the company was forced to reorganize and the value of equity was substantially written down. Preference shares, which the PUC had authorized to be issued at $75 in 1916, received only $46.20 in no par value shares; common shares, which were initially authorized for issuance at $40, received only $30.[36]

How then can the reorganization that took place in Halifax be explained? The payout streams revealed in Table 5-4 indicate that the reorganization led to a substantial change in the amount of fixed interest payments relative to dividends. From 1911 to 1915, before the take-over, interest accounted for only 21 per cent of the total payments to capital. From 1920 to 1925, interest payments accounted for 100 per cent of payouts. This was the result of a substantial change in the debt-equity ratio. Between 1911 and 1915, debt accounted for only 30 per cent of total capital subscribed. As of 1917, debt accounted for about 43 per cent of capital.[37] It was an even greater percentage of the reproduction cost less depreciation property value determined by the PUC – about 59 per cent.

While the Nova Scotia Tramways and Power Company take-over increased the debt component of the capital stock, the final percentages were, if anything, low in comparison to other major street railway and power companies operating in Canada at the time. In 1911, debt accounted for 42 per cent of the capital of the British Columbia Electric Railway; 51 per cent for the London Street Railway Company; 56 per cent for the Quebec Railway, Light, Heat, and Power Company; 56 per cent for the Saint John Street Railway Company; 50 per cent for the Sherbrooke Railway and Power Company; and 55 per cent for the Winnipeg Electric Railway Company. The take-over in Halifax then can be ascribed to an attempt to provide a debt-equity ratio more in keeping with the inherent risk of the undertaking – a ratio which the conservative management of the existing company had not been willing to recognize.

Table 5-3

Annual Yield Earned by the Halifax Electric Tramway Company Limited, 1901-14

	Net earnings/ total capital subscribed plus surplus[1]	Net earnings/debt plus market value of equity[2]		Net earnings less interest/value of equity subscribed plus surplus[1]	Net earnings less interest/market value of equity[2]	
		Per cent				
1901	7.68	8.02		10.10	10.40	
1902[3]	6.15	6.09		6.24	6.54	
1903	6.09	6.52		6.73	7.22	
1904	7.93	9.00		9.66	10.90	
1905	6.47	6.87		6.74	7.67	
1906	7.80	8.60		8.59	10.14	
1907	7.84	9.22		9.07	11.14	
1908	8.05	9.52		9.10	11.46	
1090	8.53	9.46		8.74	11.12	
1910	9.15	9.81		8.84	11.46	
1911	9.44	9.30		8.16	10.56	
1912	9.37	9.15		7.78	10.30	
1913	9.62	9.54		7.93	10.77	
1914	9.23	9.50	9.14[4]	7.59	10.70	10.2[4]
Average	8.10	8.61		8.23	10.03	

1 Columns 1 and 3 measure annual return based on capital subscribed.
2 Columns 2 and 4 measure annual return based on market value of equity when defining the capital base.
3 For further notes, see Table 5-2.
4 Uses price in note 6, Table 5-2, to value equity.
SOURCE Houston, *Annual Financial Review* (Toronto: various years).

Of course, the consolidation was not a financial success. But that probably was the result of the failure of the company to develop hydro-electricity and of the inflation that increased costs rapidly between 1917 and 1920. Both were the result of unforeseen circumstances brought about by the war. Capital became expensive towards the end of the war, and hydro-electricity itself was finally developed in 1922 by the province which then supplied the Halifax company (Armstrong and Nelles, 1976, p. 130). Perhaps just as important, the regulatory system adopted by Nova Scotia was cumbersome when it came to adjusting rates to reflect sudden changes in costs. When the 1916 rate base was decided, the rate of return granted the company was not inadequate by legislated standards. Net earnings were $332,773 on a rate base determined as $3,450,000 or 9.6 per cent. Thereafter, gross earnings continued to increase until 1922 (see Table 5-4) but net earnings did not. It was not until 1922 that the regulatory agency, worried about the health of the Nova Scotia Tramways and Power Company, began a two-year process of re-evaluating the rate base. Nevertheless, the company did remain solvent during this period.

Regulation in Nova Scotia did not lead to the bankruptcy crisis that elsewhere resulted in public ownership. The new form of regulation, while imperfect, nevertheless managed to adjust to changes in the environment that required recontracting.

The problems that beset the Halifax tramways and power sector were not felt in the telephone sector. From its inception in 1914, the Maritime Telegraph and Telephone Company grew steadily. Table 5-5 presents the number of telephones served, gross and net revenues, and the capital base of this company. Table 5-6 contains several different measures of the profitability of the company. Column 1 indicates that the dividend yield remained at 6 per cent until 1925 and then grew to 8 per cent by 1928. Column 2 provides a weighted average of the capital cost of both equity and debt – using yields on par value. It increases from 6 to 6.8 per cent over the period. Columns 3 through 5 provide alternate measures of the net earnings relative to the capital base. The Nova Scotia PUC allowed 8 per cent on the value of property; however, the company had a substantial return

Table 5-4

Earnings, Dividends and Interest Payments of the Halifax Electric Tramway Company Limited, 1900-16; and of the Nova Scotia Tramways and Power Company Limited, 1917-25

	Gross earnings	Net earnings[1]	Interest	Dividends
		Dollars		
1900	232,766	104,631	30,000	40,000
1901	251,644	109,232	30,000	40,000
1902	314,160	126,217	30,000	47,291
1903	365,374	124,562	30,000	68,621
1904	379,464	167,523	30,000	70,659
1905	370,368	138,774	30,000	75,635
1906	387,517	171,808	30,000	84,910
1907	405,452	176,508	30,000	87,592
1908	424,618	189,905	30,000	87,058
1909	447,579	207,973	30,000	85,129
1910	477,109	230,474	30,000	98,000
1911	502,399	245,525	30,000	112,000
1912	539,953	253,393	30,000	112,000
1913	605,933	268,924	30,000	112,000
1914	645,241	269,818	30,000	112,000
1915	718,840	331,753	30,000	112,000
1916	759,726	332,773	20,889	112,000
1917	859,667	241,647	110,080	62,026
1918	998,702	259,876	123,899	124,644
1919	1,258,501	211,510	144,618	62,364
1920	1,461,039	87,630	202,526	–
1921	1,446,639	181,638	204,781	–
1922	1,419,471	320,687	207,647	–
1923	1,393,979	317,698	218,034	–
1924	1,299,371	277,135	217,940	–
1925	1,344,098	384,728	216,925	–

1   Net earnings is gross revenues minus (operating expenses plus taxes).
SOURCE   Houston, *Annual Financial Review* (Toronto: various years).

on investments, and neither the revenue therefrom nor the investments were considered in establishing operating revenues. Column 3 uses both sources of revenues less all taxes to calculate the yield and therefore could exceed the allowed return. This measure increases from 7.3 per cent in 1914 to 9.1 per cent by 1929. Column 4 uses just operating revenues (excluding miscellaneous and investment revenue) before federal income tax. Column 5 makes a correction for federal tax for the years 1920-29. The before-tax yield commences at 5.8 per cent in 1914 and reaches 9.0 per cent in 1926. The after-tax yield increases to about 8.5 per cent in 1926. In light of the margin of error in calculating income tax and the capital base, the latter is not excessive relative to the 8 per cent regulatory standard. Under the regulatory system in effect, the Maritime Telegraph and Telephone Company gradually increased its profitability to the maximum allowed.

In Nova Scotia then, the independent regulatory tribunal performed the required function during the crisis that beset the industry with its transformation from thermal to water power. Arrayed on one side were those who believed that a new company had to be encouraged to develop hydropower. On the other were city leaders who wanted the best possible terms extracted from the franchise holder. Complicating the process was the acquiring firm's desire to recapitalize the company and to change the debt-equity ratio dramatically to reflect more closely industry standards. This change led to substantial fear that recapitalization involved "watering" and would only serve to increase consumer elec-

Table 5-5

Financial History of the Maritime Telegraph and Telephone Company Limited, 1914-29

	Number of telephones	Gross revenue	Operating plus other revenue less tax[1]	Capital base[2]
		Dollars	Dollars	Dollars
1914	17,763	631,687	186,743	2,571,219
1915	19,142	675,677	189,616	2,556,591
1916	20,621	738,697	205,995	2,648,087
1917	22,173	813,483	201,895	2,923,421
1918	24,636	953,847	192,686	3,228,491
1919	26,406	1,209,472	243,147	3,567,482
1920	29,163	1,417,430	305,158	4,300,384
1921	30,421	1,469,999	339,071	4,541,157
1922	31,183	1,487,712	357,034	4,688,135
1923	31,977	1,531,470	378,887	4,671,815
1924	32,745	1,477,026	374,570	4,645,726
1925	33,052	1,529,670	423,228	4,772,700
1926	33,917	1,568,924	433,983	4,713,615
1927	34,870	1,626,119	446,039	4,736,657
1928	36,445	1,718,239	455,598	4,849,989
1929	38,262	1,852,252	469,866	5,193,169

1 This is defined as gross revenue less operations costs, maintenance expenses, federal, provincial, and municipal taxes, and miscellaneous expenses.

2 Capital base is taken from plant and property accounts less reserves for replacement. Each year's figure is adjusted downward by the discrepancy between this estimate for 1914 and the PUC evaluation for that year.

SOURCE   Houston, *Annual Financial Review* (Toronto: various years).

tricity, gas, and railway rates. The regulatory agency, with its emphasis on used and useful capital invested, successfully arbitrated the conflict.

New Brunswick

A second Maritime province, New Brunswick, also adopted a formal regulatory tribunal at about the same time as did Nova Scotia. New Brunswick passed an act to establish a Board of Commissioners of Public Utilities in 1910.[38] The legislation resembled the 1909 Nova Scotia legislation. Utility rates were to be "reasonable and just." New Brunswick already had legislated certain regulatory powers, but only over telephones. The *Telephone Act* allowed expropriation by the government at the amount invested plus 10 per cent. Rates could not be increased if earnings exceeded 8 per cent of the amount invested.[39] The new act of 1910 brought all utilities furnishing street railway service, heat, light, water, power, and telephone service within the jurisdiction of a board.

The New Brunswick regulatory agency was created in response to complaints that arose essentially from residents

of Saint John about the New Brunswick Telephone Company.[40] Between 1904 and 1910, the Bell subsidiary had purchased a number of independent telephone companies and thus had developed greater control over the industry, making more formal regulation important to municipalities who no longer saw competition as able to perform a regulatory function.

The New Brunswick PUC set about its first rate hearing in 1911, not by focusing on the rate base, but by examining whether the rates were "reasonable" – because the latter was specified in the enabling legislation as the criterion to be used and not the former. The Commission accepted the rates filed by the telephone company in 1912 with only one exception (Armstrong and Nelles, 1986, p. 281). It is clear from the early decisions of the Board that the interests of both consumers and investors were seen as being the same. The PUC's chairman in 1920 stated:

> While there is no better asset a utility can have than a contented public, the converse is true, that the public cannot expect good service unless it pays adequate rates. The true interests of a public utility and the true interests of the public are identical . . . the public must be prepared to secure to the

Table 5-6

Rate of Return Earned by the Maritime Telegraph and Telephone Company Limited, 1914-29

	Dividend yield[1] on common stock	Weighted average yield[1]: equity plus debt	Return on capital base using net operating plus other revenue less tax[2]	Return on capital base using operating revenue[3]	
				Before federal tax	After federal tax[4]
			Per cent		
1914	6.0	6.0	7.3	5.8	
1915	6.0	6.0	7.4	6.0	
1916	6.0	6.0	7.8	6.7	
1917	6.0	6.0	6.9	6.6	
1918	6.0	6.2	6.0	5.6	
1919	6.0	6.2	6.8	5.0	
1920	6.0	6.4	7.1	6.6	6.1
1921	6.0	6.4	7.5	6.5	6.2
1922	6.0	6.4	7.6	6.8	6.4
1923	6.0	6.4	8.1	7.3	6.8
1924	6.0	6.4	8.1	8.0	7.5
1925	6.0	6.4	8.9	8.7	8.2
1926	6.5	...	9.2	9.0	8.5
1927	7.5	6.4	9.4	8.9	8.4
1928	8.0	6.7	9.4	8.8	8.4
1929	8.0	6.8	9.1	8.7	8.2

1   Calculated on par value.
2   See Table 5-5 for definition of capital base and operating plus other revenue.
3   The income concept used here is the same as for column 3, except that miscellaneous revenue and dividend or interest income are excluded.
4   Federal tax is apportioned to operating revenue on basis of percentage of operating revenue to operating plus other revenue.
SOURCE   Houston, *Annual Financial Review* (Toronto: various years).

utility a sufficient sum to carry on its work and to pay a reasonable return upon its investment.[41]

Thus the New Brunswick Commission was able to give private capital the same sort of protection that Nova Scotia did; even though it did not create the same elaborate rate-base regulatory system found in its sister maritime province.

Throughout this period the enabling legislation continued to focus on the responsibility of the PUC to adjudge whether rates were "unreasonable, insufficient, or unjustly discriminating." Even the revised act of 1927[42] makes no mention of the powers of the Board to determine a rate base. Nevertheless, the reproduction cost standard also emerged here. As of 1927, the New Brunswick Supreme Court ruled that it had been "definitely settled" that reproduction and not original cost was the most satisfactory method to determine value of service.[43] A short time later, the New Brunswick Board of Commissioners of Public Utilities attested to its own use of this measure:

It is an established principle that the valuation must be as of the time of the rate determination, and in such determination

of value the 'reproduction new' cost less observed depreciation of the electric plant of the company used and useful rendering service by it must be considered.[44]

Even so, common sense was allowed to prevail since the courts also supported consideration of other methods when the Board saw fit.[45]

The New Brunswick Supreme Court later confirmed the ability of the Board to handle inflationary periods in a flexible fashion. In 1949, the Supreme Court ruled a prudent investment standard could be applied since "it would be a fallacy to fix a rate base on reproduction new cost less depreciation during a time of abnormally high prices."[46]

Alberta

Alberta was the third province in which an active regulatory commission emerged at an early date (1915) to regulate private utilities.[47] The PUC followed essentially a prudent investment standard based on historic costs.[48] This standard could be adopted because the regulatory act was passed when both the province and its utilities were relatively young. Thus actual investment could be readily determined. When there is a long period between a utility's inception and the onset of regulation, there is more difficulty in ascertaining whether there was inflation of capital without taking stock of actual investment.

The Alberta Board, like its Nova Scotia counterpart, was able to arbitrate difficult renegotiations between Alberta cities and the utilities that served them. For example, the Canadian Western Natural Gas, Light, Heat and Power Company, which served Calgary with a subsidiary, the Calgary Gas Company, ran into considerable contractual problems with the city between 1916 and 1921. The city challenged the franchise rights of the company only to have the Court of Appeal and the Supreme Court rule that the company's franchise rights extended over the entire city.[49] In 1920, the company applied for higher rates (dividends had been 2 per cent in 1917 and 1918, but were suspended in 1919, 1920, and 1921). Since no agreement could be reached, the matter was referred to the Alberta Board of Public Utilities Commissioners. A price increase from 35 cents per million cubic feet (MCF) to 48 cents for domestic consumption was granted. In doing so, the Board ruled that the company was entitled to earn 8.5 per cent on total capital invested – which it set at $6,350,000.[50] Although the company listed its property at $10,864,034, this was sufficient to cover the fixed interest costs and to

re-establish the company's credit – at least with the debenture stockholders. Table 5-7 outlines the course of the Canadian Western Natural Gas, Light, Heat and Power Company's debenture stock prices on the London market, and the difference between its yield and that on London gilts between 1917 and 1924. The latter measures the risk that bondholders viewed as inherent in the company. During the contract crisis, this premium increased; but the traditional differential was re-established shortly after the PUC ruling.

The Alberta PUC also used a prudent investment standard to govern the Northwestern Utilities' exclusive franchise contract to supply gas to Edmonton. This company received a 10 per cent net return after deducting sinking and depletion costs and operating expenses.[51]

Thus, at an early date, the Alberta PUC had adopted a standard that ensured the private utilities in that province would receive a "fair return" on fair value and accordingly provided the means by which contract renegotiations could be effected without transactions failure.

Conclusion

The problem with *ex ante* franchise contracts for the regulation of natural monopolies is that they cannot easily handle recontracting. Because of the nature of the utility

Table 5-7

The Price and Yield of the Debentures of the Canadian Western Natural Gas, Light, Heat and Power Company, 1917-24

	Average price of CWNG[1] debenture stock	Realized debenture yield	Yield on gilts	Difference
	£	Per cent	Per cent	Per cent
1917	77.44	6.46		
1918	77.38	6.46	4.20	2.26
1919	74.44	6.72	4.80	1.92
1920	59.50	8.40	5.50	2.90
1921	42.75	11.70	4.90	6.80
1922	58.50	8.55	4.40	4.15
1923	72.50	6.90	4.50	2.40
1924	75.50	6.62	4.30	2.32

1   CWNG – Canadian Western Natural Gas, Light, Heat and Power Company.
SOURCE   de Zoete, *The de Zoete Equity Gilt Study: A Study of the Relative Performance of Equity and Fixed Interest Investment from 1919 to 1984*, 30th annual edition (London: de Zoete and Bevan, January 1985), p. 22; and Annual Report for 1925 of the International Utilities Corporation, in Houston, *Annual Financial Review* (Toronto: 1925).

industry, what initially started as a large-numbers bargaining situation quickly degenerated to a small-numbers situation. The long-lived, immutable characteristics of investment in the industry make contractual failure costly. The ability of the Canadian legislatures to expropriate without compensation means public enterprise may be chosen as the way to internalize contractual failure more often than in a country like the United States where the state was constrained directly from confiscation during renegotiations.

The modern regulatory tribunal, with its extensive rate-making power based on rate-base regulation, emerged in the United States to handle the complex recontracting problems associated with the utility industry. As this chapter indicates, this form also developed in Canada, and in three provinces it served to diffuse recontracting crises. But this form of regulatory tribunal was not selected by all jurisdictions to resolve the regulatory problem. Indeed, its appearance was the exception not the rule. And as was demonstrated in Chapter 4, it existed at the federal level, but this did not serve to prevent the regulatory crisis that beset the Canadian railways during World War I. Succeeding chapters describe the different types of regulatory contracts that evolved in the utility sector as both federal and provincial governments grappled with recontracting problems in water, gas, electricity, telephones, and transit service.

6 The Evolution of the Regulatory Contract in the Nineteenth Century

There are three industries in Canada where municipalities began contracting in the 1800s with private utility companies for the provision of utility services. These were central water plants, gas distribution networks, and urban transit systems. Each industry began with *ex ante* franchise contracts. These were contracts for a given length of time, for the duration of which the terms were fixed at the beginning. Each contract met with different problems.

In the case of waterworks, the state had the greatest difficulty in revising the regulatory contract that would satisfy the varied demands for water in Canada's newly emerging urban centres; and consistent with the hypothesis presented in Chapter two, public enterprise was adopted as the solution, *faute de mieux*. In the case of gas plants, the solution to growing state demands for recontracting was the adoption of a type of voluntary regulation. In the transit industry, the *ex ante* franchise contract with its attendant limited opportunity for periodic revision was maintained. The crisis that led to a dramatic modification in the regulatory contract used for transit systems did not occur until the inflationary period of World War I. Each of these industries is examined in turn.

In the end, three different frameworks emerged. None involved the formation of the type of independent regulatory agency that was to emerge in the twentieth century, because the prerequisites for this institution had not yet been established. On the other hand, in only one of the three instances was the original franchise-type contract maintained. The contractual problem was too complex for this simple instrument to solve, except in what increasingly came to be very unique circumstances.

Water and Municipalization

By the mid-1800s, Montreal and Toronto had emerged as Canada's two dominant metropolitan areas. The provision of water via central collection systems was originally left to private enterprise. This did not endure. First Montreal, then Toronto moved to a publicly owned system as a result of contractual failure. Contrary to nationalization in the railway sector, this failure was not associated with opportunistic behaviour. It arose from externalities and the inability of public authorities to devise an optimal pricing –

cum-taxation – system to deal with these externalities. The pricing problem could have been resolved, as it was eventually, by the imposition of a water tax on all homeowners; but the public authorities faced a constraint when it came to using their coercive taxing power to "benefit" a privately owned utility – even one with whom the state had contracted for a needed public service. At least part of the problem can be ascribed to an immature political system which had not devolved adequate taxation powers from provinces to municipalities.

Modern centrally supplied waterworks offered two advantages to Canadian cities. First, they provided a continuous supply of water to replace wells that were either drying up or were becoming a health hazard. Second, they promised a supply of water for hydrants to protect against the ever present danger of fire – a danger which constantly reared its head. Major fires occurred in Winnipeg in 1875, in Ottawa in 1900, and in Toronto in 1904. The Great Chicago Fire of 1871 provides the best-known example of the extent to which the wooden buildings of nineteenth century North American cities could quickly succumb to fire. For both reasons, but primarily because of the threat of fires, municipalities such as Toronto, Montreal, and Winnipeg contracted with private companies to build waterworks systems.

Contrary to the emphasis that came to be placed at a later stage on controlling the rates the natural monopolist could charge, the early franchises in this industry were more concerned with the quality of service, because the waterworks at first possessed little monopoly power. Wells and water-wagons that circulated through the city offered competition to a centrally distributed system and restricted the returns that a waterworks could be expected to earn. Indeed, returns were such that private companies could sometimes not be found to construct and operate the systems. In 1845, Quebec called for tenders for a water system from the private sector, and, in 1850, Hamilton did the same; but in neither case was the prospect for profits sufficient to attract private bids (Armstrong and Nelles, 1986, pp. 31-32).

In 1842, Toronto granted a private franchise to the Toronto Gas, Light, and Water Company – a company organized by Albert Furniss, who also owned the gas franchise in Montreal. Furniss asked for a city guarantee to pay for gas for 100 street lights at £6 a piece and a corporate charter that allowed the excavation of public streets. He offered to provide a waterworks if the city would guarantee to pay £250 a year for 21 years for five hydrants. The city's insurance agencies promised to pay half of the city's annual costs for the hydrant system for five years (Jones and McCalla, 1979, pp. 302-03).

In the early period, the waterworks business was risky. A locally owned company that had purchased the Furniss Toronto company went bankrupt in 1853 and the works reverted to the Montreal entrepreneur. In the 1860s, a successor – the Metropolitan Gas and Water Company – failed, and once more the works were returned to Furniss. It was not until 1872 that Toronto finally purchased the assets of the private company from Furniss' estate (Armstrong and Nelles, 1986, pp. 17-18).

The same transition from private monopoly to publicly owned waterworks took place in Montreal. Montreal's first waterworks was provided in 1801 by the Company of Proprietors of the Montreal Water Works, which was organized by James Frobisher of fur-trading fame (Armstrong and Nelles, 1986, p. 12). Throughout the 1840s, Montreal became gravely concerned about the rising toll from major fires and considered the advantages of a municipally owned waterworks. The privately owned waterworks was offered to the city, and the latter obtained legislative approval to buy it in 1843; but it was not until 1845 that the city concluded the transaction.

These were not the only two cities that started with a privately owned water system, then switched to public enterprise. Vancouver, Calgary, and Winnipeg all originally contracted with private companies, but had expropriated them by the turn of the century. While the preferred contract for water supply was, at the outset, with the private sector,[1] this did not last.

A change in the nature of the regulatory instrument can occur for a number of reasons. Unspecified contingencies may be so numerous that a franchise contract will fail and internalization is required to regularize recontracting. Opportunistic behaviour can emerge on the part of the state, which makes it an unreliable partner, or on the part of firms, which makes the state's task so difficult that it chooses a publicly owned corporation with whatever imperfections it possesses as the alternative to a regulatory system that has broken down. None of these explanations, however, is compelling in the case of water systems. Toronto's experience can be used to illustrate why the reason for the choice of public enterprise must be sought elsewhere.

Disagreements between Toronto and Furniss' company began almost from the outset. Conflicts developed over Furniss' disruption of city streets, over the adequacy of water pressure for fire protection, and over water quality – the city had located a sewer outlet in 1845 adjacent to the waterworks intake. City growth was the most pressing problem: with it came the need to expand the system and to build new reservoirs to support greater pressure for hydrants. But this was a costly undertaking, and the city found it difficult to accept the price increases that were required. In 1868, the water company renegotiated the hydrant contract for $5,000, up from the previous $1,000. In 1870, the city went to arbitration only to have the figure set at $6,750 per annum (Jones and McCalla, 1979, pp. 304 and 314).

While disagreements occurred, they do not appear to have been so great that the failure of the *ex ante* franchise contract can be ascribed to them. An acceptable arbitration procedure seems to have been adopted by the late 1860s, at least for the repricing of hydrants. Nor was there a basic failure in controlling rates charged by water and gas works. Throughout this period, the cities exerted continuous regulatory control over the gas and water utilities through their own contracts with the companies. What with fire protection, street lighting, and illumination of public buildings, the city often was the largest customer of the utility. The city offered private purchasers protection by specifying in their own contract with the utility the maximum price that could be charged private customers.

It is true that the timing of the transition to publicly owned waterworks might have been related to the changing fiscal capacity of the municipality. While a municipal system was considered in Toronto both at the outset and later, financial considerations played an important role in the decision to rely upon private monopoly. In 1840, when the waterworks contract was first let, Toronto was uncertain of its ability to raise money in London financial markets for the water system. In the end, Toronto's costs for the Furniss project amounted to only 6 per cent of the projected capital costs of the project had they been built by the city. In the 1850s, the city had just received permission to build a municipally owned gas works when the crash of 1857 severely constrained its borrowing capacity (Jones and McCalla, 1979, pp. 304 and 312). However, the maturing of Toronto's borrowing status that accompanied its growth was only a necessary, not a sufficient, condition for the establishment of public enterprise in this field. Even if fiscal capacity was an important factor, it is still necessary to ask why municipalization occurred in this sector and not elsewhere.

It is also difficult to ascribe the municipalization of waterworks to opportunistic behaviour. Little opportunism was exhibited by both sides during renegotiations. In Toronto, Furniss did not adopt a strategy that would make it difficult for buyout – as the street railway barons in Vancouver, Winnipeg, and Montreal would do almost 60 years later. Indeed, Furniss was more than willing to sell to local entrepreneurs – which he did twice, first in 1851, then in 1858 – only to have to repossess the works when the new owners went bankrupt. He also offered to sell the works in 1854 and 1856 to Toronto when the issue of municipal ownership arose (Jones and McCalla, 1979, p. 307). In turn, the political milieu offered him considerable protection from competition by a municipally owned waterworks. In both 1857 and 1872, the enabling legislation for a city-owned system specified the private company had to be purchased before operations could commence. When the city terminated buyout discussions with the private company in 1873, the ratepayers defeated a bylaw that would have allowed the city to raise money for its own waterworks – a decision that was interpreted to mean the voters wanted the city to come to terms with the private company. Finally, it should be noted that the purchase price eventually arranged was not confiscatory. Although the waterworks were evaluated at $186,500, a price of $220,000 was agreed upon (Jones and McCalla, 1979, pp. 318 and 320). The difference reflected the franchise value of the works – as it should have, if all rights were being duly compensated.

While the transition to public enterprise in the case of waterworks was not accompanied by the same type of opportunism that was exhibited in the railway case, it was the result of a contractual failure as discussions surrounding the transition indicate. The state proved unable to devise a pricing system that reflected the externality that the waterworks provided. Pressure available for hydrants depended upon the size of reservoirs and the strength of pipe. A system that was adequate for fire-fighting needs might be too expensive for household needs. Miscalculation of demand elasticity would leave the utility with fewer customers than anticipated when the contract was originally signed. More importantly, householders that did not connect to watermains, but who had hydrants located nearby, obtained fire-protection benefits from the system. Since private companies could not fully capture the value of the externalities created, they therefore had trouble providing optimal capacity.[2] They built systems that were essentially tied to household needs and not the higher pressures required for fire-fighting.

The solution would have been to pay the company an adequate fee for the hydrants and to have the city impose a tax to cover this fee. But general taxes at an early stage would have discriminated against those very large sections of these cities that were not supplied with water. The power to impose discriminatory taxation was slow to be included in

city charters of the time. Finally, forcing homeowners, who could do so, to connect to the water system would allow the externality to be captured, since rates were lump-sum and water usage was generally not monitored. The province, however, was unwilling at first to grant this coercive power even to municipally owned companies. The failure, then, that arose in this industry, was a failure in the political process that was slow to devolve needed powers on municipalities.

When Montreal sought legislative approval in 1843 to purchase the private waterworks, the assembly insisted on inserting conditions that water taxes could not be imposed on householders not served with water and denied the city the power to force homeowners to connect with city mains.[3] If the city faced problems with devising an optimal rate structure, it was all the more difficult for private companies to do so.

The same pricing problem existed in Toronto as in Montreal. When Toronto city council debated the problems associated with the supply provided by the private company in 1853, the option of allowing this company to collect water rates from all homeowners was raised but not implemented. The importance of this power was emphasized when provincial enabling legislation for a city-owned waterworks in 1857 stipulated that the city could not levy a general water tax until the private company was purchased.[4] These general powers of taxation were regarded as being of critical importance for the financial success of the waterworks. The same terms were included in subsequent legislation in 1872 that this time led to the Toronto municipal take-over.[5]

Toronto and Montreal were not the only municipalities where the pricing problem arose. In Winnipeg, an exclusive franchise to supply water for a 20-year period was given to a privately owned company in 1880. The primary reason for the city's interest in a waterworks was the threat of fire. The company, in return for its franchise, was to supply hydrants and "furnish free of charge to the city, to the full extent of the resources and powers of their works, all water requisite for the extinction of accidental fires" (Artibise, 1975, pp. 208-09).

Discontent surfaced in 1886 over the adequacy of a water system for fire protection, but the company was found to be meeting its obligation under the franchise contract. Little could be done unless the city was willing to aid in expansion of the size of the system. The company offered to do so itself, if the Council made water connections compulsory.[6] The city was unwilling to take action because it lacked political support. When a plan to establish its own waterworks was put before Winnipeg electors in 1892, the measure was defeated (Artibise, 1975, pp. 210-11). It was not until 1898 that Winnipeg finally bought the company.[7]

Under coaxing from the Fire Underwriters Association, the city then built a high pressure system in 1905 to serve the downtown section. This system was paid for by special assessments on the properties so protected. Thus the problems of assessing an appropriate price for services rendered was only solved after the taxing power of the municipality was brought into play with municipalization. The taxation and pricing problems were contentious issues since, as late as 1905, only 60 per cent of Winnipeg households had water connections (Artibise, 1975, p. 350, fn. 27).

The choice of public enterprise, then, was closely connected with a public good or externality-pricing problem. Substantial externalities both in the form of improved sanitation and fire protection were associated with the establishment of a waterworks system. Devising a taxation-based pricing system, however, that would transfer sufficient funds to the private utility to build the required capacity was beyond the ability of the state. In effect then, it was this constraint, rather than opportunistic behaviour on the part of either party to the negotiations, that led to the adoption of municipally owned waterworks in both cities.

The reason for this failure is not clear; the existence of a potential solution is not at issue. The law could have required homeowners to connect with the private system. A fixed charge could have been levied on all homeowners and transferred to the company – to effect a two-part tariff system. Perhaps it was simply that the mores of the time would not countenance the use of what were then considered to be extraordinary powers to benefit a private company. But more likely, the coercion implicit in such actions required a counterweight to ensure that the prices paid were fair. Without coercion, homeowners were free to avoid payment by not purchasing the service. With coercion, an institution that would guarantee fair prices was required. In the 1850s, the legal infrastructure for regulatory boards had not developed. The process of creating the regulatory board had started in the second half of the century in the United States with judicial rulings on what the state could regulate; but it took between 20 and 40 years before the preconditions required for the effective operation of state commissions as contract arbiters could be created. These regulatory options were unavailable at this time to the Canadian municipalities that were trying to reformulate the regulatory contract with the private firms that then operated the waterworks systems. Thus, the requirement that there be some form of political control over rates led to the choice of municipalization, because the power of coercion was being used, and because the political system has always provided a mechanism for the adjudication of equity issues.

Voluntary Regulation in the Gas Industry

Regulation can, in some instances, occur without the necessity of a public agent to negotiate a contract with the monopolist. As Chapter two suggests, where the users are sufficiently small in number, they often do so by themselves. This was the case with the gas industry in Toronto and Montreal. In both cases, a cooperative company emerged that was intended to prevent exorbitant gas rates from being charged without requiring the modern independent regulatory tribunal.

The early regulatory contracts in this industry and elsewhere proved unwieldy, because of their failure to provide a mechanism for the state to reopen the contract. Generally, recontracting occurred only when growth forced the company to request a modification of its legislative charter because of increased capital requirements or when unforeseen events brought on bankruptcy. An alternative, the sliding-scale arrangement described previously, was available; but it was used relatively infrequently. One example of its use, however, is provided by the evolution of the regulatory process governing the Toronto gas industry.[8]

The development of a cooperative company as a means of overcoming the contractual problem was followed in both Montreal and Toronto in response to the same forces. The Montreal Gas Light Company was organized by A. Furniss in 1836. This company negotiated its first contract with the city for street lights in 1841. But by the mid-1840s, discontent over the rate structure surfaced in city council. Although Furniss offered to sell his gasworks to Montreal, there was little public support for intervention in what was a product consumed mainly by the well-to-do. Instead, the New City Gas Company was formed. Its charter specified that no person could hold more than 500 shares or cast more than 20 votes.[9] The Furniss company was purchased shortly thereafter by this new company.

In Toronto, the Consumer's Gas Company (Consumer's Gas) received a perpetual though not exclusive contract to supply gas to Toronto in 1848. It was organized as an alternative to Furniss' Toronto Gas, Light and Water Company essentially as a shareholders' cooperative. In order to ensure automatic adjustment of rates to costs, its charter forbade the company from paying dividends of more than 10 per cent. In the same year as its incorporation, it took over the Furniss company. By 1850, Consumer's Gas had 369 customers and 300 shareholders.

The history of Consumer's Gas in Toronto illustrates that, even here, recontracting required a gradual modification of the form of regulation. Over the course of 50 years, the regulatory contract, which was written first to restrict dividends, was modified to cover earnings, struggled with defining the optimal debt-equity ratio, and almost foundered on the extent to which maintenance expenses were to be allowed to fund renewals rather than just repairs. Nevertheless, the recontracting process did not break down and result in public ownership as it did later for electricity and street railways in Toronto.

Both the sliding-scale contract and the threat of entry brought Consumer's Gas prices down rapidly in response to dramatic declines in costs. The entry threat first arose in 1851 when a group of dissident shareholders approached the government of the Province of Canada for a new charter to incorporate the Metropolitan Water and Gas Company.[10] Consumer's Gas brought its own rates down from $5.00/MCF in 1849 to $3.00 in 1855, following a brief dip to $2.50 in 1854.

Throughout this period, the municipality continued to be a major purchaser of gas and, with hard bargaining, served to regulate company profits. In times of depression like the early 1860s, gas street lamps were disconnected. Private consumption also was highly income elastic. As a result of the 1860s Depression, gas production in Toronto did not exceed its 1860 level until 1870. The gas company was a monopoly but it had little market power. The existence of substitutes like kerosene, whose production in Canada was rapidly expanding as the oil fields in Petrolia were developed, and the obviously high income elasticity of the demand curve for gas during the Depression of the 1860s, provided an adequate regulatory function.

The next threat of entry came not from the private but from the public sector. In the early 1850s, the *Ontario Municipal Act* was amended to permit municipalities to erect their own gas and waterworks – but only with approval by two-thirds of ratepayers. When prosperity returned in the 1870s, Consumer's Gas earnings averaged over 10 per cent of book value and the imperfections in the regulatory contract that only restricted dividends to 10 per cent became obvious. As long as both earnings and dividends were less than 10 per cent, there was no public outcry. But when earnings went above 10 per cent, even though dividends did not, agitation for a municipally owned system developed in 1874.

The company turned to the provincial government for protection and succeeded in having legislation passed that required cities to purchase a gas company's total assets before a municipal system could be constructed. The city was required by the restrictions in an 1877 bill to purchase

from a private company all "rights, franchises, privileges, and easements" in addition to the plant itself before it could build its own plant. As such the Toronto gas company was able to protect itself from public competition. Because it possessed a perpetual franchise, expropriation would have been very costly since the price to be paid would have to include the capitalized value of a stream of future earnings.

With the advent of the 1880s, Consumer's Gas introduced the new "carburetted water gas," which had been developed by Lowe in the United States. The average cost of gas fell from $1.08 in 1879 to 80 cents/MCF by 1885 and average rates were reduced from $1.86 to $1.37. But earnings remained above 10 per cent.

Toronto reacted in two ways. First, it sought to stimulate competition by encouraging the development of electricity. In 1884, the city council awarded part of its street lighting contract to the Toronto Electric Light Company (Toronto Electric). Second, it began to negotiate with the Toronto gas company for a limitation on the reserves (retained earnings) that the company could maintain. An agreement to this effect was not reached until 1887 when Consumer's Gas applied to the Ontario legislature for permission to expand its capital stock from $1 million to $2 million. In the resulting negotiations, the company obtained its desired increase, but only after agreeing to put all funds received from selling stock above par into a reserve fund (Armstrong and Nelles, 1984, p. 198). Such a fund could never exceed half of paid up capital; if it did, rates were to be cut so as to reduce the reserves to the maximum allowed level.

Even this modification did not satisfy the public. In 1888, it was reported that Consumer's Gas had voided the intent of the new arrangement by raising part of the new capital required via debt – thereby preventing its reserve fund from surpassing the stipulated limit.[11] Stipulating the size of the reserve fund was inadequate without specifying the debt-equity ratio that the company would follow. Once more foresight proved to be inadequate. Partly because of this new conflict, the city subsequently opposed the attempt by Consumer's Gas to begin producing electricity (Armstrong and Nelles, 1986, p. 82). It thereby maintained the possibility of regulation via competition as opposed to regulation via contract.

The appropriate debt-equity ratio was not the only reason for conflict between the city and the company. The size of the annual surplus that went into the reserve fund depended on costs. Considerable acrimony developed over the size of maintenance reserves charged as costs by the company. Disagreement arose as to whether they were being used, not only to maintain, but also to improve plant, and should therefore be part of capital expenditures. There was nothing unusual about the use of operating surpluses for investment – both the Grand Trunk and the Canadian Pacific did likewise. The reason is that the difference between the two is often difficult to discern in practice. Most expenditures extend the life of equipment. The difference between maintenance and investment then comes down to an arbitrary choice of period to divide one from the other. Given the nature of the regulatory contract in this instance, this problem gave rise to constant disagreements from 1888 to 1891.

Throughout the 1890s the debate between the city and Consumer's Gas continued. The urgency given to revising the contract was tempered by the ever-increasing competition that electricity offered to gas production. The city was also constrained in its options by the cost of expropriating the gas company. Even though the company's invested capital was only $2 million, the city's auditor estimated expropriation might cost up to $17 million because of the gas company's perpetual franchise (Armstrong and Nelles, 1984, pp. 203-04).

During this time, the company stood ready to renegotiate the contract; it offered to link gas rates to dividend rates, or to pay a fixed percentage of profits to the city. However, its contract with the city was not revised until 1901, when the gas company once more required an amendment to its charter for an expansion in its authorized capital. Eventually, the company agreed to limit its reserve fund to $1 million plus the premiums received on stock. More importantly, the city purchased $10,000 in stock and received a seat on the board of directors (Armstrong and Nelles, 1984, p. 212). With this partnership, relations were normalized.

The Toronto Consumer's Gas Company was one of the few regulatory success stories in Ontario – at least in relative terms compared to the fate of the Toronto Electric Light, the Electric Development, and the Toronto Street Railway companies. In these cases, contract renegotiations led to public ownership. The reasons for the success in the case of gas may be attributed to several factors. First, the gas company was partially protected because of its perpetual franchise.[12] Second, gas was never perceived as being quite so essential as electricity, either for commercial use or household illumination. For a far longer period, it remained the domain of the rich. Third, the competition provided by electricity and the sliding-scale contract served to reduce gas rates over time. The spirit of vengeance that characterized Toronto's contract renegotiations in electricity and tramways, a spirit bent on appropriating previously earned surplus, did not emerge with the same intensity in the gas sector.

Even though the company had a perpetual franchise, recontracting did occur. When additional authorized capital

stock was required, the company sought an amendment to its charter. The clauses giving the required increase in capital were usually accompanied by the imposition of other clauses that imposed new regulatory restrictions, for concessions always came during these recapitalizations. In these negotiations, both parties were constrained from taking extreme positions. Expropriation was too costly for the city; the gas company could not simply walk away and leave the contract unrevised, because in a rapidly growing community serious service problems and lost profit opportunities would have resulted. Finally, the fact that the gas company had started essentially as a consumers' cooperative and lauded itself for this tradition no doubt facilitated compromise.

Tramways and Regulation by Contract[13]

The first age of the tramways extended from 1860 to the early 1890s with horses providing the motive power. Regulation was imposed via *ex ante* franchise contracts. These contracts were revised and then superseded with the same type of contract when electrification of the tramways occurred in the 1890s. Notwithstanding the problems that arose with the franchise contract, this method of regulation must be adjudged to have been successful since basically the same format was used to regulate the second phase of the industry from 1890 to 1920.[14]

In both Montreal and Toronto, the original contracting process for horsedrawn tramways took place between 1859 and 1861. In Montreal, three groups competed for the franchise, which was finally awarded to the directors of the Montreal and Champlain Railroad. In 1860, Toronto received representations from an English contractor who was then building the Milwaukee street railway, engaged in prolonged debates over the terms of the franchise through the summer of 1860, and finally, having determined the conditions it wanted imbedded in the franchise, drafted the final terms of the contract in March of 1861. While Toronto was faced with only two tender offers, its contract terms were similar to those which Montreal had received in more competitive circumstances.[15]

These franchise contracts specified the streets to be served, required city approval of construction plans, and imposed certain pavement and maintenance obligations upon the companies. The Montreal franchise was for 40 years; but after 20 years, Montreal could purchase the works for a price to be arbitrated plus 10 per cent. The Toronto contract was for 30 years, and the acquisition price at the end of the term was also to be established by arbitration. The contract in the latter case was automatically renewed if the purchase option was not exercised.

The terms in both these contracts indicate there was more concern for service and public safety than for controlling monopoly rent. Profits did not seem a certainty at the outset and it was difficult to predict the value of the franchise. The technology was new; so too was the extent of the market, since many customers could still walk rather than take the tramway. Therefore, the need to constrain profits had little importance. Nor did municipal experience with the waterworks franchise contracts suggest a need to do so. Even though Montreal and Toronto had either municipalized or were engaged in considering the transfer of waterworks from private hands to the public domain by 1860, this was being done to provide optimal service levels. It was not to capture rents.

The profitability of transit service during the Depression of the 1860s was such that public priorities did not change. In the mid-1860s, dividends were suspended in Montreal; by 1869, the Toronto Street Railway Company was put into receivership. Moreover, for at least a period of time in the 1870s, competition developed in Montreal for the City Passenger Railway from omnibus companies operating on routes that were not covered by the original franchise.[16]

Initially, public complaints about the street railways were directed primarily at the level of service, the lack of progress being made in extending lines as the cities grew, and whether the street paving obligations were being met. Gradually the matter of profits and fares came to the fore. Montreal had shown considerable tolerance when it waived some of the original contract terms during the Depression conditions of the 1860s. Extensions specified in the original contract were deferred, as were certain tax and street paving obligations. However, with improved circumstances in the early 1870s, Montreal moved not only to recoup its past debts but also to capture part of the revenues of what was becoming an increasingly profitable operation. The city passed a bylaw requesting annual payment of $20,000 or about 12 per cent of gross revenue for the year. While the company opposed this levy, negotiations were commenced because the franchise was to expire in 1880. No progress was made by this date and the franchise was extended in 1880 without agreement on new financial terms for a period of five years. In 1885, the new agreement was finally reached that promised an annual payment of $1,000 per year for the first five years, rising at five-year intervals to $5,000 during the last interval. The new 25-year lease that was granted the City Passenger Railway Company carried an expiry date of 1910.

In Toronto, relations with the Toronto Street Railway Company deteriorated over the period. Continuous litigation during the 1880s over the company's pavement obligations generally were settled in favour of the company.

The company tried and failed to get its franchise changed to a perpetual basis. In 1886, a strike by the car men produced considerable public antipathy to the Toronto Street Railway Company. In 1890, the ratepayers of Toronto voted to acquire the company, as was their right under the original franchise. It was purchased in 1891. The city did not operate the street railway system for long, however. In both Winnipeg and Toronto the expiration of the horsedrawn tramway franchise coincided with the introduction of the new electric railway systems. As in Winnipeg, Toronto negotiated a franchise for the new technology with a Mackenzie company – after receiving tenders from a number of parties.[17]

The *ex ante* contract continued to work in this sector because the bargaining process had not been reduced to a small-numbers bargaining situation.[18] Just as the first set of franchises were due to expire, new technology removed the advantage that the horsedrawn incumbents had and opened the bidding to competing parties, all of whom had roughly equal opportunities to win the new contract. In the end, Toronto benefited from the competition. The new franchise specified an annual paving tax of $800 per mile of track, a 30-year term (expiring in 1921), fares of 5 cents per passenger, minimum wages and maximum hours for employees (Armstrong and Nelles, 1977*b*, pp. 39-40). In addition to the mileage pavement tax, the city was to receive a graduated tax of 8 per cent on gross receipts up to $1 million escalating to 20 per cent above $3 million.[19]

Almost immediately, disagreements over the paving clause began. The disagreement reveals more about the difficulties of writing a contract than about the venality of the parties concerned – though local newspaper accounts understandably focused on the latter. As part of the terms of both the 1861 and the 1892 franchises, Toronto exacted a per-mile tax to pay for paving and a promise to keep the pavement in good maintenance. The difficulty was that maintenance costs depended upon the type of material used in construction – and the latter was not specified. The city, of course, had the incentive to skimp on construction costs, because that would place the maintenance burden on the transit company. The transit company had the incentive to demand high construction standards.

The optimal decision (fixed cost versus maintenance) could not be specified a priori. Little experience was available in advance as to the wear and tear that would be caused by street railways. Moreover, the nature of the services going under and using the city streets was changing sufficiently rapidly that flexibility was required. During the first period, the horsedrawn transit company complained that cedar blocks placed in sand provided an inadequate foundation. A partial solution was arranged that placed the maintenance burden equally on the two parties. Finally, just prior to the expiration of the contract in 1889, the company agreed to a tax of $600 per mile so as to limit its maintenance obligations.

In the case of the electric street railway, Toronto exacted both a tax ($800 per mile of single track) and a pavement maintenance obligation. Unfortunately, it was more concerned with extracting surplus from the monopoly franchise, and it neglected to take past experience into account in writing the contract. Conflict on the quality of the foundation for the pavement began even before construction. The city wanted to install cobblestones on sand; the company wanted an underpad of concrete (Armstrong and Nelles, 1977b, p. 123). The company offered to do the job itself – but only if the $800 tax, which was meant to cover paving costs, was withdrawn. Apprehensive of the company providing an inferior paving job, the city was not willing to modify the franchise contract. In the end, it went ahead with the paving itself. As a result, the pavement obligations of the company and its performance continued to be a matter for concern during subsequent years.

Montreal's desire to electrify the tramway system had to overcome the problem that a new contract had been renegotiated in 1886 with the horsedrawn system. The city, however, called for tenders in 1892 for an electrified system and accepted from those submitted that of the horsedrawn company – the Montreal Street Railway Company. This company agreed to pay one-half of snow cleaning on streets operated, and a percentage of gross receipts amounting to 4 per cent on the first $1 million, an additional 2 per cent for each increment of $500,000 up to $3 million, and 15 per cent above $3 million.[20]

The bargain struck during these franchise negotiations varied considerably. For instance, Winnipeg received only 5 per cent of gross revenues in the 1892 contract, and those payments would not start until 1902; the Halifax Electric Tramway Company paid only 4 per cent of gross revenues plus a $1,000 tax for an overall rate of about 4.6 per cent of gross revenues in 1902; as of 1902, Montreal received 6.2 per cent of total revenues (8.7 per cent if snow removal fees are included);[21] and the Toronto Railway Company paid 13.9 per cent of its gross revenues in 1902 to the city.[22]

In spite of some problems, the second phase of contracting was completed much to the satisfaction of all concerned. The cities were able to replace one technology with another. They carefully considered their requirements and put the franchise out to competitive bidding. During the 1890s, there still existed the large-numbers bargaining situation

that the *ex ante* franchise contract requires as a prerequisite. These conditions, however, were to change in the next phase of development.[23] Nevertheless, in this period and in this utility sector, regulation via contract and not via independent tribunal enjoyed a modicum of success.

Conclusion

The independent, quasi-judicial tribunal that regulates most utilities today has become the agent that writes, monitors, and renegotiates frequently (usually on an annual basis) the contract between consumers and utilities. It is not the only method by which regulation of prices can be accomplished. In gas, water, and transit, the original instrument chosen was a fixed-term, *ex ante* contract. Conditions were specified in advance and fixed for a period of anywhere from 10 to 40 years. No formal mechanism for adjustments, other than tort law and reference to the courts, was available. Of these three sectors, this form of contract continued only in transit operations.

In both gas and waterworks, alternate forms of regulation evolved. In both gas and water, arm's-length contracts were superseded by internalization. But the form of the internalization differed. In gas, consumers essentially began their own company, and then adopted sliding-scale provisions that were meant to facilitate rate adjustment without renegotiation of the franchise contract. That this type of contract emerged should probably be ascribed to the initial conditions. In a monopoly situation in which only a small number of consumers exists, it is not unusual to find a contract being made directly between consumers and producers. This was the initial situation in the gas industry. As the number of gas consumers increased relative to the number of gas owners, the terms had to be modified; for at this stage, the interests of owners and consumers diverged. There were also a number of unforeseen problems that developed with the contract. A clause which restricted dividends had to be rewritten to include earnings on equity, which in turn required specification of debt-equity relationships and the division of funds between maintenance and investment purposes. Nevertheless, modifications were made that permitted this type of contract to handle changes in the environment.

In the case of water supply, internalization of the regulatory contract between consumers and producers was accomplished via municipalization. Parallel to the situation in gas, consumers provided the water production facilities themselves; but in this instance, they did so via a municipally owned company, because the taxing power of the state was required to provide optimal levels of service. Externalities associated primarily with fire protection, but also with sanitation, prevented the *ex ante* contract with a privately owned utility from functioning well.

These histories indicate that it is simplistic to suggest that regulation can be accomplished without the modern regulatory agency. Rather, they lead to an understanding as to why alternative forms have generally disappeared. Just as many arm's-length markets have been replaced as firms have been expanded to effect transactions internally, so too has the arm's-length regulatory contract been replaced, because this form of regulation has often been unable to cope with recontracting problems. It was unable to adapt to changes in the environment as well as has the modern regulatory tribunal.

The next chapter focuses on studies of adaptation during the period between 1890 and 1920. The transit and electric power industries of British Columbia, Manitoba, Quebec, and Ontario all commenced with *ex ante* franchise contracts. While there were similarities to the way new regulatory institutions developed, there were also differences. The changes that did occur provide us with a better understanding of the reason for contractual failure in business-state relationships.

7 British Columbia: Honour and Circumstance; Regulation by Independent Tribunal Avoided

Writing in 1944, A. W. Currie emphasized the novel aspects of the rate-making process imbedded in the 1943 report of the Public Utilities Commission (PUC) on the rates charged by the British Columbia Electric Railway Company Limited (BCER). What is more remarkable than the 1943 decision itself was the relative infancy of the Commission form of regulation in British Columbia. Whereas many other provinces had adopted a form of regulatory commission between 1906 and 1920, British Columbia did not adopt continuous regulation until 1938.[1] The reason was not that the same recontracting crises that beset other utilities were avoided in British Columbia. Here, as elsewhere, a municipal movement developed that focused on the excessive level of rates and the inadequacy of service being offered by the electric utility and the street railway under *ex ante* franchise contracts. But in contrast to other jurisdictions, the contractual process did not so deteriorate that it had to be internalized either via the creation of public enterprise or via a modern regulatory tribunal. An ad hoc arrangement for reopening contract negotiations during the term of the franchise sufficed.

A number of factors led to this result. The most important was a well organized company strategy that succeeded in deflecting opposition forces. The London-based company carefully developed support in the provincial legislature with an adroit campaign that stressed the importance of foreign capital for British Columbia's development. It also organized its affairs in such a way that a public take-over by the city of Vancouver would have been extremely costly. Finally, it adeptly moved to take advantage of an unexpected quirk of fate. An "accidental" legal ruling occurred at the peak of the populist movement that helped the company to escape from the jurisdiction of a local regulatory tribunal. As a result, the Vancouver electric and gas utilities essentially escaped regulation by an independent tribunal until the late 1930s. The tramway operations, on the other hand, attained a new and more flexible contract that allowed for a more frequent renegotiation of fares in response to cost changes than the original franchise contract had permitted.

The British Columbia experience then serves to stress that contractual failure with the *ex ante* franchise contract is not inevitable. The *ex ante* franchise contract between state and utility was not always supplanted as contractual problems developed. The West Coast situation also demonstrates that the state may in these circumstances act with no venality, and the utility may devise a strategy that serves to protect itself from the unwanted exercise of confiscatory power by the state. Nevertheless, the role played by accident or luck was sufficiently important that the British Columbia experience cannot be used to draw general conclusions about the adequacy of the franchise contract to adapt successfully to unforeseen contingencies.

Historical Development (1896-1917)

The BCER[2] emerged in 1897 out of the consolidation of Victoria, Vancouver, and New Westminster railway interests that had gone bankrupt in the mid-1890s. The initiative for the reorganization was provided by London interests and was encouraged by a provincial government intent on providing services to its emerging but still small urban centres. Throughout this period, the company continued to be run from London (Roy, 1973, pp. 239-40).

The new company possessed a relatively broad charter: with the rights of its predecessors, the right to serve areas not yet organized as municipalities, to enter other businesses, and to merge with other similar enterprises. The company was also protected by a clause in Vancouver's municipal charter that prevented the city from building a municipal competitor without first purchasing the private company.[3]

By 1901, the company had consolidated its position by renegotiating its franchises with Vancouver, changing them from licenses that were written on a street-by-street basis with varying termination dates to a comprehensive contract with a common termination date of 1919, and a lower revenue-sharing arrangement (Armstrong and Nelles, 1986, p. 98). This meant the railway would not have to recontract continuously with the city as each licence came due.

From an early stage, the company assiduously cultivated support at the provincial level. When the British Columbia premier of the period (McBride) travelled to London for his frequent visits, the directors of the BCER made a point of seeing him (Roy, 1972, p. 244). When he was considering the establishment of a PUC in 1914, the importance of British capital investment in British Columbia influenced his decision to the contrary (Armstrong and Nelles, 1986, p. 207). Assiduous lobbying gave the company sufficient influence with the private bills committee of the legislature that it could offset some of the thrust of populist pressure that eventually emerged in Vancouver as elsewhere. For example, when Vancouver attempted in 1900 to remove the buyout clause in its charter, the company was able to block this initiative.

The company also reduced the number of actual and potential competitors and thus made it difficult for the city to renegotiate the regulatory contract using the threat of new contracts with outsiders. Large-numbers bargaining situations did not reduce themselves to small-numbers renegotiating situations just because capital was immutable and long-lived. The process involved one of merger activity that made regulation by franchise contract more difficult.

A separate company, Vancouver Power, was organized in 1898 to develop hydro-electricity. Shortly thereafter, it was merged into the BCER. More damaging was the competition that developed with the Vancouver Gas Company. A rate war developed in 1902 that was eventually resolved by the BCER's purchase of the gas company in 1904.

Just as these consolidations in the electricity and gas sectors contributed to a strategy of self-defence, so too did BCER's move to expand transit service beyond Vancouver. Forty- and 50-year franchises were obtained by the BCER from South and North Vancouver (Roy, 1973, p. 252). The company also managed to obtain a perpetual franchise in 1908 to serve one of the towns outside of Vancouver. The larger the system, the greater would be the cost to any municipality of expropriation. Vancouver ratepayers would have had to bear all of the costs of expropriation without incurring all of the benefits – a classic externality problem. The long franchise lives that the company obtained would have increased the cost of expropriation even further.

The strategy of the BCER to surround Vancouver with a system of street railways was facilitated by the influence the company had built up with the provincial government. Perpetual franchises were received in 1908 from the provincial government for two areas under its control. When Vancouver annexed these areas in 1911, it requested these franchises be changed so that they would expire with the other Vancouver franchises in 1919. Stressing the need to protect its rights, the company refused to consider a change. Once more, in its negotiations with the province over this

issue, the London-based company stressed the need to maintain good relations with U.K. capital markets – a point that was well-taken in light of Vancouver's failure to float a bond issue at this time (Roy, 1973, p. 256, fn. 42). While the provincial cabinet initially recommended that the franchise be modified, pressures from the company eventually led the government to drop the matter.

Where the BCER was not initially protected by a historic buyout clause, as was the case with Victoria, it lobbied extensively to obtain one. In 1909, the company offered rate reductions and the promise of a major expansion, and obtained such a protective clause. Subsequently, the BCER baulked at its promise to build a new line to the sparsely settled Saanich peninsula; later, it responded to pressure from the British Columbia premier and finished construction of this line. This was a costly venture, since the line turned out to be unprofitable and was eventually abandoned in the 1920s (Roy, 1972, pp. 252-53).

During the early years, Vancouver politics began to exhibit the same tendencies seen elsewhere. Some politicians came to see the regulatory contract as inadequate. As early as 1906, Vancouver ratepayers overwhelmingly accepted the principle of municipal ownership of utilities (Armstrong and Nelles, 1986, p. 154, fn. 37). Little happened, however, until the province took a greater interest in the whole issue of regulation. In 1912, a Royal Commission on Municipal Affairs recommended the creation of a PUC.[4] This was in the midst of the period when regulatory commissions were being created in both the United States and eastern Canada. After extensive consultations between the government and the BCER, during which it was once again stressed that British Columbia needed "the goodwill of the British investing public far more than it does a Public Utility Commission," the question of a regulatory commission was dropped (Roy, 1971, p. 5, fn. 8).

While fending off the regulatory initiative, the BCER moved to renegotiate its franchises – both with Vancouver and its suburbs. Its strategy was to consolidate all franchises into a common expiry date substantially after the 1919 deadline it faced in Vancouver, in order to reduce the probability of a crisis if negotiations were left to the last moment prior to the expiration of each franchise. The company requested a 30-year franchise and a 5.25 per cent guaranteed rate of return (Roy, 1973, p. 255). Since the municipalities could not come to a joint agreement, these negotiations proved unsuccessful.

The company was alert for threats from the private as well as the public sector. Although most competitors had been absorbed around 1900, a new firm emerged by the end of the first decade that offered serious competition. In 1901, Vancouver businessmen organized the Stave Lake Power Company whose objective was to develop cheap hydropower for industrial power users. Eventually, Montreal interests reorganized the company as the Western Canada Power Company (WCP) in 1909, and developed a plant shortly thereafter. In 1913, the BCER reached an agreement with its competitor, whereby the BCER surrendered the industrial sector in Vancouver to this company and, in return, obtained a cheap contract for bulk power (Roy, 1973, p. 257). The final threat from the WCP was eliminated with its purchase by the BCER in 1920.[5]

With its consolidation policy, its ability to absorb competitors, and its strong political position, the BCER reached its zenith in terms of its profitability between 1909 and 1911. The price of ordinary deferred stock reached a maximum at this time (see Table 7-1). While dividends continued at a constant rate until 1914, and traffic peaked in 1913, shareholders had already begun to discount future earnings streams by 1913. Over the next four years, the value of the stock plummeted and dividends were discontinued. These financial difficulties resulted from a severe reduction in ridership occasioned both by a general depression in business conditions that arose in British Columbia before the outbreak of World War I and by the arrival of jitneys on the city streets. Jitneys were a type of taxicab that roamed the city streets, often just ahead of the street railways, picking up passengers. By 1916, the BCER annual report estimated the loss to jitneys at about $350,000 – an amount more than sufficient to have paid the dividends that had been suspended on ordinary and preferred shares.

Renegotiation of the Regulatory Contract

The political climate was altered during this period with the election of a Liberal government in 1916 – a government with at least some Vancouver members who had developed a following by arguing for lower tramway and electrical rates. By 1917, Vancouver was lobbying for repeal of the protective clause that would allow it to go into direct competition with the BCER without purchasing the latter. Anticipating success in this endeavour, Vancouver took out an option on a nearby source of hydro-electric power.

The company's response to the rising political attacks changed, as the directions of the thrusts against it varied. Between 1914 and 1915, it canvassed other street railways, asking for information on how regulatory agencies might work (Armstrong and Nelles, 1986, pp. 207-08). In the spring of 1915, the company even prepared a draft regu-

Table 7-1

Profitability and Traffic of the British Columbia Electric Railway Company Limited, 1905-27

	Yearly mean price of deferrred ordinary stock[1]	Dividend rate on par value	Passengers carried[2]
	£	Per cent	
1905		6.0	10,352,451
1906		6.0	12,395,582
1907		7.5	16,281,766
1908	129.0	8.0	21,328,180
1909	132.0	8.0	25,183,739
1910	145.5	8.0	34,476,804
1911	143.5	8.0	46,541,448
1912	144.1	8.0	62,154,166
1913	127.8	8.0	71,973,822
1914	114.5	8.0	63,429,023[3]
1915	54.5	–	46,330,096
1916	48.5	–	43,021,598
1917	32.8	–	43,234,384
1918	36.0	–	52,853,373
1919	42.9	6.0	53,316,288
1920	50.0	6.2	60,692,708
1921	53.8	6.2	67,932,527
1922	74.0	6.2	67,441,903
1923	94.0	6.5	67,692,851
1924	105.0	6.5	68,252,634
1925	114.5	8.0	69,779,475
1926	137.0	8.0	72,547,367
1927	170.0	8.0	75,113,022

1 The average of the high and low reported for the year in the various annual reports of the BCER.
2 From 1913 onward, the Railway Statistics differentiate between total passengers carried and fare-paying passengers. The numbers here are for fare-paying customers.
3 The Railway Statistics records 52,754,380 for the year 1914.
SOURCE Annual Reports of the British Columbia Electric Railway Company Limited as reported in Houston, *Annual Financial Review* (Toronto: various years) for 1905-15; and Canada, House of Commons, *Sessional Papers*, Railway Statistics, various years, for 1916-27.

latory bill to put forward should it be necessary. Soon the BCER redirected its activities to try to get the jitney threat removed. It did so by approaching the provincial government to regulate jitneys, by petitioning the city to restrain jitneys in return for a reduction of electric lighting rates, and by causing jitters in the London stock market about investing in British Columbia by publicizing the jitney problem. The provincial government, finding itself divided on the issue, empowered municipalities to regulate jitneys, while refusing to do so itself (Roy, 1972, pp. 247-48). But Vancouver was in no mood to restrict the jitneys, since the electric transit franchise was due to terminate in 1919 and competition from the jitneys was performing a regulatory function that the fixed-term *ex ante* franchise contract in effect did not.

With the initiation of the debate in 1917 on the protective buyout clause, the company offered to sell out to the British Columbia government – of course, on favourable terms in the absence of the clause's repeal. The company's offer placed pressure on the provincial government, since it forced British Columbia to face the issue of the cost of following the public ownership route – a cost which, given wartime exigencies, was too great for the public purse to bear. Moreover, the company's offer made it difficult to characterize the utility as intransigent and uncooperative.

While the city ultimately succeeded in rescinding the protective buyout clause, it won a Pyrrhic victory. As angry messages from the London financial community descended on the provincial government in Victoria, the company was able to emphasize the support it possessed overseas in the British financial community. Vancouver squandered its political credits at this time, because its scheme was uneconomic, and the city did not proceed with it. In the midst of the squabbling, a railwaymen's strike in the summer of 1917 brought the operations of the railway to a halt. The various crises led to the creation of a Royal Commission to examine the operations of the BCER.

The Commission in late 1917 recommended that the jitney problem be resolved by constraining competition from these taxis, that electric rates be reduced, and street railway fares be increased so as to reduce the amount of cross-subsidization that was occurring between the two, and that a permanent PUC be appointed.[6] Vancouver accepted a fare increase to 6 cents in 1918, subject to eventual approval by a PUC.[7] A *Public Utilities Commission Act* was then passed that guaranteed the BCER a fair rate of return and gave the PUC the scope to regulate publicly owned utilities.[8]

In the midst of these events, unforeseen circumstances rendered the provincial action void. A 1919 amendment to the federal *Railway Act* had stipulated that any railway or telephone company whose lines crossed those of a federally chartered company fell under federal jurisdiction. After having this pointed out to them by a CPR solicitor, the BCER turned to the federal Board of Railway Commissioners and obtained the 6 cents fare it had been seeking from the city. The province promptly abolished its PUC,[9] having decided that it had too much independence and was an unnecessary expense now that it had little to do (Roy, 1971, pp. 12-13).

Outraged by the loss of local control occasioned by this set of events, the city of Vancouver, supported by the BCER, lobbied the federal government and had an amendment passed that voided federal control.[10] The amendment gave the company a year's grace under its newly acquired federal rate structure. The company then lobbied the provincial government not to create another PUC. In addition, it sought to have Vancouver agree to the new fares by threatening to obtain a federal charter, declaring the BCER to be "a work for the general advantage of Canada." This declaration would bring it back under the jurisdiction of the Board of Railway Commissioners.[11]

Faced with this threat, Vancouver negotiated a new franchise contract with the BCER. A 6-cent fare was confirmed and arbitration procedures that could be invoked at three-year intervals were adopted. In turn, the BCER agreed to reduce its lighting rates from 6 cents to 5 cents/kw.[12] When the dust finally cleared, the company had succeeded in retaining freedom in setting its gas, light, and power rates, while providing for a mechanism to adjust street railway fares to reflect changes in costs.

With the implementation of the new higher transit fare and a return of passenger traffic after the war, the company's fortunes rebounded (see Table 7-1). Once more dividends were paid – 6 per cent starting in 1919, then increasing to the prewar level of 8 per cent by 1925. The company's ordinary stock, which had peaked at £144.1 in 1911 and then fallen to £32.8 in 1917, had returned to £137 by 1926. Regulation then served to normalize conditions to a pre-World War I basis.

Conclusion

In British Columbia, the original franchise contracts were found wanting. On the one hand, they failed to place any restriction on electrical rates; on the other, they provided no efficacious means of recontracting prior to the termination of the franchise. In British Columbia, however, the crisis in renegotiations did not come until World War I when the regulated company, suffering from a loss in ridership and escalating costs, found renegotiation in its own interest. A regulatory board was chosen to facilitate a closer equation of prices in both electricity and tramways with their respective costs; but through a quirk of fate this form of governing instrument was allowed to lapse. In its place, a mechanism was adopted that permitted more periodic renegotiations to take place on the tramways operations.

In British Columbia, the transactions failure associated with the franchise contract never became so recriminatory that public enterprise was a serious candidate for the choice of regulatory instrument. And while a regulatory tribunal was tentatively adopted, it was discarded at the first opportunity for a substitute that required less ongoing supervision of the industry. More importantly, the mechanism by which electrical rates would be controlled was extremely ill-defined. Implicitly, negotiations over tramway fares were to be tied to electrical rates – as they had in the first set of negotiations after 1919.

British Columbia offers an example of a situation in which contractual renegotiations were pursued with the minimum of threat from the state. Opportunism by the state, while always feared by the BCER, was avoided. In part, this was the result of a successful strategy pursued by the company. A protective buyout clause had been inserted in the city of Vancouver's charter at an early stage in the company's history. The BCER then acquired a pattern of franchises that made it costly for Vancouver to expropriate in light of existing law on the requirement of compensation for going value. The company also acquired competitors, so that, by the time the protective clause was removed in 1917, the alternatives available to the city, other than direct ownership, were limited. And the company's lobbying served it well amongst provincial politicians in stressing the need to placate British capital markets by not interfering with, regulating, or expropriating its operations.

As important as company strategy was, the result cannot be ascribed solely to the company's actions. The attitude of the political participants cannot be ignored. British Columbia had strong ties to England. For example, the province did not adopt the North American standard of driving on the right until the 1920s, preferring instead the British norm. Roy (1973, p. 240, fn. 2) has referred to the prevalent attitude as involving a colonial mentality. This should not be regarded as a demeaning description. British Columbians, especially senior politicians, were anglophiles. As such, British institutions and constitutional practice formed an important set of norms on which behaviour was based. Not the least of these was the custom of Common Law that protected private property and contractual freedom. It is significant that throughout the shifting political regimes between 1894 and 1921, the various provincial governments always offered protection to the BCER. While the post-1916 Liberal government may have revoked the protective buyout clause that had been inserted in Vancouver's charter in 1895, it replaced it with a PUC that was made responsible for establishing a fair return on a fair valuation. When circumstances led eventually to its replacement with the *Passenger Rates Act* of 1922, a "fair and reasonable return" was embodied as part of the legislation (Roy, 1971, p. 19).

Attitudes are influenced by economic as well as political and cultural tradition. In this respect, no doubt, the ability to compromise found in British Columbia would have been influenced by the province's somewhat tenuous geographic and financial position. With a resource-based economy subject to even greater variability than the rest of Canada, British Columbia's financial position was never comfortable. For example, a shortage of provincial revenues was accepted as a pressing argument for failing to consider the establishment of a PUC in 1912. In this situation, British Columbia could less afford alienating British capital than Ontario, which had begun to tap New York capital markets at an earlier date, and which exhibited much greater tendencies to confiscate the rights it had granted private utilities.

The political participants in British Columbia were not the only parties to exhibit good faith during most of the renegotiations that took place. The BCER also showed itself capable of goodwill gestures that encouraged compromise. Roy (1973) recounts how most decisions of the company were made by the London Board of Directors. But commitments made by the local manager without prior Board approval during difficult negotiations were generally upheld. The Saanich line outside Victoria was built against the better judgment of the Board of Directors after the Premier argued that such an action was important for the company's image in light of an implicit commitment made by local management. When the local manager agreed to a rate equalization for a Vancouver suburb, the Board accepted the policy for short-run policy purposes, even though it objected in principle and had not given prior approval (Roy, 1973, pp. 247-48 and 253).

Finally, events in British Columbia were unmistakably influenced by unforeseen circumstances. The accidental legal decision that temporarily removed the BCER from local control was fortuitous for the company. It placed considerable pressure on the city to come to a new agreement with the company. As such, it emphasizes the important constraint that was placed on civic populism by the Canadian federal system. There were other more senior levels of government to which utility companies could appeal.

The theory of regulation developed in Chapter two suggested the regulatory contract was likely to develop certain contracting problems. It also noted that with the particular leeway available in Canada for opportunistic behaviour, transactions failure during the recontracting exercise could very well result in the internalization of the contracting process via the creation of public enterprise. Only case studies can reveal the likelihood either that transactions will be allowed to reach a crisis stage or that the state will act in a venal fashion. British Columbia's experience demonstrates that the state need not be viewed as possessing a basic character flaw. Similarly, the utility need not be regarded as a passive participant. British Columbia never appeared bent on confrontation; and the utility was extremely adept at reading the political winds. Nevertheless, the example developed in this chapter does show that a crisis occurred at the expiry of the franchise in 1919. That it was resolved without the establishment of a modern regulatory tribunal or municipalization was probably as much the result of a quirk of legal fate, as it was of the reasonableness of the various parties concerned.

At the provincial level, the transition from the franchise contract to an independent regulatory tribunal generally lagged behind events in the United States. In the electrical and tramway sectors, the transition did not take place at all in British Columbia and Quebec (except for the street railway company in the latter), occurred slowly in Manitoba and Alberta, and was superseded by nationalization in Ontario. In Bell Canada's case, the evolution was more rapid. By 1906, Bell Canada was brought under formal regulatory review. Interestingly, the transition was accompanied by a change in political jurisdiction.

Bell Canada managed the evolution of the regulatory process to its own advantage. It successfully voided the constraints of the franchise contract by disposing of its competitors. When its very success in this regard forced a change in the state's chosen regulatory instrument, it managed to have a weak form of regulatory tribunal chosen as a substitute. As in the case of the BCER and its avoidance of regulation by tribunal, chance and good fortune played a considerable role in the final choice of a regulatory instrument.

Historical Development

The Bell Telephone Company of Canada (Bell) received a federal charter in 1880[1] that was revised in 1882 with a declaration that the company was "a work for the general advantage of Canada" (Armstrong and Nelles, 1986, p. 72). At the same time, Bell obtained rights from Ontario and Quebec to string wires and erect poles because, even with a federal charter, regulatory jurisdiction was not clear at this time.[2]

Initially, Bell faced competition both from existing companies and from potential entrants. Both were gradually eliminated. On the one hand, Bell grew by purchasing local telephone companies that had been operating with equipment provided by Bell's forerunner. Bell also moved to block the expansion of far more powerful rivals than the local exchanges. As in the United States, the telegraph companies offered potential competition both because they operated with alternative technology and because they already had entered or were potential entrants to the telephone

industry. In the United States, this was resolved when Western Union and Bell reached a patent agreement that essentially left the telephone business to the latter. In Canada, Bell simply bought out the telephone plants of the telegraph companies. It acquired Maritime telephone exchanges from Western Union.[3] The fledgling telephone plant of the Montreal Telegraph Company was also purchased. Finally, companies that were not purchased were attacked for patent infringements. The policy quickly eliminated most of the competition. By 1881, Bell's general manager claimed that "we now have the entire field in Canada" (Armstrong and Nelles, 1986, p. 70). While not perfectly accurate, it was close to reality.

Competition was only severely restrained; it was not eliminated by these strategies. The Toronto Telephone Manufacturing Company continued to manufacture telephones and in 1885 successfully challenged Bell's Canadian patents on the basis that Bell had not fulfilled the requirement of the *Patent Act* that specified patents be used for manufacturing in Canada (Armstrong and Nelles, 1986, p. 73). In order to counter the threat this offered, Bell embarked on a strategy of consolidation, more intense price competition, and pre-emptive investment in long-lines construction. In Dundas, Peterborough, and Port Arthur, Bell offered free service to eliminate a competitor.[4] In Winnipeg, Bell set up a dummy corporation, that competed with a private rival until the latter was driven from the market (Armstrong and Nelles, 1986, p. 108). By 1886, the Toronto Telephone Manufacturing Company was acquired by Bell.

As it grew, Bell, like the BCER, developed an acute sense of local politics. It ensured that local interests were represented in its regional subsidiaries. This not only made the subsidiaries more responsive to local concerns but also made it difficult for local complaints to picture the subsidiaries as tools of central Canada. British Columbia was "organized from the start by autonomous though friendly interests, the New Westminster and Burrard Inlet Telephone Company" (Armstrong and Nelles, 1986, p. 109). The Nova Scotia Telephone Company was organized in 1886 with 33 per cent Bell ownership. By 1887, a similar situation evolved in New Brunswick with the creation of the New Brunswick Telephone Company. Control over both maritime companies was maintained through a large minority stock position and equipment supply contracts.

With the threat of entry from telegraph companies eliminated, Bell turned its attention to another potential source of competition. The railways, with their rights of way, could potentially link non-Bell local exchanges. In 1885, Bell began the process of contracting with the railways to use their rights of way, and for the exclusive right to put telephones in train stations. But it still had to deal with an indirect threat from the CPR. In 1888, the Federal Telephone Company started operations in Montreal. Since, it was financed by the CPR's backers – amongst others, Sir Donald Smith and Sir William Van Horne – this entrant could not be treated lightly. Bell's solution was to purchase the upstart – at a substantial premium. The advantage of this arrangement was spelled out by Bell's Canadian manager:

> . . . we are assured of the cordial support and cooperation of these people, who to all lookers-on appear to own Canada. We would be enabled to advance rates in Montreal to a point which would, in a few years, repay all this outlay. We must shortly go to Parliament for an increase of capital, or must issue new Bonds to replace those now maturing in 3 years, and it would be impossible for us either to sell Stock or issue Bonds if we are engaged in a competition with the Canadian Pacific Railway (Armstrong and Nelles, 1986, p. 112).

Even though Bell acquired many of its competitors during this period, it never eliminated the threat of entry. In order to protect itself further, Bell devised an entry blockading strategy of negotiating exclusive franchises with local governments. Partially as a response to the possibility that the Federal Telephone Company would also enter the Toronto market, Bell negotiated an exclusive franchise with the city of Toronto in 1891. Bell agreed to pay 5 per cent of its gross revenue for five years to the city; to charge, at maximum, rates of $50 for business and $25 for dwellings; and to place wires underground in downtown areas. It had succeeded by 1905 in negotiating exclusive franchises with 36 municipalities in Ontario and Quebec (Armstrong and Nelles, 1986, p. 110).

As a result of Bell's strategies, competition or potential competition that provided a meaningful constraint upon Bell was substantially eliminated by the mid- to late-1890s. Bell's success in buying out local exchanges and in neutralizing both the telegraph and railway companies removed this threat. In doing so, Bell also removed the alternatives available to public authorities during the recontracting process. As such, the opportunity for contractual failure increased. But it was Bell, not the public authorities, that tried to take advantage of the situation. In 1896, when the franchise with Toronto came up for renewal, Bell refused to renegotiate and applied to the federal government to increase Toronto's rates.[5] It was Bell that sought to void the type of municipal regulation that was acceptable to it in 1891 – a time when the exclusion of rivals from the Toronto market was more important from its point of view.

While the city appealed to the federal government to disallow the new rates and the federal government did so, the company continued its old rates, but charged *new* subscribers higher prices. The federal government admitted it could do nothing about this. As a result, considerable pressure developed from municipal governments for some form of regulatory review. By 1900, 140 municipalities submitted a petition to the federal Parliament for a more effective scheme of regulation. In the meantime, Toronto tried another approach and attempted to exert control over Bell's placement of poles. The matter went to court in 1901 and was resolved in Bell's favour by the Judicial Committee of the Privy Council in 1904. With the Privy Council ruling that the company's federal charter superseded municipal and provincial government regulation, Bell was almost completely freed from local control (Armstrong and Nelles, 1986, p. 165).

That still left municipal ownership of competing systems as an alternate device for regulation. The economics of a municipal system that had to compete with Bell were less than promising, and although Toronto considered this option, it abandoned it in 1904. Ottawa did the same. In 1902, ratepayers in this city voted in favour of a publicly owned system. Ottawa city council ruled out a municipal alternative, considered supporting an alternative private company, and then finally renegotiated a contract with Bell in 1907 (Armstrong and Nelles, 1986, p. 166).

The municipal alternative turned out to be unpalatable because of Bell's almost exclusive control of long-distance intercity lines. With Bell's control of long lines firmly established by the early 1900s and its exclusive contract with the railways, adoption of a franchise contract with anything but a Bell subsidiary promised considerable difficulties. The experience of the Lakehead cities of Port Arthur and Fort William served to emphasize the consequences of trying the alternate approach. Here a municipal system was constructed. But Bell refused the new company access to the CPR station. Appeal was made to the Board of Railway Commissioners, but its decision in 1904 upheld Bell's contract with the railway. A connection was allowed, but only if damages were paid to Bell.[6]

This was not the only ruling that the Board of Railway Commissioners would make that severely restrained recontracting with other companies. A local company would have little chance of succeeding if it could not gain access to the long-distance trunk lines controlled by Bell. Bell granted such access very selectively. In 1908, an amendment to the

Railway Act made the Board of Railway Commissioners responsible for adjudicating disputes between Bell and independent telephone companies.[7] Eleven companies applied to the Board in 1911 for arbitration of this issue. The Chief Commissioner, in his decision, observed that "competition in connection with telephones never appealed to me" and ruled that the independent companies would have to pay 15 cents per call in addition to the regular charge (Armstrong and Nelles, 1986, p. 203). As a result, independent telephone companies were placed at a considerable disadvantage relative to Bell exchanges, and competition from this source was effectively constrained.

Bell's success in freeing itself from local regulation led to a vigorous response from two sources. In Toronto, the city council passed a resolution advocating federal operation of long lines. In Montreal, the mayor of Westmount, who had originally been stirred to activity by the Quebec legislature's removal of local control over the Montreal Light, Heat and Power Company, began organizing a group of municipalities to lobby provincial and federal governments to develop more effective control of utilities (Armstrong and Nelles, 1986, pp. 142-46). He joined forces with Toronto by pointing out that the problems the latter had with Bell were similar to those developing in the electrical utility sector in Montreal.

As a result of a growing perception by Ontario and Quebec municipalities that local control was being lost, the Union of Canadian Municipalities was formed in 1901 as a lobby group. Initially, the Union had some success in opposing applications from utilities for federal charters that would void local control. In 1902, it succeeded in thwarting the attempt of Mackenzie's Toronto and Hamilton Railway Company to get a federal charter, by winning the right to have a clause included in its charter that required it to submit to local regulation (Armstrong and Nelles, 1986, pp. 144-45). In this activity, the Union received provincial support. The Ontario government passed legislation in 1907 voiding all franchise rights acquired by utilities which thereafter secured declarations of general advantage from Parliament.[8]

The leaders of the municipal movement could count on considerable support. By 1903, their members numbered over 100. Many amongst them came to see municipal ownership as the only vehicle through which local control could be exerted (Armstrong and Nelles, 1986, pp. 144-45). An additional force, the Canadian Independent Telephone Association, which was spearheaded by Francis Dagger, a British telephone engineer, also lobbied for federal government involvement in long-distance telephone lines. In 1903, this pressure forced the Liberal government to amend the *Railway Act* so as to designate the Board of Railway

Commissioners as arbitrators of railway station connections.

With the 1904 Privy Council ruling firmly establishing federal control over Bell, the federal government was persuaded in early 1905 to begin a full-scale investigation of the telephone industry. A Select Committee of the House of Commons was created to examine the alternatives for regulating the telephone industry. Bell was caught by surprise but quickly organized to defeat the local forces. Most of its opponents argued for some measure of local control, or public ownership. Bell was not without influence. Many of the central players had close connections to Bell. The Chief Commissioner of the Board of Railway Commissioners, who ruled against the Lakehead municipal telephone company in 1904, had previously been president of the Bell-controlled New Brunswick Telephone Company. The Leader of the Opposition had been Bell's counsel in the Maritimes. Halfway through the hearing process, the Postmaster General who chaired the Select Committee was replaced by the lawyer who had been representing Bell in the hearings (Armstrong and Nelles, 1986, pp. 166-72).

Bell was able to dispose easily of the threat of federal ownership of long lines. The Canadian Prime Minister, Laurier, was not disposed to nationalization.[9] Bell focused instead on influencing the type of regulatory authority that was likely to emerge from the hearings. In the end, the *Railway Act* was amended to bring the federally chartered telephone companies under the Act. Rates were made subject to approval by the Board of Railway Commissioners (Armstrong and Nelles, 1986, p. 174, fn. 36). Municipalities could supervise at most the placement of wires and poles. Moreover, while the Railway Commissioners could order interconnections, these were made subject to compensation and were constrained not to create "undue or unreasonable injury to or interference with the telephone business of such a company."[10]

The regulatory system that resulted did not threaten the dominant position that Bell had created for itself. The 1904 decision on railway station access and that in 1911 on independent telephone company interconnection further protected Bell from competing companies. The prevailing philosophy was that the telephone system was a "natural monopoly." The Board of Railway Commissioners explicitly stated their distrust of competition. Moreover, while the Board, from the very beginning, asked whether the company was in satisfactory financial condition, it showed no inclination to adopt the rigorous U.S. standard that required establishment of a rate base and then a decision on the fair rate of return (de Grandpré, 1970, p. 30). In the first set of rate hearings after the 1906 legislation, Bell had submitted a new set of tolls that standardized rates. While it argued that a fair return should be provided, it did not advocate calculation of a rate base, only the recognition that costs had gone up and so too should revenues. In what must be one of the most peculiar dispositions of any rate case, the matter was resolved by accident. The Commissioner responsible for the decision died and the new rates were allowed to stand without change (Armstrong and Nelles, 1986, p. 202).

The implicit standard that emerged was one based on an incremental revenue criterion that accepted the legitimacy of costs as of the date at which regulation was initiated. In 1912, the Board evaluated another Bell rate application and found that the company was in a satisfactory financial condition and did not therefore need to adjust rates.[11] In effect, the Board adopted what came to be called the "prudent investment" standard – except it never evaluated the reasonableness of the initial investment as was done in Nova Scotia. It ruled that revenue should cover operating costs, maintenance, provision for depreciation and a just and reasonable return to investment.[12]

Conclusion

In the end, Bell was saved from possible expropriation in central Canada, because it was able to escape from having to negotiate its regulatory contract at the municipal level. It was in Toronto, not Montreal, where the greatest pressures originated: where the street railway had been briefly nationalized in the early 1890s, where Bell's local franchise came under severest attack, where the public-power movement evolved in the first decade of the twentieth century, and where the city council came to advocate public

ownership of telephone trunk lines. That Bell avoided having to recontract with public authorities in a political jurisdiction that clearly distrusted private capital and that was willing to use whatever means available to remove private capital can be attributed to the federal charter of Bell. Whether this was obtained with unusual foresight or by good luck is not very important. In the end, it sufficed.

The judicial battles over jurisdictional control took place at a time when changes in technology and the nature of the product supplied made these particularly difficult issues. At its birth, telephone service was a local product. Telegraphs still dominated the transmission of long-distance messages. By the beginning of the twentieth century, however, long-distance lines were in place and becoming increasingly important. Local control alone or regulation was neither optimal nor feasible – as Bell was quick to point out when it argued that fixed costs so dominated its cost structure that it was impossible to determine the division of costs between local and long-distance service.

Irrespective then of Bell's refusal to negotiate franchises at the local level, a regulatory crisis, which developed over jurisdictional control, was not unexpected. Such a crisis also developed in the United States. In Canada, the crisis was concluded quickly, though not necessarily effectively, by the Privy Council decision when the supremacy of federal authority was determined. Jurisdictional control may have been decided at this point, but the question of fairness remained unresolved. Local interests still had to be satisfied that their concerns would be considered by a federal regulatory agency. When westerners perceived this would not occur with a federal bureaucracy based far away in Ottawa, they turned to a different regulatory instrument. This is the subject of the next chapter.

9 Manitoba: Public Enterprise Accompanied by Regulation

In Manitoba, as elsewhere, the original franchise contracts developed inadequacies that, by the early part of the twentieth century, led to pressures for renegotiation. Manitoba, however, chose a uniquely Canadian solution. It adopted both public enterprise and regulation. Between 1905 and 1910, Manitoba nationalized the telephone system in the province and authorized Winnipeg to establish a municipal electrical plant to compete with the privately owned Winnipeg Electric Company. Subsequently, a PUC was established primarily to regulate these state-owned utilities.

The Manitoba telephone nationalization was associated with two aspects of contract failure: both opportunism by the state and the inability to write a particular contract that cross-subsidized some consumers. At the same time, it demonstrates that the strategy to avoid nationalization, which worked for Bell in eastern Canada, was not sufficient elsewhere. No one business strategy can be called upon to protect long-lived immutable capital in the face of an acquisitive state.

The creation of a publicly owned electrical utility was also accompanied by opportunism on the part of the state. This episode illustrates how, even in the face of the loss of an exclusive franchise because of entry by a public utility, a private utility need not be driven out. There were three reasons for this. First, an effective business strategy was followed by the private utility. Second, outside constraints, imposed by federal control of Manitoba water resources, helped the private company. Third, a regulatory structure was established that served to restrain competition from the public utility. Together, these factors allowed the private utility to coexist with the publicly owned utility.

In the first chapter, it was argued that the choice between a regulatory tribunal and nationalization would be affected by their relative costs. Moreover, it was claimed that the different constraints placed on opportunistic government behaviour in Canada as compared to the United States would lead to a lower cost (at least in the short run) for nationalization and thus more state-run utilities. It is, therefore, significant that opportunism on the part of Manitoba can be found in its dealings with the privately owned utilities in both sectors.

But the Manitoba case study emphasizes a second reason for relative cost differences in the two instruments. When federal influence in a state is so pervasive that it makes provincial regulation difficult, the relative costs for a province of choosing the regulatory, as opposed to the public enterprise, instrument will be increased. Manitoba found itself in a situation where federal charters of both the telephone and the power generating company removed both from meaningful local regulation.

The choice then of the state-run utilities in both the telephone and electricity sectors can be rationalized within the framework presented previously – with the modification added that the federal system also influenced the relative costs of the two policies. What is truly unique, however, about the events in Manitoba is that a regulatory agency was subsequently chosen to monitor the activities of the state-run utilities. This shows the advantages of this agent for administering, monitoring and arbitrating the contract between the state and a natural monopolist – in cases where the monopolist is both publicly and privately owned.

The Expropriation of Bell Canada's Manitoba Operations

The loss of Bell Canada's Manitoba assets to a provincial government intent on the development of a publicly owned telephone system may be said to have been partially the result of Bell's strategy to avoid local control in its central Canadian markets. So successful was Bell in avoiding local control in central Canada, that Manitoba felt compelled to take the only action available to it if it was to have a measure of local control – that of nationalization. Nationalization was accomplished by the use of a stratagem that threatened the confiscation of Bell property through the use of provincial taxing power.

After the 1904 Privy Council ruling that confirmed federal jurisdiction over Bell, Ontario populists chose to try to redress the loss of the local authority's right to negotiate the regulatory contract by exerting political pressure in Ottawa. Manitoba, separated by greater distances from the nation's capital, followed a different route – that of public ownership. The difference was probably the result of western sentiments that a regulatory board based in Ottawa might be able to appreciate local concerns in Toronto or Montreal, but was unlikely to be cognizant of those arising much further away on the Prairies.

At the same time as the federal government established a Select Committee to study the problem of regulating the telephone industry in early 1905, the province of Manitoba's Private Bills Committee recommended that the province consider a publicly owned telephone system (Mavor, 1917, p. 16). By November, Premier Roblin announced the government was committed to the public ownership of telephones. In early 1906, another committee was struck and a bill for the creation of a public system was introduced and passed.

The province sought legal advice on whether it could expropriate Bell's Manitoba properties, but was informed by counsel that Bell's federal charter protected it. The federal government took the same position (Armstrong and Nelles, 1986, pp. 178-79). Moreover, when the province approached the federal government for power to expropriate, it was turned down (Mavor, 1917, p. 17). Nevertheless, the provincial government was given legal advice that the province could exploit its power by imposing a discriminatory tax on Bell's business. The legislation that was introduced in March provided both for a discriminatory tax and for a joint provincial-municipal system. While the discriminatory tax measure was later withdrawn, the government in effect had revealed that it possessed a trump card it could play whenever it wished.

At first, political support for the provincial government's policy was less than overwhelming. In municipal plebiscites held in the fall of 1906, many of the municipalities voted against building locally owned exchanges to link with provincial long lines (Armstrong and Nelles, 1986, p. 188). Within a year, this had changed. A provincial election in early 1907 was fought and won with a major campaign theme of publicly owned telephones. Construction of provincial long lines was commenced. By the fall of 1907, the provincial government was also building a local exchange in Winnipeg. Throughout the 1907 political campaign, the opposition favoured the same policy of public ownership, so strong was public support for the idea. Much was made of the possibility of providing lower telephone rates both for farmers and for users in smaller towns.

In the fall of 1907, Bell conceded and sold its plant to the provincial government for $3.5 million in 4 per cent Provincial Bonds, or for about $3 million taking into account the discount then existing on such bonds (Mavor, 1917, pp. 29-31). The face value consisted of about $3.2 million depreciated plant value plus 10 per cent for forced sale. Evidence

confirms the amount paid was approximately the reproduction value of Bell's investment.[1] Of course Bell would have been entitled to the capitalized value of future profits if it had been treated fairly according to the law, since its franchise was in effect perpetual. That it did not continue to press its case in this regard might partially be attributed to its own need for funds during the financial crisis that beset North American capital markets in 1907 (Armstrong and Nelles, 1986, p. 183). Much more important was Bell's recognition that it might end up with assets worth even less than replacement value, because of "ruinous competition" from the government system. The government lines were already under construction. Moreover, the Manitoba Premier had already shown his disposition to use the tax system to discriminate against private companies. Bell's general manager summed up the reasons for the sale:

> If we are sure of losing money in Manitoba through competition with the Government, I think that with $4,000,000 or whatever price we might receive, in our pockets, we would be better off than conducting ruinous competition without the $4,000,000[2] (Armstrong and Nelles, 1986, p. 184).

There is, therefore, a parallel between the telephone nationalization in Manitoba and the creation of public enterprise in the rail sector at the federal level. In both cases, the state was able to use power not available to the private sector in order to coerce a company into divestment of its long-lived immutable assets. It is less obvious, however, that Manitoba acted in quite the same opportunistic manner as the federal government. For one thing, Manitoba was not a direct party to the original contract that had been written in Ottawa when Bell's charter was first granted. Indeed, it could very well be argued that Bell was indirectly responsible for the events in Manitoba – by its search for protection from a recontracting process in Ontario that threatened to break down because of the strong civic populist movement in Toronto. But if that is the explanation for the choice of instrument in Manitoba, the connection between action and reaction is sufficiently indirect that the type of venality or deception implicit in the use of the phrase "opportunistic behaviour" is certainly lacking. What can be said is the strategy that worked for Bell in one jurisdiction had ramifications in another that could not be undone given the time and the place.

The Manitoba nationalization does demonstrate that no one strategy for private utilities was sufficient to protect them in their dealings with the state. A federal charter, such as that possessed by Bell, could deflect municipal attempts at expropriation; but it could not prevent them where a provincial government was intent on choosing a regulatory instrument that provided more local control. In the end, the threat of discriminatory taxation and the predatory deep pocket of the public purse in Manitoba served to force Bell to sell its Manitoba operations.

It should also be noted that the failure of the recontracting process in Manitoba was associated with the attempt to achieve a public goal that is difficult, though not impossible, to accomplish with a privately owned utility. In Manitoba the political process adjudged lower rates and rate equalization to be more important and pressing than in central Canada.[3]

While a regulatory agency may use subsidies to lower all rates or may set rates to favour specific users, there is an administrative cost of using this type of governing instrument that may be larger than when the same policies are implemented by a state-owned corporation. The government may be able to monitor the subsidy requirements more easily when it has direct access to the books of a publicly owned utility. It may have less difficulty in directing a Crown corporation to adopt a rate structure that meets certain equity goals but involves cross-subsidization.

This oft-repeated argument for the choice of a publicly owned entity for the provision of service cannot be given much credence in light of the situation that subsequently developed in Manitoba. The creation of a public telephone company in Manitoba was not accompanied by a careful accounting of the subsidies involved in government ownership. If anything, government ownership was used to obfuscate the true cost of government policy. During the first three years of ownership, the accounts of the government's telephone company were distorted so as to conceal the true cost of government operations. No depreciation expenses were charged and maintenance was included in capital expenses. As a result, the government operation was made to look profitable when it was not, and rates were reduced in early 1909. By 1911, however, the true state of affairs was finally revealed when the Telephone Commission that ran the publicly owned telephone company, somewhat to the chagrin of the government, charged all maintenance and reconstruction expenses to revenues and showed a considerable deficit, which in turn precipitated a political crisis.

Mavor has calculated that the deficit on government telephone operations rose from about $12,000 in 1908, to $15,593 in 1909, to $16,000 in 1910, and to $220,000 by 1911. So too did the loss per telephone. At the beginning of 1908, there were about 14,000 telephones; by the beginning of 1911, 29,748. Thus the subsidy per subscriber provided by public funds increased from about 85 cents to $7.40 over the period.[4]

This sequence of events might be used to suggest that the choice of the public instrument was crucial to subsidization, not because of monitoring advantages, but because of the increased possibilities for disguising subsidies with the use of the public corporation. The latter is important when the population at large (over 460,000 in Manitoba as of 1911) is subsidizing a relatively small number of users (less than 30,000). But events do not support this argument. The possibilities for deception were relatively limited; as deficits mounted, they became easier to detect and too costly for the government to ignore.

A Royal Commission was appointed in early 1912 to investigate the Telephone Commission, but not to examine the extent to which the deficits that had arisen were the result of government directives and policy. Its *Report* criticized both the operations and the accounting practices of the Commission. Faced with finding a way to extricate itself from an embarrassing situation that was going to require an increase in telephone rates, the government created a Public Utilities Commission (PUC).[5] The public telephone system was thereafter run by a single Telephone Commissioner under the supervision of an advisory board (one of whom was the Public Utilities Commissioner).[6]

The new PUC granted rate increases that removed most of the deficit by the end of 1913 and reduced the subsidy to about $1.15 per subscriber. Just as important, under the aegis of the Public Utilities Commissioner, accounting systems were adopted that more closely reflected costs (Mavor, 1917, pp. 127-29). Regulation then became the instrument used by the government to control its publicly owned telephone system.

Competition between Private and Public Utilities in the Electrical Industry

The Winnipeg Electric Railway Company emerged by the turn of the century as a privately owned company with a monopoly in the electricity, gas, and public transit sector in Winnipeg. Originally formed by Mackenzie and Mann of Canadian Northern famed as the Manitoba Electric Street Railway Company, it obtained the Winnipeg franchise in 1892 to build an extensive electric railway to replace the previous horsedrawn operation that had been run by another company.[7] Its charter specified that it could also produce and sell light, heat, and power.

During the succeeding six years, the Mackenzie street railway company moved to consolidate all utility operations in Winnipeg. By doing so, it removed potential competitors and made the contracting process with the state into a small-numbers game. In 1894, it bought out the rival street railway (Armstrong and Nelles, 1986, p. 94). In 1895, the Manitoba Electric Light Company (chartered in 1880) lost its Winnipeg municipal contract and was eventually forced by economic circumstances to merge with the Winnipeg Electric Street Railway in 1898. With this acquisition, Mackenzie acquired a charter that allowed his company to distribute power anywhere in the province without the consent of municipalities (Rea, 1975, p. 75). In 1900, another important competitor was purchased – the North West Electric Company. Mackenzie also developed a gas plant to serve the Winnipeg market. In 1902, cognizant of the advantages of hydro-electric power, Mackenzie joined with the Ogilvie Milling Company's backers and developed a hydro-electric project on the Winnipeg River, only 60 miles from Winnipeg, which started producing power in 1906. In 1904, the resulting distribution company (the Winnipeg General Power Company) was merged into the street railway company to form the Winnipeg Electric Railway Company (Armstrong and Nelles, 1986, p. 96). In turn, the Winnipeg Electric Railway Company controlled through stock ownership the generating company (the Winnipeg River Power Company, later to become the Manitoba Power Company). Thus, as was done in Vancouver, private competition was reduced by merger, consolidation, and by pre-emptive investment.

In response, Winnipeg tried to regain a measure of local control. The 1892 franchise with the street railway stipulated that, after 1902, 5 per cent of gross revenues and a levy of $20 per car had to be paid to the city; but there was no provision for control of electricity or gas rates. The franchise was to last 35 years (expiring in 1927), at which time the city had the right to buy the company at a price to be fixed by arbitration. If the city did not do so, the franchise was to be extended for five-year intervals (Rea, 1975, p. 75). The original contract then gave the company considerable freedom; but when it became highly profitable, and as the alternatives facing the city were reduced, a demand for recontracting emerged. The first steps were taken in the field of electrical generation, since it was here that the original franchise offered the least protection to the public.

Like the case with the telephone sector, the division of responsibilities between the federal and provincial governments presented peculiar problems to the province of Manitoba with regards to its choice of regulatory instrument. The federal government still administered the allocation of the Manitoba watershed. While the Winnipeg Electric Railway Company operated with a provincial charter, the electrical generating subsidiary possessed a federal charter. The Bell case as to the paramountcy of provincial or federal regulation was already winding its way through the courts in 1902, but with the Privy Council's decision of 1904, it became clear that the provincial powers were severely limited in the case of a federal charter. This meant the choice of a provincial regulatory board for Manitoba was not a viable option. While a regulatory board might rule on the appropriateness of the rates charged to Manitobans by the Winnipeg Electric Street Railway Company, it was not within its powers to control the rates charged this company by its federally chartered power-generating subsidiary.

Since Mackenzie's acquisition strategy had removed alternate private parties with whom the state might negotiate franchise contracts, and since regulation via tribunal was unsuited to the task, the regulatory route chosen was the development of a municipally owned power plant. But first, the state had to exercise its power to abrogate the protection it had offered to attract private investment in the first place. In Manitoba, like Ontario, legislation had been passed that promised buyout protection if public plants were built.[8] Winnipeg attempted in 1902 to have this removed, but was rebuffed by the province. In 1906, the city was finally successful in obtaining the requisite modification of its charter to build a municipal plant, including the removal of the protective buyout clause. A generating plant was constructed after some delay, a distribution system erected, and municipal power began to flow in 1911. Thus, in Manitoba, the protection offered the initial investor was removed at the behest of the province's capital city. Moreover, when Mackenzie offered to sell his plant to the municipality, he was rebuffed (Armstrong and Nelles, 1986, p. 156). Therefore, as in Ontario, the choice of public enterprise in Manitoba was associated with the abrogation of contractual commitments made by the state to protect capital originally committed by private investors to the industry.

In contrast to the power generation sector, a strategy of franchise proliferation, extension, and consolidation served to protect the capital of the street railway company. During the period 1900-10, Mackenzie followed a franchise extension strategy similar to that which was adopted in both Vancouver and Montreal by the street railways. In 1905, the Suburban Rapid Transit Company, which served the western suburbs of Winnipeg, was purchased. In 1908, the Winnipeg, Selkirk and Lake Winnipeg Railroad, which operated in the northern suburbs, was acquired. Franchises for some 17 municipalities were eventually consolidated under the Winnipeg Electric Railway Company. The exclusive Winnipeg franchise had a termination date in 1927, but the others had dates between 1932 and 1943. In each case, the contract specified that the municipality could buy the railway plant at termination or extend the franchise. Of course, with the judicial requirement that expropriation value would have to include "ongoing" concern, this meant that expropriation by Winnipeg would force Winnipegers to subsidize residents of surrounding municipalities, because the capitalized value of future profits in the surrounding systems would be factored into the purchase price. As was the case elsewhere, this strategy served to increase the cost of expropriation.

The railway extensions not only served to protect the railway franchise; they also were used to protect the gas and electricity business of the private utility. The company agreed to suburban rail extensions only if the municipalities bound themselves to long-term contracts to purchase gas and electric power. As such, it pre-empted these markets and protected itself to some extent from potential competition from the Winnipeg-owned electrical utility (Winnipeg Hydro).

When the city obtained the right to build its own utility in 1906, it in turn tried to constrain the Mackenzie company's ability to distribute power in the city by challenging its right to string wires therein. The legal case was commenced in 1906 with the company claiming it had these rights under the charter of the Manitoba Electric, Light, and Gas Company that it had absorbed. In 1912, the Judicial Committee of the Privy Council ruled in favour of the company.

While private capital won this skirmish, it had not won the war. The municipal utility lowered its rates to 3.33 cents/kwh in 1911 with the first delivery of its hydro-power. The Winnipeg Electric Railway Company was forced to match the new rates, dropping its rates from the previous level of 7.5 cents/kwh (Rea, 1975, p. 78). Mackenzie offered to sell his company to the city in the same year; while an agreement was reached with the mayor, the city council rejected the offer. Thereupon, Mackenzie apparently found a New York syndicate willing to purchase the company, but only if the street railway franchises were given additional protection (Nelles, 1976, pp. 468-69).

To do this, seven private bills were introduced in the legislature that, in effect, would have acquired all remaining suburban railway franchises for the Winnipeg Electric Railway Company and made them perpetual. While Winnipeg opposed these bills, it did not have strong representation in the 40-member legislature where only four members represented the city in spite of the fact that it contained one-third of Manitoba's population (Rea, 1975, pp. 79-82). The rural members supported the package, because it promised transportation to the metropolitan area for many of their districts. Thus, the city appeared likely to lose its fight with the local monopoly as a result of the latter's resort to a different political constituency.

At the same time as these private bills were before the legislature, the province submitted its PUC Bill which had emerged from the telephone controversy. It was here that Winnipeg felt it had even more to lose. While all private utilities were to be controlled, public utilities would only come under the Board if it was done on a voluntary basis. But if they were brought under the Board, the latter could fix their rates. During the course of debates, the private company was adamant that the publicly owned utility's rates were unfairly low and that a regulatory commission would be expected to remedy this situation. Winnipeg thus feared that, with only a slight modification in the Bill, their hard-won low electricity rates might be lost.[9]

In the end, a compromise was reached.[10] The private bills were modified so that the perpetual franchise was avoided, but the suburban railway bills were passed. In turn, the city agreed to place the municipal utility under the Board, with the provision that the latter was not allowed to raise the rates of any utility against its wishes (Manitoba, 1939, p. 197). Thus, a regulatory body was created that controlled the private sector and could at least wield powers of moral suasion over the public utility.

The effect of the new regulatory structure was to moderate the rivalry between the public and private sectors. The PUC Commissioner managed to obtain cooperation between the two utilities in Winnipeg by getting them to share each other's poles (Nelles, 1976, p. 470). In a related capacity, as a one-man Royal Commission to examine the feasibility of extending public power through the province, he rejected the idea of a Manitoba version of Ontario Hydro (Armstrong and Nelles, 1986, p. 195). Nevertheless, a small rural publicly owned system was created in southwestern Manitoba in 1919. Its losses, however, constrained the enthusiasm for an Ontario Hydro-type venture in subsequent years. Finally, the PUC exerted moral pressure on the Winnipeg municipal utility to increase its rates. Gradually its rates crept up to those of the private utility (Nelles, 1976, pp. 471-72).

The PUC also served to reduce the contractual problems that faced the street railway's operations. Its 1915 *Report* noted that unreasonable demands for service were often made and that it was the Commission's duty "to withstand attempts to oppress a public utility through the medium of the Commission." Finally, when the railway appeared before the Commission in 1919 looking for relief from the rapid inflation in costs that had squeezed the profits of most Canadian utilities, the Manitoba PUC granted an interim increase and then proceeded to evaluate the capital stock using the reproduction cost basis that was widespread in the United States.[11] Thus, by 1920, Manitoba's PUC had evolved into a tribunal that, at least when it came to setting tramway rates, protected private capital from the type of opportunistic behaviour that forced the Grand Trunk into bankruptcy.

The other threat to the private utility – that from publicly owned power – was constrained by a different force. As in the British Columbia case, it came from the peculiar federal nature of Canada. Contrary to the British Columbia case, it arose not from a peculiar quirk in federal railway legislation; in Manitoba's case, it came from the power the federal government exerted over the development and use of hydro sites in the province.

Before 1930, the federal government administered the rivers, lands, forests, and mines of Manitoba for the general advantage of the Dominion. From 1909 onward, the Department of the Interior oversaw the efficient use of the Manitoba watershed. Under its jurisdiction, regulations were created that gave strict control over stream flows and all technical and operational matters. These regulations stipulated that new sites were to be developed only after existing sites had reached their full potential. In addition, sites were reserved for exclusive use.[12] The result, as tidy and efficient as it might have seemed in the eyes of its creators,[13] was that the Winnipeg Electric Company (renamed in 1924) gained exclusive access to a large, cheap source of power that gave it a cost advantage.

The public and private electrical utilities had already begun to work hand in hand in the mid-1920s. A "gentleman's agreement" was reached that meant existing customers, except for large industrial users, would not be allowed to switch accounts. This served to stabilize competition (Manitoba, 1939, p. 195). In 1925, the public utility found itself short of power and agreed to buy power from the private utility. In return, a further agreement was reached to divide up markets. Essentially the city-owned utility was given Winnipeg's inner core, while the private utility was assigned the suburbs (Armstrong and Nelles, 1986, p. 301). The cooperation between the two was extended well into the 1930s by federal actions.

The Winnipeg River remained the principal hydro source until the 1950s. The first two leases (given to the Winnipeg Electric Street Railway's generating subsidiary in 1904 and Winnipeg Hydro in 1906) had been let before a comprehensive federal development plan was created. When a comprehensive plan was finally formulated by the Department of the Interior, it required the abandonment of the private company's site for the development of the new plant at Seven Sisters Reach. The private company was thus requested to abandon its original rights in return for rights at

the new location. In turn the next, but smaller, development of Slave Falls was to be reserved for Winnipeg Hydro. The net result was to leave the private utility with 70 per cent of the available horsepower (Nelles, 1976, pp. 475-78).

The Winnipeg Electric Company, having been informed of the plan, duly applied for the Seven Sisters Reach's project in 1927 (Nelles, 1976, pp. 475-76). Initially, the Premier of Manitoba opposed the application because his United Farmers' party had espoused public ownership of power. He eventually relented when it became clear that the province did not have the power to expropriate the power-generating subsidiary because of its federal charter; and if the site was developed by the province, there was not enough demand in the smaller publicly owned distribution systems for the new generating capacity. Finally, the Department of the Interior strongly argued the efficiency case for sequential and exclusive development of hydro sites – a case which, because of the requirements of abandoning the private company's previous site, gave the Seven Sisters Reach's site to the Winnipeg Electric Company.[14] In the end, the Premier relented, but did obtain an arrangement that guaranteed all the power that the provincial rural electric system needed for $13.80/kwh.[15]

Opposition immediately developed at both the municipal and provincial levels. However, the Winnipeg City Council, divided much more clearly into opposing business and labour factions since the 1919 Winnipeg General Strike, narrowly defeated a motion to request Winnipeg Hydro to make its own application. The Department of the Interior, therefore, did not formally have to adjudicate two opposing applications. Still, pressure was exerted on Ottawa by Manitoba federal Members of Parliament to prevent private development at Seven Sisters Reach. In the end, the Premier had to lobby Ottawa to approve the plan that the Department of the Interior had proposed. Approval was granted in August 1928 (Nelles, 1976, pp. 475-78).

This agreement served not only to consolidate the Winnipeg Electric Railway's control over electricity; it also served to solidify its hold over the transit business, for it came just as its lease on the latter was coming to an end in 1927. From 1922 onward, the company had tried to get extensions of its franchise. It was met with fierce opposition in Winnipeg where the General Strike of 1919 had created irreconcilable factions. The business community, aided by the passing of control of the company to local interests from Mackenzie in 1919-20, and worried about the general threat to private property from militant labour groups, increasingly supported the company. But this support was not sufficient to carry the council when the matter of a new transit contract was discussed. On the other hand, with the Seven Sisters Reach's development, the company possessed a long-term franchise that gave it control of a major share of electrical generating capacity for the foreseeable future, and the temptation to take over the street railway business was reduced. With the requirement that expropriation would have to pay for ongoing value, the new generating capacity with its long-lived franchise would have substantially increased the costs of expropriation.

Two events then served to affect the regulatory environment in Manitoba. The first was the creation of a formal regulatory agency in 1912 followed by its 1920 regulatory decision to allow the revenues of the private electrical street railway to be based on a reproduction cost basis. The second was the Department of the Interior's decision to reserve the Seven Sisters Reach's development for the privately owned Winnipeg Electric Company – a decision finally ratified in 1928.

The impact of each of these events can be evaluated by examining the price history of the Winnipeg Electric Railway Company's equity and debt. Table 9-1 contains the average price of the common stock (column 1), and of one of the debt issues (column 4). Dividend yield on the par value of common stock and realized yield on debenture stock are listed in columns 3 and 5, respectively. Finally, the U.S. yield on long-term corporate bonds is provided in column 6 for comparison to the Winnipeg Electric Company's long-term debt yield.

The three periods 1905-12, 1912-20, and 1920-29 are characterized by very different results. Prior to Winnipeg's city-owned development being brought into operation in 1911, the Winnipeg Electric Railway Company saw its net earnings yield, its dividend rate, and the price of its common stock increase continuously. In the second period, the yield, the common-stock price, and the debenture price fell steadily. Both competition from the city-owned development (Winnipeg Hydro) and the inflation of the late war years negatively affected the profitability of the private company. Whatever influence the moral suasion of the regulatory agency might have had after 1912 on the rates charged by Winnipeg Hydro, it was not sufficient to offset the effects of inflation in the latter part of the period.

With the regulatory agency's adoption in 1920 of the traditional rate base standard, the price of the privately owned company's debt began to recover. The differential between the yield on this debt and U.S. long-term corporate bonds, which had reached a peak in 1920, declined to a plateau by 1924. On the other hand, the price of common stock continued downward until 1924. It then rose dramatically until 1928, as the implications of the allocation of the

Seven Sisters Reach's project were digested by the stock market. Thus the regulatory system staved off the bankruptcy threat, but it was the federal government's role that injected value back into the equity holdings of the company.

Conclusion

In the introductory chapter, it was argued that the first *ex ante* franchise contracts between the state and a private utility has many of the characteristics of relationships that are likely to develop severe difficulties during recontracting exercises. Because of this, an alternate form of contract – one that provides for more continuous recontracting – is required. With the appropriate legal environment that constrains the state from opportunistic behaviour, the independent regulatory tribunal can serve this purpose.

That discussion, however, did not recognize the particular problems that can arise in a state where jurisdiction is divided between federal and provincial governments. Evidence of these problems emerged during the transition from the *ex ante* franchise contract in Manitoba. In Manitoba, as elsewhere, the terms of the original franchise contract had serious shortcomings; but by the time political pressures arose for renegotiations, the incumbents in both the telephone and the electrical industry, through aggressive acquisition strategies, had removed most competitors from the industry. The prerequisites necessary for a franchise auction had disappeared because of the transition to a small-numbers bargaining situation.

As advantageous as regulation by tribunal might be in these circumstances, it had one significant defect. It was not available to local authorities because of federal charters possessed by the key participants.[16] This left publicly owned instruments as the only choice open to the province – if local regulation was to be implemented.

Regulation did evolve at a later stage, not to control privately owned utilities, but to act as the government's agent to control the state-run utilities. The Manitoba example, then, provides a different reason for the emergence of regulation; though its emergence is still related indirectly to the contractual problem previously outlined. In Manitoba, a PUC served to resolve problems, in both the telephone and the electric sector, that had arisen because of the presence of public corporations. In the telephone sector, the regulatory agency was chosen as the mechanism to permit rate increases when public subsidies had reached unacceptable levels. In the electrical utility sector, regulation was seen by the private sector as the instrument that would control opportunistic behaviour on the part of

Table 9-1

Financial Statistics of the Winnipeg Electric Railway Company,[1] 1905-28

	Average price of common stock, Toronto[2]	Net earnings to par value common equity	Dividends yield on par value of common stock (100)	Average price of perpetual consolidated debenture stock[3]	Realized yield on consolidated debenture	U.S. yield on 30-year corporate bonds[4]	Difference columns 5 and 6
	Dollars	Per cent	Per cent	Dollars	Per cent	Per cent	Per cent
1905	165.2	9.86	5.0				
1906	174.9	11.17	6.5				
1907	157.4	12.01	8.0				
1908	154.6	13.14	10.0				
1909	177.8	14.39	10.0	103.00	4.37	3.77	0.60
1910	183.4	15.58	10.0	104.75	4.30	3.80	0.50
1911	222.9	18.51	11.5	106.26	4.24	3.90	0.34
1912	231.8	16.75	12.0	103.25	4.36	3.90	0.46
1913	201.7	14.07	12.0	99.00	4.55	4.00	0.55
1914	197.6	11.05	12.0	95.00	4.74	4.10	0.64
1915	...	5.51	9.5	86.94	5.18	4.15	1.03
1916	97.7	5.61	0	76.25	5.90	4.05	1.85
1917	55.4	1.69[5]	0	67.94	6.62	4.05	2.57
1918	48.0	0.98[5]	0	64.50	6.98	4.75	2.23
1919	43.0	1.08[5]	0	65.50	6.87	4.75	2.12
1920	32.8	6.56[5]	0	49.75	9.04	5.10	3.94
1921	37.8	3.84[5]	0	50.00	9.00	5.17	3.83
1922	37.2	3.51[5]	0	67.88	6.63	4.71	1.92
1923	33.6	2.75[5]	0	75.75	5.94	4.61	1.33
1924	29.3		1.0	81.25	5.54	4.66	0.88
1925	46.2	2.28[6]	2.0	82.25	5.47	4.50	0.97
1926	52.7	4.44[6]	2.0	79.25	5.68	4.40	1.28
1927	76.1	6.09[6]	2.0	83.75	5.37	4.30	1.07
1928	112.8	4.52[6]	2.0	89.50	5.03	4.05	0.98

1 The Winnipeg Electric Company after 1924.
2 This is the average of the monthly high, low quotation, where both were available for a month.
3 This was secured by a trust deed whereby the whole of the company's assets and properties were mortgaged.
4 The 30-year yield was chosen as being closest to the term of the debenture stock.
5 After depreciation.
6 After depreciation; before deducting "additional depreciation" but after "deferred and undistributed charges."
SOURCE Columns 1, 3 and 4, Annual Reports of the Winnipeg Electric Railway Company, Houston, *Annual Financial Review* (Toronto: various years); and column 6, United States, Bureau of the Census, *Historical Statistics of the United States: Colonial Times to 1957* (Washington, D.C.: U.S. Department of Commerce, 1960).

the state by eliminating ruinous competition emanating from low prices charged by the public power company. The problem that regulation was called upon to resolve in both sectors originated from the state's adoption of public ownership because of a failure of the initial contractual regulatory process.

This failure, however, did not arise solely from opportunistic behaviour by the state. Rather, the private sector had adopted strategies that made the transition to regulation by tribunal difficult or impossible. Bell's success with its federal charter meant Manitoba could hope for little local control over telephones except by nationalization. Mackenzie's Winnipeg Electric Railway Company, with its overlapping railway franchises and its perpetual electricity franchises protected by federal charter, left Manitobans with little choice but to seek a local solution through the creation of publicly owned utilities.

Regulation became the method used to control the public corporations – both to ameliorate the government's own short-run tendency to use the public corporation to achieve patronage goals in the telephone industry and to deflect the criticism that the publicly owned electrical utility was engaging in unfair competition. In the latter case, the federal government also exercised an important constraint. Through its control of Manitoba rivers, it was able to regulate access to the source of hydro-power and this had the side effect, intended or otherwise, of ensuring that the private utility would maintain its position relative to the public company.

The choice of instrument, then, in Manitoba can be ascribed to both business strategy and the nature of the federal state. The former led to the choice of the public option by the state; the latter restrained its use in one sector. But the political milieu cannot be ignored in this process, for the Manitoba situation, just described, resembled that of British Columbia very closely. In the latter case, the public ownership route was rejected on both practical (lack of fiscal capacity) and ideological grounds. Similarly, it resembled the situation that developed in Ontario. In Ontario, telephones remained beyond local control, but the publicly owned electrical utility system swallowed up private competitors to obtain a greater share of the market than was achieved in this period in Manitoba.

The difference between Manitoba and British Columbia lies partially in the different attitudes exhibited toward monopoly and the willingness to choose public ownership. Manitoba had from its inception been willing to expend public monies to redress the perceived wrongs of monopoly. It had led the fight against the monopoly possessed by the CPR – a monopoly that had been created by the federal government. Manitoba sought to stimulate the growth of competing railways through land grants and by aiding the cooperative grain movement. In the latter case, it eventually established a government-controlled grain-elevator system. Its policies in the telephone industry were similar. The telephone sector appeared to move beyond local control when the federal government assumed regulatory control. This time Manitoba chose public enterprise to re-establish a measure of local regulation. A local regulatory tribunal was no longer an option given the 1904 Privy Council decision on Bell. Manitoba's actions in power generation were similarly motivated by an uncertainty as to the jurisdiction of a local regulatory body in light of the federal charter of the generating subsidiary of its Winnipeg Electric Railway Company.

That Manitoba did not move as far as Ontario did in the electrical utility sector can be ascribed to several factors. First, the same scandals involving private utilities that served to arouse public indignation in Ontario in the 1890s did not emerge in Manitoba.[17] In contrast, the public outcry that did occur was directed at government mismanagement of the grain-elevator system and the telephone industry. Second, there was not the same political force in support of public electrical power. In Ontario that force was manifested at the provincial level by Adam Beck who not only had a long career but who also developed a substantial following among small businessmen across southwestern Ontario. Manitoba did not possess the same number of nascent industrial communities that Ontario did. Moreover, the support from the Manitoba business community for public ownership was badly split by, and evaporated after, the Winnipeg General Strike. As time passed, the goal of protecting the private-enterprise system increased in importance relative to the need to control monopoly power. Moreover, by the time the schism had developed in 1919 between owners and workers, the regulatory system had moved to an American style fair-return-on-fair-value basis, and control of monopolies seemed to be well in hand. Finally, the federal government exerted more control at an earlier stage in the development of electrical power in Manitoba than it did in Ontario.

Thus political culture was an important determinant of institutional choice. The same economic problems can be resolved with a variety of solutions. When one choice is unavailable, there are substitutes the state can choose to modify the manner by which the objectives of the regulatory franchise are met. Manitoba chose nationalization, partly because the franchise option and regulation by tribunal had been voided, partly because opportunistic behaviour on the part of the state made this a relatively inexpensive option.

In both cases, the utility faced arbitrary changes in the nature of the contract – for which it was not compensated. Nationalization may, therefore, partly be ascribed to its lower relative cost. But in the case of Manitoba, the likelihood that taste mattered cannot be ignored since the political culture accepted nationalization so frequently.

The Manitoba case also demonstrates that a regulatory agency may be chosen, not just for control of private utilities. In this case, it became a vehicle by which two publicly owned utilities were monitored. Its function was not so much to place a ceiling on prices; rather, it was to set a floor for them. As such it should be interpreted as one of the means by which the somewhat new form of organization – a government corporation – was monitored. The regulatory agency offered some of the same advantages for control of publicly owned as it did for privately owned utilities. In addition to these advantages, the government could, through the appointment of an independent regulatory agent, deflect undue pressures for inefficiency which were characteristic of many publicly owned utilities when first created.

10   The Creation of Ontario Hydro: The Franchise Contract Repudiated

During the first two decades of the twentieth century, the electrical utility industry in Ontario was transformed from one with a substantial private component to one where the Crown corporation, Ontario Hydro, dominated both production and distribution. Starting as a quasi-regulatory agency that purchased power and then redistributed it for purchase by municipally owned systems, Ontario Hydro became the dominant producer of hydro-power by the early 1920s.

As in the case of the nationalization of the Canadian railways, the creation of Ontario Hydro and its subsequent performance has been cloaked in an ideological rhetoric that has obscured the significance of the events surrounding nationalization. Propounded by a progressive movement, supported by succeeding generations of voters since 1907, it has come to be a symbol of the uniqueness of the Canadian approach to economic development – an example of the state's positive role in promoting the industrial process and cooperating with business. Symbols, however, tend to obscure reality. A careful examination of the circumstances surrounding the creation of Ontario Hydro, shows the state was anything but successful in its relations with those who had actually pioneered in the electrical utility process.

The theory presented here suggests that the creation of a public enterprise like Ontario Hydro should have been associated with a crisis in business-government relations and the exercise of opportunistic behaviour by the state – what has been referred to as a transactions failure. This was the case. Transactions failures arose for the reasons outlined in the first section of this work. Imperfect foresight was exercised in stipulating conditions in original franchises granted to monopolies. Technical change gave rise to the need for recontracting. During that recontracting exercise, the ideology of the public-power movement was used to justify opportunistic behaviour that voided the protection offered investors in the original agreements – without compensation. This was exactly the type of behaviour that the U.S. Constitution constrained. In Canada, the supremacy of the legislature allowed it to ignore contractual commitments that would have been protected in the United States. In those circumstances, it is not surprising that private capital was eventually displaced and nationalization resulted.

The end result was similar to that found in the railway sector – the creation of a large public enterprise as a regulatory instrument. There were, however, important differences. In the railway case, a regulatory agency, acting at the behest of the government, adopted a confiscatory rate policy that contributed significantly to the bankruptcy of the carriers that were eventually nationalized. In Ontario, the government, acting more directly both through its agent, Ontario Hydro, and by the passage of legislation, voided previous commitments it had given to protect privately owned capital from state expropriation.

Historical Development

The Demise of the Franchise Contract

In the last two decades of the nineteenth century, electricity emerged as a new energy source in competition with gas for illumination purposes. During this period, there were a number of separate electricity-generating firms in most urban areas competing for public franchises. Toronto was no exception.

In 1881, the Toronto Electric Light Company (Toronto Electric) was incorporated and received a token street lighting contract from city council in 1884. Finding competition from gas too intense, the company offered itself for sale to the Consumer's Gas Company of Toronto (Consumer's Gas) in 1888, only to be rejected because the gas company found the terms too high and favoured competing generating technology from Westinghouse (Armstrong and Nelles, 1986, p. 80).

During this early period, Toronto tried to sustain the competition that existed among the various utilities. It attempted to maintain the conditions that made the franchise contract viable. When Consumer's Gas applied to string wires in 1889, the city refused, thus keeping the gas company out of electricity. It also tried to cultivate competition between companies in the lighting field. In 1889, the city signed two contracts – one with Toronto Electric and one with the Toronto Incandescent Electric Light Company – giving a 30-year franchise to each and promising to issue no more franchises. In order to provide for recontracting should the competitors disappear, a provision was included to void both franchises if the two companies amalgamated.

Until the mid-1890s then, Toronto was served by several competing companies: two of which produced electricity and one which produced a substitute (gas). It is not surprising then that municipalization did not receive widespread support. As late as 1895, Toronto voters rejected a municipal lighting-plant. But matters were to change shortly thereafter. The city soon found the franchise terms that were meant to maintain competition could be circumvented. In 1894, Toronto Electric, which had previously restricted itself to arc lighting, entered the incandescent field in direct competition with its rival. Competition led to amalgamation in 1896; though, to avoid annulling the 1899 franchise agreements, the two companies retained a separate legal existence under a single management. The city, somewhat belatedly, challenged the amalgamation. The companies, claiming that this tardiness sanctioned their actions, eventually won their case in 1905 (Armstrong and Nelles, 1984, pp. 205-06).

Restrictions upon competition did not always originate just from strategic behaviour on the part of the utilities. Sometimes state action helped to consolidate the position of the incumbents. Consumer's Gas managed to have an upper limit placed on the price that could be charged by a newly chartered competitor in 1853. The price was sufficiently low that it blocked entry to the gas sector. The same result occurred in the electric railway industry. In 1895, the province of Ontario effectively reduced the threat of entry into the transit sector when it passed legislation governing new charters of street railways. Dividends were limited to 8 per cent and limits placed on fares. While the two electric railways serving the city cores of Toronto and Montreal may have been profitable, this was not the case with entrants. Entry was really only possible by opening new lines to serve suburban municipalities. But such service, with its lower density, required higher fares, and was only marginally profitable. For example, the suburban Montreal Park and Island Railway went bankrupt in 1898. Years later, in 1911, Toronto financed the Toronto Civic Railway to serve its suburbs, but it ran at a deficit. Thus, Ontario legislation effectively blocked private entry from all except the incumbent railway after 1895. Gradually, this railway surrounded the city with a number of suburban railways, none of which paid any franchise fees. They were amalgamated as the Toronto and York Railway in 1907 (Armstrong and Nelles, 1986, pp. 130-31).

As competition for franchises disappeared, an even greater problem emerged. The franchise contract, such as that possessed by the Toronto Street Railway, contained no arbitration procedure – except for reference to the courts for interpretation of the terms of the original contract. Moreover, the issues that could be so arbitrated were not resolved in a very satisfactory manner. In the period between 1898 and 1910, the city of Toronto used this route to try to force the Toronto Street Railway to expand its system in order to serve new sections of the city. But the city failed here, as in the case of Toronto Electric, when it turned to the courts for arbitration.

The Toronto railway's franchise had given the city the right to specify route extensions. In 1898, the company received legal advice that it did not have to make extensions beyond the city's legal boundaries as of the date of the franchise. Since Toronto had grown rapidly via annexation of suburbs during this period, this offered Toronto particular difficulties. The matter was finally taken to court in 1909 and 1910, and the Judicial Committee of the Privy Council upheld the company's position (Armstrong and Nelles, 1986, p. 132).

While the Toronto Street Railway appears at first glance to have been obstinate, the confrontation had its roots in poorly specified terms of the 1892 franchise contract that was drawn up by the city. A street railway's profitability could be seriously eroded if the density of ridership declined. Because of Toronto's smaller size relative to Montreal, the Toronto Street Railway had trouble maintaining the same traffic density (riders per car-mile) as Montreal. In the 1890s, the manager of the Toronto company was given strict instructions to cut down on car mileage so as to increase earnings per car-mile – with reference being made to the higher earnings being made in Montreal compared to Toronto (Armstrong and Nelles, 1986, pp. 124-25).

Apart from its smaller population, Toronto differed from Montreal in another important aspect. The growth rate of its population from 1890 to 1921 was higher. Part of the reason for this was that Toronto had annexed a large number of suburbs between 1890 and 1898. Montreal did not.[1] As a result, Toronto's emphasis on the need to expand the transit system is understandable. Equally so was the company's concern that expansion of its system into newly developing suburbs would reduce density and profitability.

At the core of the company's concern with profitability was the tax rate in the original franchise. Compared to the rate used in Winnipeg, Montreal, and Halifax, the percentage of gross revenues paid in Toronto was high. It was also high by United States standards. Table 10-1 compares the tax burden for the Toronto Street Railway to that imposed on U.S. street railways between 1915 and 1918. Toronto had negotiated a franchise tax that, with growth in revenues,

Table 10-1

A Comparison of the Burden of Taxes on the Toronto Street Railway Company and the United States Electric Tramways, 1915-18

	United States[1]			Toronto[2]		
	Revenue taxes	Pavement and other	Total	Revenue taxes	Pavement and other	Total
	Per cent					
1915	6.40	3.21	9.61	15.25	3.78	19.03
1916	6.33	2.68	9.01	15.23	3.61	18.84
1917	6.27	2.40	8.67	15.42	4.20	19.62
1918	6.47	2.10	8.57	16.03	5.05	21.08

1 D. F. Wilcox, *Analysis of the Electric Railway Problem* (New York: 1921), p. 81.
2 Annual Reports of the Toronto Street Railway Company, Houston, *Annual Financial Review* (Toronto: various years).

generated a tax rate more than double the United States average. If the Toronto railway system had been expanded, the traffic carried would have been subject to the high tax contained in the franchise agreement. This was not the case for separately created subsidiaries such as the Toronto and York Radial Railway. Thus, the original franchise contract no longer suited the circumstances that prevailed in 1900. The two parties, however, were unwilling to compromise. The city was as much at fault as the company during these negotiations, because it insisted that the original franchise terms be applied to any extensions that were brought into the city (Frisken, 1984, p. 242). More importantly, no arbitration procedure existed to impose a new contract. While the courts could interpret the clauses of the original contract, they could not devise a solution to the problems that developed.

The franchise contract, therefore, proved inadequate because of its lack of flexibility. It also fell into disrepute because of scandals associated with its original award. In 1894, when the contract of Toronto Electric came up for renewal, the company was approached by the Chairman of the Fire and Light Committee for money to buy votes. While the extortion came from public-office holders and not the company, the cause of the corruption lay in the process. This process, therefore, fell into disrepute. But further revelations arising from a judicial inquiry implicated the Toronto Street Railway. Its agent spent considerable sums of money during the tender hearings (Armstrong and Nelles, 1977*b*, pp. 42-45). These scandals, brought to public attention by inquiry and press reports, served to weaken the *ex ante* franchise as a viable regulatory instrument; for as soon as the public perceived the terms of the contract could be affected by corruption, the moral imperative to observe the terms subsequently was substantially reduced.

It is difficult to know whether corruption in the letting of these contracts was any greater in the 1890s than in previous periods. The increased profitability of many utilities by the turn of the century suggests that there may have been more leeway and a greater incentive to corrupt the negotiations. Moreover, there was a certain perception at this time that corruption in big business was endemic. This attitude fueled the progressive movement (McCormick, 1981). The revelations in Toronto would have confirmed the fears of those of its citizens who were following the revelations of a new brand of U.S. journalist – the "muckraker."

By the first decade of the twentieth century, the franchise contract was no longer regarded as an adequate regulatory instrument in Toronto. The companies in each of the telephone, electricity, and transit industries had so consolidated their positions that competitive bidding was no longer an option. Bell had refused to renegotiate its exclusive franchise in 1896, because it no longer had to worry about a competitor. The two Toronto light companies had merged. The Toronto Street Railway had developed suburban franchises that ringed the city. In each case, there was no outside party left upon whom the city might call. The preconditions for transactions failure had emerged.

When Toronto turned to the courts, as it did with the electric light merger or the Toronto Street Railway's refusal to build extensions into the newly annexed suburbs, it consistently lost. Toronto also tried to regain a measure of control over Bell by challenging the latter's right to string wires; it lost this battle too. Only in the case of the gas company was Toronto successful in modifying the terms of a franchise contract. In electricity, transit, and telephones, the courts blocked Toronto's efforts to negotiate new terms that recognized the increased profitability of the utilities that were serving its citizens. A new regulatory framework was therefore bound to emerge. What was adopted, however, was public ownership, and not the independent regulatory tribunal that proved so popular in the United States.

The Private Sector

The transformation of the electric sector in Ontario from one that mixed public and private enterprise to one dominated by the public sector evolved slowly over the first two decades of the twentieth century. By 1900 electric lighting plants abounded in many localities, but were generally supplied from local steam-run plants. The thrust to develop the huge potential of the Canadian side of Niagara Falls did not seriously get under way until 1900. In 1899, a franchise was granted to the Canadian Niagara Power Company,[2] in 1900, to the Ontario Power Company, and, in 1903, to the Electrical Development Company. The first two were American-owned and focused primarily on the export market. The latter was Canadian-owned and linked indirectly via its principals to Toronto Electric and the Toronto Street Railway. The most well-known of the principals was Mackenzie, also an organizer of the Canadian Northern Railway, the gas company in Vancouver, and the Winnipeg utility conglomerate. Table 10-2 presents the maximum allowable horsepower provided by each franchise, the power actually developed in 1906 and 1910, and that exported to the United States in the latter year. The export orientation of the first two companies is evident.

Each of the franchises stipulated the maximum allowable horsepower and the term – 50 years with three subsequent renewals of 20 years each. Payments to the government of Ontario were based on a sliding scale. For example, the Electrical Development Company was required to pay a flat rental fee of $15,000 plus $1.00/HP for power generated between 10,000 and 20,000 HP, $0.75/HP from 20,000 to 30,000 HP and $0.50/HP above 30,000 HP (Mavor, 1925, pp. 30-31). In return, the government, through its agent the Niagara Falls Park Commissioners, covenanted not to enter into direct competition in the generation of power.

The Electrical Development Company was pioneered by substantially the same investors involved in the Toronto Electric and the Toronto Street Railway Company. Both of these companies had expanded rapidly during the 1890s; and though a new steam-generating plant was in place by 1900, it was clear that it would shortly be inadequate given the burgeoning demand for electricity. The Electrical Development Company, therefore, was formed with these two customers being the source of demand justifying the large capital investment required.

The franchise system adopted at first for hydro-generation in Ontario had some of the same problems that franchises in other areas experienced. The pace of change made the initial terms of the contracts obsolete. In the case of the power-generating stations, the state had little idea of the long-term potential of Niagara Falls, partially because of the uncertainty associated with the long-distance transmission of electricity, partially because of the failure to appreciate that domestic demand would expand long before the expiration of the franchises and require a redirection of power that was initially contracted for export. The initial terms of the contract, which extracted relatively low franchise fees,[3] quickly became outdated.

Problems with the franchise of Toronto Electric emerged for slightly different reasons. While it was offered for sale to the city of Toronto in both 1907 and 1913-14, the city rejected it on both occasions. One of the reasons given was

Table 10-2

Hydro-Generating Capacity at Niagara Falls, 1906 and 1910

	Maximum allowable HP	Developed HP		HP exported to the United States
		1906	1910	1910
Canadian Niagara Power Company	100,000	40,000	46,000	46,000
Ontario Power Company	250,000	50,000	52,000	35,000
Electric Development Company	125,000	37,500	42,800	10,000

Source   Column 1, J. Castell Hopkins, *The Canadian Annual Review of Public Affairs* (Toronto: Annual Review Publishing Company, 1905), p. 286; column 2, Hopkins, *Canadian Annual Review* (1906), p. 173; and columns 3 and 4, Hopkins, *Canadian Annual Review* (1910), p. 409.

that municipalization would have involved taking over the contract to purchase power from the Electrical Development Company at rates that were regarded as unduly high. The power contract with Toronto Electric was for 25 years; with the Toronto Street Railway, for 18 years.[4] Once again, the problem was one of lack of foresight. The initial franchises did not envisage the development of alternate power sources, nor that the service being offered would become so widely used that its price would garner so much public attention. Electric lights were in their infancy in 1889 with incandescent lights just beginning to replace arc lights. Electric railways in 1891 were still having to overcome difficult technical problems, which made their success anything but assured. As such, little importance was attributed at the time to the necessity to control profits. By the middle of the first decade of the twentieth century, the profitability of the enterprises led to demands for renegotiation of the franchises. Between 1900 and 1910, the Toronto Street Railway averaged 8.4 per cent on net worth (common stock plus surplus) while Toronto Electric averaged 9.3 per cent (Hall, 1968, pp. 58-59). In a capital-intensive industry where 4 per cent was regarded as the capital cost of the government,[5] these returns suggested private franchises were costly to the consumer.

The contractual agreement with the generating company by each of these two Toronto distributors meant that direct control of both could still leave consumers paying higher prices than complete regulation of the entire system would provide. The contracts themselves do not appear inordinately long, since they were being given to encourage capital that was both immutable and long-lived and therefore subject to capture should opportunism develop. But the mere existence of the contracts substantially complicated the needed renegotiation process, since it widened the number of parties that had to become involved.

Emergence of Ontario Hydro

As the American-owned generating plants were being built at Niagara Falls, a populist movement for the public provision of power gained momentum. Support came from both Toronto and the smaller towns of southwestern Ontario. Manufacturers from large and small towns alike supported the movement, since they saw it as a source of cheap power. The Toronto group was worried that a monopoly would gain control and be insufficiently regulated. The smaller town manufacturers worried that, while Toronto because of its size would obtain hydro-power, they would have to continue to rely upon higher cost steam-generated

power. The movement, however, was not restricted to manufacturers alone. The notion of a cheap source of illumination appealed to most municipal ratepayers. Indeed, when elections were held in 1907 to ratify the public system that emerged, the vote was 28,333 in favour of 10,199 against in the industrial centres of western Ontario.[6]

The first phase of the public power movement culminated in the "Berlin Convention" of 1903 that essentially handed the task of organizing, which had until then been informal, to a committee of mayors. Shortly thereafter, the Ontario legislature created the Ontario Power Commission, whose task was to collect data on costs and to evaluate the possibilities of municipalities joining together to supply themselves with electricity. After the evaluation stage, if ratepayers in participating municipalities approved, a permanent Board of Commissioners was to construct a transmission system (Nelles, 1975, p. 245). Moreover, while the government handed out the last power-generating franchise in 1903 to what was to become the Electrical Development Company, it reserved 62,500 HP for purchase by the municipalities at prices to be set by the government (Mavor, 1925, p. 33).

In its first phase, the Hydro-Electric Power Commission of Ontario (Ontario Hydro) was essentially a distribution company. The enabling legislation was passed in 1906, but the participating municipalities did not ratify the contracts required by the legislation until early 1907. In 1907, bids for power from the Niagara producers were solicited; Ontario Power, the American-owned company, won with the low bid. In 1908, the contract for the transmission lines was let. The first power reached Berlin in 1910. By 1910, 10 municipalities were receiving some 2,500 HP; by 1914, some 75 municipalities were receiving 77,000 HP; and, by 1916, 191 municipalities were receiving 167,000 HP (Nelles, 1975, p. 363).

Although the Commission started as a distribution company, it was given some control over the private sector. It could decide whether the generating plant or the output of private companies was required and acquire either for its own purposes.[7] Initially, at least, it tried to use these powers to dictate to the Electrical Development Company the territory in which it could sell – restricting it only to Toronto (Mavor, 1925, pp. 89-92). The second phase of Ontario Hydro saw it move into the generation of power. In 1914, Ontario Hydro purchased a generating plant on the Severn River, in 1916 on the Trent, and in 1917, it purchased the generating capacity of Ontario Power at Niagara. It then proceeded with construction on Queenston Heights – the Chippewa Creek project that was essentially completed in 1921.

Opportunism

The Conmee Clause

During the evolution of Ontario Hydro, the state reneged on two contractual obligations it had made to the private sector. In 1899, a term, known as the Conmee clause, was inserted in the *Ontario Municipal Act* that was intended to prevent municipalities from expropriating, either directly or indirectly, private capital committed to gas, electric light, or waterworks.[8] Before municipalities could create their own companies in these spheres, they were required to purchase any existing private companies at a fair price, which was to be decided by arbitration.

It was under the protection of this clause that Toronto Electric began to organize efforts to bring electricity from Niagara Falls to Toronto. After initial attempts to buy power from the American-owned Niagara Falls Power Company failed, its principals obtained a franchise in 1903 for generation of electricity at Niagara Falls and transferred the franchise to the Electric Development Company (Mavor, 1925, pp. 30-31). The work at Niagara proceeded and by 1906, the cornerstone for the power-generating station was laid. At the same time, a transmission line was constructed from Niagara Falls to Toronto that would provide power to the Toronto Street Railway and Toronto Electric. Power first reached Toronto via this line in December 1906 – power to supplement the steam electric plants that had already been built.

Unfortunately, the protection Parliament offers from political opportunism can also be removed. As long as the provincial government had no direct interest in hydro production, it was willing to constrain the arbitrary use of municipal authority. As it moved into the ownership area itself, however, it removed the protection offered by the Conmee clause. In 1906, the first *Hydro Act* was introduced into the legislature. The Conmee clause was declared not to apply to municipalities obtaining power from the Commission (Mavor, 1925, p. 53). As such, the city of Toronto no longer had to offer protection to the private capital that had been invested to serve the city. Toronto then entered into a contract with the Hydro Commission and proceeded to build its own distribution system in competition with Toronto Electric.

Repeal of the Conmee clause allowed Ontario Hydro to proceed without having to bear the expense of expropriation. With its establishment in 1906, it faced a difficult problem. The privately owned Electrical Development Company had both generating capacity, a transmission system to Toronto, and a distribution system in Toronto Electric and the Toronto Street Railway. The other major consumer of power was Hamilton, which was served by another private company – the Hamilton Cataract Power Light and Traction Company. The latter had pioneered the long-distance transmission of power in Ontario when it opened its plant in 1898 with a 35-mile line from the Niagara escarpment to Hamilton. Together, Toronto and Hamilton could not be allowed to remain outside the system. Estimates presented to the government in 1906 of the potential horsepower requirements for the Niagara District had indicated Toronto and Hamilton would account for about 48 per cent of the total demand.[9] If these two markets were left to the private sector, scale economies at the generating level would be lost.

Expropriation of these private companies was felt to be too costly. Throughout the period, successive Ontario premiers were acutely aware of the potential costs of a state-owned company. In 1902, as the debate raged over the nature of public intervention, Ross, the Liberal premier, expressed concern about the use of the public treasury to benefit towns in a geographically limited part of Ontario. In 1905, the new Conservative premier, Whitney, worried about the expense of having to buy out existing concerns – envisaged to be between $5 and $25 million (Nelles, 1975, pp. 239 and 260). Provincial expropriation was therefore not feasible and would have to be done by the individual municipalities. But the original *Hydro Act* required municipal councils to approve bylaws authorizing contracts with Ontario Hydro before it could serve an area. Thus, there was some pressure to minimize the cost to municipal ratepayers so that they would approve the contracts. Repeal of the Conmee clause did exactly that.

The Electrical Development Company at this time ran into acute financial difficulties. It found itself unable to raise capital from financial markets that were increasingly leery of expropriation. While the government was short-tempered with those who claimed that expropriation without compensation might take place, pointing out that the *Hydro Act* specifically promised compensation for expropriation,[10] it seemed not to understand the fear of the financial community that expropriation could come equally from unfair competition – from a government-owned company that was not required to bear the same costs as a private company. One concern, voiced at the time, was th e fact that the Hydro Commission did not pay municipal tax (Mavor, 1925, p. 220). The financial crisis of the Electrical Development Company continued until 1908, when the company was formally folded into the Toronto Power Company, which in turn was controlled by the Toronto Street Railway. By doing so, the future of the generating plant was guaranteed on the basis of the markets offered by the Toronto Street Railway and Toronto Electric.

Throughout the debate as to the appropriate role of private and public bodies, both sides appeared to have been willing to consider a compromise – to adopt a mixed system with private ownership subject to regulation. In 1906, Ontario Power offered to build a transmission system for the government, retailing power at rates to be set by the Commission (Nelles, 1975, p. 270). In 1907, before Toronto voted on the necessary bylaw to contract with the Hydro Commission, Toronto Electric offered to enter a voluntary sliding-scale type regulatory arrangement, with a fixed 8-per-cent dividend and with surplus going to reduce rates (Mavor, 1925, p. 104). In the same year, those in control of a faltering Electrical Development Company offered the government two alternatives: to rent its existing system at cost plus a fair return, or to go into a partnership with the government again at cost plus interest. The government also gave consideration to a partnership. In 1908, the Premier of Ontario hoped he could work out a merger between Ontario Power and the Electrical Development Company, so that the transmission line would be constructed by a private company. Mackenzie, one of the principals behind the Toronto Street Railway, was willing to suggest that capital costs could be reduced if the government guaranteed the bonds of the company (Nelles, 1975, pp. 282-89). In 1913, Mackenzie once more offered to sell the assets of both the Toronto Street Railway and Toronto Electric at appraised value. While there seems to have been little disagreement over the value, the city rejected the offer – as they had in 1907 – because of a contract between the aforesaid companies and the Electrical Development Company said to be at $35/HP for 30 years.[11]

Yet all of these private overtures came to naught. The state in the end was unwilling to compromise. Backed by the power of the ballot box, the head of the Ontario Hydro-Electric Power Commission, Beck, pushed his advantage. The end result was the creation of a commission which not only could buy power but which also was given a regulatory role that expanded substantially over time.

The Power Generating Clause

The second instance of opportunism occurred as Ontario Hydro moved into the power generation field during World War I. The Ontario government violated its contractual obligation that it not enter into competition with the Electrical Development Company in the field of power generation. The clause in the original franchise read:

The Commissioners will not themselves engage in making use of the water to generate electric, pneumatic, or other power except for purposes of the Park, provided that in case the said Commissioners . . . at any time may have granted to any other

person or corporation license to use the waters of the said Niagara or Welland Rivers, and by reason of failure of such person . . . to carry on the works so licensed, the . . . Commissioners find it necessary to forfeit said license and to take over said works, this clause shall not prohibit said Commissioners from operating such works for the generation and transmission, sale or lease of electricity or power (Mavor, 1925, p. 118).

With the purchase by Ontario Hydro in 1917 of Ontario Power and its generating facilities at Niagara Falls, the protection afforded the Electrical Development Company was specifically voided.

It should be noted that Ontario Hydro's transition from that of a distributor of electricity to that of a producer with its concomitant breaching of the Electrical Development Company's franchise was accomplished during the emergencies of World War I. Ontario Hydro's chairman used the crisis to the best of his advantage. First, by charging the private company with exporting illegal quantities of power to the United States, and by having a Commission of Investigation focus public opprobrium on the company, Beck effectively undercut any sympathy that might otherwise have existed for the private sector. That the power exports were supporting U.S. munitions contracts with Britain and that Ontario Hydro was making similar exports reduced the credibility of his contentions – at least in hindsight. But at the time, as Nelles has noted "the war itself, confused matters and exaggerated feelings" (Nelles, 1975, pp. 362-75). Whatever the characterization of the actions of Ontario Hydro's chairman, there is little doubt that they served to effect the final transition of Ontario Hydro to a fullfledged large producer of energy. As with the railway case, public need was adduced as reason for ignoring previous public commitments that had been made to those willing to invest in long-lived immutable capital.

The franchise clause that was voided in 1916 was meant to protect the privately committed capital at the generating level from the same sort of unfair competition that the Conmee clause had tried to restrict at the municipal level. It was not long before events illustrated just how one-sided competition can become when the publicly owned company can use the power of the state to favour itself.

Between 1916 and 1918, the escalating demands for power generated by World War I strained the power-generation capacity at Niagara Falls. At the time, substantial exports were being made to the United States – much of it going to aid the war-effort. Beck, as head of Ontario Hydro, called upon the federal authorities to cut back on such exports and publicly decried the exports of the Electrical Development Company. Even while doing so, it appears that

Ontario Hydro was actually exporting considerably more power than the privately owned Canadian company. Beck's position with Ottawa was that his own company should be permitted to continue exports (at the higher American prices), but that the private companies should be cut back. Beck used his political power and threatened to run Hydro candidates in a forthcoming federal election. In the end, Ontario Hydro had its way and the federal authorities redirected to Ontario Hydro the power the private companies were exporting. As Nelles has pointed out, cancellation of exports removed one of the few supports the private company could rely upon, and this elimination "would in time throw them into complete dependence upon the commission" (Nelles, 1975, pp. 367-71).

Protection from Judicial Review

What was striking about these episodes was the Ontario government's reluctance to use the courts to adjudicate the claim of the aggrieved private interests. At an early stage, the government appended clauses to various *Hydro Acts* that prevented the adjudication process from being used, as they had to, given the strict constructionist rulings of the Canadian judiciary. In the Acts of both 1906 and 1907, the public was enjoined from bringing any action against the Commission "without the consent of the Attorney General for Ontario." Thus, the political authorities could choose whether to permit the courts to exercise constraint directly on the validity of actions by its agent, the Ontario Hydro-Electric Power Commission. This did not fully resolve the issue. At first, an indirect challenge to contracts entered into by municipalities with the Commission was still possible. When the mayor of Galt refused to sign a contract, legislation was enacted in 1909 stipulating the contract "shall be treated and conclusively deemed to have been executed by the said Corporation of the Town of Galt."[12] Moreover, at the same time, another clause was enacted that stipulated that any other actions being brought questioning contracts with the Commission were to be "forever stayed" (Mavor, 1925, pp. 114-15 and 138).

While appeal was made of this attempt to place the contracts beyond the power of the courts, the judiciary confirmed the supremacy of Parliament. Justice Riddel concluded:

> This legislation is within the limits fixed by the *British North America Act* and so is perfectly valid. I have not to tell the Legislature what to do; I am a creature of the Legislature – though not a subservient creature. If the Legislature says it is your duty not to try such and such an action, it is my duty not to try it. I am here to carry out the laws (Nelles, 1975, p. 292).

Contrary to the situation in the United States, no constitutional protection was available for the sanctity of contracts, if the legislature chose to override such contracts. The Canadian judiciary made it clear that no protection was afforded private property from confiscation in such a situation. In a related action, Justice Falconbridge observed:

> We have heard a great deal recently about the jurisdiction of the Province, a good deal of complaint about the exercise of its powers; but there is no doubt that the highest authority has declared that within its own jurisdiction it is supreme; in fact, while it seems rather severe I suppose there is not any doubt it has been conceded in recent cases that if the Legislature had chosen to confiscate – the word that is used – the farm of the plaintiff without any compensation they would have a perfect right to do it in law, if not in morals (Nelles, 1975, pp. 292-93).

After the Ontario Hydro-Electric Power Commission had taken over the Ontario Power Commission and had made plans to develop new power itself at Niagara, the Ontario government also passed legislation to validate the breach of contract that protected the Electrical Development Company in its original franchise. The following clause was appended to the legislation[13] enabling Ontario Hydro to begin construction:

> The exercise of the powers which may be conferred by or under the authority of this Act or any of them, shall not be deemed to be a making use of the waters of the Niagara River to generate electric or pneumatic power within the meaning of any stipulation or condition contained in any agreement entered into by the Commissioners for the Queen Victoria Niagara Falls Park (Mavor, 1925, p. 140).

Once again the legislature simply removed the protection afforded private capital with no compensation, and thereby prevented any recourse to the protection afforded by the courts.

The last recourse of the principals of the Electrical Development Company and the Toronto Power Company in both 1909 and in 1916 was to the federal authorities for disallowance of the provincial legislation. Here the private interests faced two handicaps. Other acts of the legislatures of both Ontario and Great Britain had removed some contracts from the purview of the courts unless agreed to by the Attorney General (Nelles, 1975, p. 299). Second, while the federal government prior to 1900 might have followed a policy of disallowing provincial acts which involved injustice, this had subsequently changed (Mavor, 1917, pp. 149-50). Finally, in 1909, the federal government was in no mood to oppose an Ontario government that had strong popular support for its position (Nelles, 1975, pp. 296-300). It was accepted that the appeal for an unjust act lay not to the federal government but to the electorate.[14] Thus, when popular support for confiscation existed, the federal government was no more immune from such pressures than the provincial government.

In 1916, the Electrical Development Company tried first to obtain a fiat to prevent Ontario Hydro from proceeding with its generating plant, but was denied the fiat by the Ontario Attorney General. When it issued a writ against the Attorney General and the Commission asking for a declaration that Ontario Hydro had no right to proceed, the courts refused to support it.[15] Finally, appeal for disallowance was made to the federal government but, as in 1909, was rejected (Mavor, 1925, p. 166).

The Disposition of the Toronto Electric Light Company and the Toronto Railway Company

By 1911, hydro-electricity was being delivered by Ontario Hydro into Toronto via the distribution system of Toronto Hydro. Yet it was more than a decade before the Mackenzie interests were acquired by the province. In 1923, the province acquired the Toronto Electric Railway Company and transferred its railway assets to the Toronto Transit Commission, the private Toronto electrical distribution system to Toronto Hydro, and kept the generation and transmission system of the Electrical Development Company for Ontario Hydro.

Elsewhere, private and public utilities were able to co-exist. In Manitoba, the private utility was given some protection from unfair competition from the Winnipeg-owned system by the regulatory board. In Nova Scotia, a provincial electricity commission was established in 1919 which developed hydro-power, then sold it to Halifax via the private distribution company, Nova Scotia Power and Tramways. In New Brunswick, a provincial hydro-electric system was formed in 1920 to develop hydro-power. But the municipal distribution system in Saint John bought power both from the existing private company and the public hydro source. As of 1929, the private utility was still supplying 30 per cent of the market (Armstrong and Nelles, 1986, p. 303).

One of the reasons that private and public plants continued to coexist during this period was the differences in technology possessed by each. The private firms in Nova Scotia, New Brunswick, and Toronto all possessed thermal plants. While more expensive to operate, they were the only ones

that could handle the peak load. Unless public authorities were willing to build thermal plants in addition to their hydro projects, they needed the private plants.

One of the reasons why Toronto Electric and its associated generating plant proved useful for a period of time was that Toronto Hydro did not have a reserve steam plant and could not easily handle peaking problems.[16] Toronto Electric continued from 1911 on as the residual supplier in this market. Table 10-3 lists the gross receipts of Toronto Electric from 1900 to 1919. They reached their peak in 1910-11. Of course sales of energy increased since pre-Toronto Hydro prices were about 8 cents/kwh, but around 4 cents/kwh thereafter. Actual kilowatt-hours sold increased from 28,180,200 in 1910 to 51,395,537 in 1915. Nevertheless, most of the growth in the system went to the public company – Toronto Hydro. By the end of the decade, less than a third

Table 10-3

Gross Receipts of the Toronto Electric Light Company, 1900-19

	Gross receipts
	$000
1900	411
1901	457
1902	526
1903	630
1904	752
1905	776
1906	900
1907	1,040
1908	1,156
1909	1,293
1910	1,529
1911	1,550
1912	825
1913	900
1914	1,275
1915	1,175
1916	1,100
1917	1,175
1918	1,300
1919	1,300

SOURCE 1900-09, Annual Report of the Toronto Electric Light Company, 1910, in Houston, *Annual Financial Review* (Toronto: 1911); and 1911-19, Christopher Armstrong and H. V. Nelles, *Monopoly's Moment: The Organization and Regulation of Canadian Utilities, 1830-1930* (Philadelphia: Temple University Press, 1986), Table 17, p. 191, estimated from Toronto Hydro-Electric System, Annual Report, 1923, p. 19.

of total revenues in Toronto went to Toronto Electric (Armstrong and Nelles, 1984, p. 225).

In Manitoba, a regulatory commission was charged with the delicate task of regulating rates in the presence of public-private competition. This was not done in Ontario where regulation of electrical rates was essentially accomplished via the Hydro-Electric Power Commission – both directly and indirectly. The rates charged by Ontario Hydro had a constraining influence on Toronto Electric. Indeed, Beck used his powers under the *Hydro-Electric Power Commission Act* to force down Toronto's rates in 1914 in opposition to the Toronto commissioners who were against the move because the local rates were already at cost.[17] Other regulatory powers were granted the Commission that were used to constrain the private sector. In 1916 and 1917, bills were passed that allowed the Hydro-Electric Power Commission to investigate the generating capacity of a private plant, fix its maximum level of production, and direct "excess current" to Ontario Hydro. Using this power, Beck forced the Electrical Development Company to direct power to Ontario Hydro in 1918.

During the decade, negotiations for the sale of the private utilities to the public sector were initiated but came to naught. In the spring of 1911, Toronto offered to buy Toronto Electric at 125 per cent of par; but Mackenzie offered 135 per cent and the company was folded into the Toronto Street Railway group. While the Electrical Development Company's hydro-power would still have had the transit company as base load, losing the private distribution system was at the time too costly.

The Toronto Street Railway was also offered to Toronto and an agreement was reached with the mayor of Toronto in 1913. But city council, at the urging of the chairman of the Ontario Hydro-Electric Power Commission, rejected the terms agreed upon. Mackenzie wanted an arbitrated price;

city council wanted to pay only actual investment plus the value of the unexpired franchise. With Ontario Hydro forcing down rates, it was in the interest of the city to wait, since the franchise value was clearly being eroded. Moreover, the outbreak of the war increased uncertainties in the financial market and probably placed the purchase beyond the fiscal capacity of Toronto. In addition, a new mayor, whose dislike of Mackenzie was so intense that further negotiations at the local level were impossible, was elected in 1914 (Armstrong and Nelles, 1984, p. 227).

As the period progressed and the franchise termination date approached, the company began to run down assets and strip excess cash from the company. Dividends which had averaged 5.7 per cent of net earnings from 1907 to 1913, were increased to 7.8 per cent between 1913 and 1917. Towards the end of the war, inflation in wage and materials costs forced the company into a deficit position. It appealed both to the city and provincial government for higher prices. But the public authorities, intent on waiting for the expiration date of the franchise, did nothing.

In other provinces, the crisis that was brought about by inflation brought a revision in the regulatory contract. In British Columbia, Manitoba, and Quebec, street railway fares were revised upwards to reflect higher costs. The same was done in many U.S. cities. As Table 10-4 shows, Toronto continued to force the Toronto Street Railway to abide by the old fares. It was not until after the take-over in 1921 that fares were increased by the amount other Canadian jurisdictions had deemed reasonable.

The elimination of the private sector in Ontario was finally accomplished in 1923. It is significant that the negotiations were carried on at the provincial level, for it was Beck, proponent of public power and head of the Ontario Hydro-Electric Power Commission, who saw no room for the private sector. Under attack almost continuously during this

Table 10-4

A Comparison of Street Railway Fares, 1915-22

	1915	1916	1917	1918	1919	1920	1921	1922
				Cents/fare				
British Columbia	5.5	4.9	5.2	5.1	6.4	6.4	6.5	6.4
Manitoba	4.0	4.0	3.9	3.9	5.0	5.6	6.0	5.9
Ontario	4.0	4.0	4.0	4.0	4.1	3.9	3.9	5.7
Quebec	4.4	4.4	4.4	4.4	5.0	5.9	6.1	6.1

SOURCE   Canada, Dominion Bureau of Statistics, *Street Car Fares and Index Numbers* (Ottawa: Department of Industry, Trade and Commerce, 1927).

period from private electrical interests in the United States, Beck saw success as involving the elimination of the interests that challenged his public-power movement. Throughout the period, even in the face of government investigations of improprieties in the finances of Ontario Hydro, he continued to garner considerable support in the provincial political arena. With the province bent on the creation of a public monopoly, the option of an alternate regulatory instrument that would ensure the continued operations of private electrical utilities of any magnitude in Ontario was never seriously considered.

Conclusion

Others have asked why Ontario, in contrast to most other North American jurisdictions, nationalized its electrical sector. After all, certain characteristics such as monopolistic tendencies were the same in Ontario as elsewhere. As emphasized in the opening section, it is not the monopolistic tendency per se that leads to nationalization, since regulation of private enterprise was adopted elsewhere to restrain monopolistic exploitation of franchises. Nor, as Nelles points out, is it easy to argue that the tendency of municipalities to own their own distribution plant led Ontario to extend ownership to transmission and power generation. American municipalities also often owned local electric utilities (Nelles, 1975, p. 222).

Nelles ascribes the result to the state of economic backwardness of the Ontario economy, and the social tensions that resulted – along with "a statist political tradition" (Nelles, 1975, pp. 223 and 305). Economic backwardness is important because, one supposes, the beneficial effects of industrialization are all the more evident in backward economies. The statist political tradition was the culmination of a long tradition of attempts by the Canadian government to influence the pace of economic development – so ably summarized by Nelles.

Such an explanation, however, is unsatisfactory. The United States too had its progressive movement supported by the same class of merchants and manufactures that lobbied for nationalization in Canada. United States interests were equally forceful in arguing for public ownership in the areas of national monopolies. In the United States, however, regulation as a form of social control evolved. While there is no denying the emotional appeal of the ideology of the Canadian progressive movement, it is difficult to argue that it was unique to Ontario.

The difference in the two countries' experience lies in the political arena – what Nelles refers to as the "statist political

tradition" of Canada. But leaving it at that is inadequate, for it would appear to imply that Canada in some sense had a preference for the government-imposed solution. The difference that has been generally ignored is that the United States had a Constitution that valued the sanctity of contract and that did not allow the political authorities to exclude their actions from review by the judiciary. In Canada, Parliament was paramount. The Ontario Hydro case illustrates how a determined legislature could void its contractual responsibilities and nullify protection normally offered to contracts by the judicial system.

Of course, tradition could still be defined in terms of choice of constitutions. But opportunities for constitutional revision are few and far between. It seems more appropriate to treat the constitution of a country as a binding constraint that rarely is changed – and then only after substantial evidence accrues that such a change is warranted.

A good case can be made that, if the courts had been able to act as a counterweight in Ontario, nationalization would not have been chosen – though it is not essential to the argument being made here. The nature of the contractual obligation of a franchise was interpreted in favour of the owners of a franchise when the judiciary was given the opportunity. For instance, the city of Toronto was prevented from exploiting the Toronto Railway Company when the courts ruled in 1906 that the company did not have to implement new service to points that were not within Toronto's boundaries at the time the franchise was given (Hall, 1968, p. 97). If it had been given the opportunity, there is every likelihood that the Electrical Development Company could have claimed compensation in 1916 for breach of contract or that the initial extension of Ontario Hydro into Toronto would have required compensation to Toronto Electric. The political process may not have been willing to bear those costs.

Such unwillingness does not mean that the public desire for the constraint of monopolies in the field of electrical utilities would have been stymied. In the United States, rulings, which protected private property from unfair exploitation by the state, led to fair-rate-of-return regulation. It seems likely that in Ontario a similar system would have evolved. It did so elsewhere. During the initial development of those industries in Ontario that have come to be classified as natural monopolies, the political pressures for intervention were not offset by judicial protection for property rights. The argument presented here is that, in such situations, the need for recontracting will occasionally be accompanied by opportunism that confiscates property. The history of Ontario Hydro bears this out.

11   Utilities in Quebec from 1890 to 1935:
Unfettered Development in Electricity Accompanied by
Cost of Service Regulation for the Transit Industry

In contrast to the experience of both Manitoba and Ontario, electricity and gas in Quebec enjoyed a degree of regulatory freedom that was almost unparalleled in North America. Public enterprise did not emerge in Quebec as a strong force in either of these two sectors. Nor did the modern regulatory tribunal gain acceptance here as a way to temper monopoly power. Regulation continued to be exercised via contract at the municipal level. In the case of the street railway system, intervention was also kept to a minimum. But when the inflationary years of World War I forced the Montreal Street Railway to the bargaining table, the regulatory contract was changed from one with a fixed price and 20-year term to a cost-plus contract that was renegotiated annually. Contrary to the fixed-term contract, the latter essentially guaranteed a constant rate of return.

It was the provincial government in Quebec that intervened to force modification of the tramway contract. This was done to prevent an impasse during renegotiations of the original franchise, an impasse which threatened the Montreal transit system. Intervention in the electricity and gas sectors did not occur because a renegotiation crisis did not develop, and bankruptcy was never an imminent threat. In most jurisdictions, state-initiated revision of the regulatory contract was aimed at placing a more effective ceiling on profits; in Quebec, it was only exercised when a floor was required.

Historical Developments in Montreal

The period between 1880 and 1900 in Quebec was marked by rapid, often frantic, development in the electrical utility sector. Competition between different U.S. manufacturers fueled a considerable expansion in the number of firms operating electrical plants. In Montreal, the Royal Electric Company (Royal Electric) was formed in 1881 to provide a central lighting station and a manufacturing organization based on Thomson technology. In order to sell equipment, the company installed plants in Ottawa, Hamilton, Halifax, Fredericton, and Montreal – only to sell out, in many cases, to local groups. While Royal Electric initially dominated the Montreal market, other firms entered the electric lighting business offering competing forms of U.S. technology (Armstrong and Nelles, 1986, pp. 76-77).

Competition existed both because of the number of electrical manufacturing concerns and because substitute products such as gas were generally available and somewhat cheaper for some purposes. Technological advances associated with "carburetted" gas that were introduced in the 1880s drove down gas prices – the other major source of illumination besides kerosene. Tests by Royal Electric, performed in 1890, indicated that gas was about 20 per cent cheaper than electric light in Montreal for domestic illumination purposes (Armstrong and Nelles, 1986, p. 78). Gas was also less expensive for street lighting purposes – though it provided somewhat dimmer illumination.

The city of Montreal made use of this competition between substitute products. Shortly after the Montreal Gas Company (the successor to the New City Gas Company) had its street lighting contract renewed, Montreal awarded a contract in 1886 for electric street lighting to Royal Electric for a five-year period (Armstrong and Nelles, 1986, p. 79). Several companies bid on this contract. Two years later, Montreal extended the electric lighting contract by increasing the number of street lights to be provided. Once more, it awarded the contract to Royal Electric. Again, there were several bidders. The large number of competitors existing at this time reduced the threat of monopoly and facilitated the process of regulation by *ex ante* contract.

During the next two decades, new companies, using new technologies, continued to enter the market for heat, light, and power. The early period was marked by a relatively atomistic market structure. But, as was the case in Vancouver and Winnipeg, mergers eventually led to consolidation. In addition, corporate interlocks developed between the largest electrical generating companies.[1]

In the gas market, competition between more than one company was rare. There was a short period in the early 1890s when the dominant firm, Montreal Gas, faced competition from another firm in the same industry. The Montreal Consumers' Gas Company obtained a federal charter (having been thwarted in the provincial legislature) and began supplying Montreal's suburbs. However, rivalry in the gas market did not last long. When the important street lighting contract came up for renewal, the incumbent, Montreal Gas, purchased the entrant and was able to obtain a 10-year extension of its contract with the city in 1895. Nevertheless, the short-lived period of competition did help the city to win lower rates and tax revenues amounting to 3 per cent of gross sales (Armstrong and Nelles, 1986, p. 101).

In contrast to the gas sector, numerous competitors emerged in the electrical generation field during the 1890s. Economies of scale were still relatively few in the thermal process that was first used to generate electricity. Montreal's suburbs were anxious to be served with electricity and eagerly offered franchises. The Temple Electric Company built a central station; the Citizens' Light and Power Company supplied St. Henri and developed hydro-electricity from a site on the Lachine Canal. The Imperial Electric Light Company, the Compagnie électrique St-Jean, and the Standard Light and Power Company all entered the Montreal market at this time.

The development of cheap hydro-power offered the greatest competitive threat to these early companies. In 1898, the Lachine Rapids Hydraulic and Land Company developed a hydro plant of 20,000 HP at Lachine Rapids (Dales, 1957, p. 104), and then gained a distribution system in Montreal by purchasing Temple Electric, Citizens' Light and Power, and Standard Light and Power. The latter was particularly valuable since it had a charter to sell electricity anywhere in Quebec (Armstrong and Nelles, 1983, p. 14). Hydro-power first entered Montreal's suburbs from this development.

Somewhat belatedly, Royal Electric via an affiliate (Chambly Manufacturing), developed its own 20,000 HP source on the Richelieu River with a 15-mile transmission line (a formidable feat at the time) to Montreal. The contract between Royal Electric and this company forbade supply of electricity to any other Montreal concern except for street railway purposes. In 1900, Royal Electric leased the Chambly facility for 50 years and sold off its manufacturing facilities to Canadian General Electric. Hydro-power was to provide the base load from this date forward in Montreal.

Starting in 1895, the Montreal utility sector experienced rapid consolidation. In that year, Royal Electric and Montreal Gas merged. In 1901, Royal Electric, Chambly Manufacturing (by then the Montreal St. Lawrence Light and Power Company) and Imperial Electric Light were combined into a new firm – the Montreal Light, Heat and Power Company (Montreal Light).[2] Senator Forget (who was also a leading figure in the Montreal Street Railway) was instrumental in the amalgamation (Dales, 1957, p. 104).

As Montreal Light was emerging as the dominant force in Montreal, a second large company began to take shape. The Shawinigan Water and Power Company (Shawinigan) developed its own source of power in the St. Maurice River Valley. Formed by Forget and Greenshields of Montreal and Aldred, an American, Shawinigan initially developed about 18,000 HP. When Montreal Light refused to buy power from Shawinigan, the latter signed a contract with a competitor, the Lachine Rapids group, for distribution in Montreal. Faced with this new threat, a Chambly plant that was experiencing difficulties, and a flood that destroyed another plant, Montreal Light purchased the Lachine Company and its Shawinigan contract in 1903. Montreal Light was able to report by 1903 that it was "supplying all the gas business in the city of Montreal, and its suburbs, . . . all the municipal lighting of the City and several of its suburbs . . ." (Dales, 1957, p. 115).

Montreal Light, therefore, commanded the Montreal market by 1904. Its legal position was fairly secure. Its 1901 charter had given it the franchise rights of its predecessors in perpetuity. It had the right to enter and use the streets of any municipality within a 100-mile radius of Montreal without municipal consent. But it did not have an exclusive franchise and competition was never completely eliminated. Inside the island of Montreal, Westmount, which housed the English Montreal community, owned its own power station and constantly led the price of power downward – at least to the residents of Westmount.[3] Outside Montreal, there were at least two other major companies – Shawinigan and the Southern Canada Power Company – serving the Eastern Townships. Over time, Shawinigan grew substantially. Shawinigan purchased the North Shore Power Company at Trois-Rivières in 1907, signed a contract with Laurentide Power for its surplus in 1915, formed the Public Service Company in 1915 to take over the Dorchester Electric Company in Quebec City, acquired in 1923 via the Quebec Power Company (formerly the Public Service Company) the Quebec Railway, Light, Heat, and Power Company, and took over the Laurentide Power Company plant at St-Féréol in 1925 (Shawinigan, 1926).

The Shawinigan group offered the greatest competitive threat to Montreal Light. In 1907, Montreal Light generated about 86 million kwh, Shawinigan 60 million kwh. By 1914, their respective outputs were 133 and 432 million kwh (Dales, 1957, p. 199). Although Montreal Light had temporarily staved off Shawinigan's entry to Montreal in 1903 by purchasing the Lachine Rapids Company, it was not until 1907 that a long-term peace agreement was arranged. This gave Shawinigan access to industrial customers in Montreal, and thereby meant this community had access to more than one supplier. By 1910, Shawinigan had an ownership position in Montreal Light, and each company had directors sitting on the other's Board (Dales, 1957, p. 58). Thereafter, Shawinigan delivered increasing amounts of power to Montreal Light.

Competition for the electrical market in Montreal also developed from another source – the Montreal Street Railway Company. In 1910, McConnell and Robert gained control of the transit company and created a new company, the Montreal Tramways and Power Company, which combined the transit operations with the Canadian Light and Power Company. The latter had been founded by Robert and had a 22,500 HP plant on the Beauharnois Canal. The power subsidiary was combined with several smaller electric companies into the Montreal Public Service Corporation serving both the street railway and several of Montreal's suburbs. By the end of World War I, it served almost 14,000 customers in Montreal (Dales, 1957, p. 112).

These two rivals continued their separate existence until the street railway had acquired a service-at-cost contract in 1919. Assured of steady returns, the McConnell/Robert interests were then willing to sell their utility operations to Montreal Light.[4] Even so, it should be noted that the competitive threat offered by the Montreal Tramways and Power Company throughout the period was relatively small. After take-over in 1925, the power plant of the latter company supplied only about 78 million kwh of 1,159 million kwh available to Montreal Light, of which 273 million kwh came from Shawinigan (Dales, 1957, p. 116).

Regulatory History

Both Montreal utility groups adopted the type of strategy to protect their franchises that was evidenced in Vancouver and Winnipeg. Montreal Light extended its services into Montreal's suburbs by offering rate reductions to municipalities in the Montreal area in return for long-term franchises. The Montreal Street Railway was covered by a labyrinth of contracts (some 30 with 14 separate municipalities). The main contract with Montreal had an expiry date of 1922, but others for Montreal were either perpetual or had varying termination dates – one as late as 1959 (Armstrong and Nelles, 1986, p. 204). Suburbs had agreements that were likewise staggered. Because Montreal did not annex suburbs as fast as Toronto did before 1900, much larger growth occurred in the suburbs of Montreal during the first decade of the century. This in turn provided greater opportunities for suburban franchise extensions by the utilities. This strategy of franchise extension helped to protect the Quebec utilities from threats of municipalization. Consolidation and franchise extensions made municipalization costly – all the more so in Montreal with its fragmented political boundaries.

The companies also sought protection by currying the favour of important decision-makers. In Montreal, the burgeoning electrical utility managed to persuade key political figures to align their own interests with that of the companies. During the competition for the 1886 contract, Royal Electric's Board voted to award $17,000 in stock for commissions. In 1888, the city's chief electrician reported little advantage to the city in establishing its own plant and was promptly hired by Royal Electric after it got the street-lighting contract. Two aldermen on the Light Committee became "prominent" shareholders in Royal Electric and later joined with other principals to develop water power on the Richelieu River. Political influence accompanied by corruption was critical in keeping the Montreal city contract for the Royal group in 1901, even though Lachine, its major rival, had submitted a lower bid (Armstrong and Nelles, 1986, pp. 83 and 106). Gifts were also bestowed on customers to develop support. Dales reports both Montreal Light and Shawinigan issued stock to customers for this purpose (Dales, 1957, p. 88, fn. 53, and p. 121).

Allegations of corruption received widespread public attention when a Royal Commission investigating the administration of Montreal in 1909 heard that aldermen had demanded kickbacks from Montreal Light (Gauvin, 1978, p. 20). But this seemed to have more impact on the city's reputation than on the need to regularize the method of recontracting. Other corrupting influences were sufficiently widespread that the utilities did not come to be singled out as the greatest threat to good government in Montreal.

During this period, the *ex ante* franchise contract did not fall into disrepute as it did in Toronto. But it was seen to suffer some deficiencies. By the end of the first decade of this century, the two Montreal utilities had fully entrenched their monopoly position and were showing signs of their profitability. As in other jurisdictions, the regulatory franchise contract now was much harder to negotiate because the number of alternatives facing the municipalities had been reduced by the consolidation movement, especially in gas and electricity. In Quebec, as elsewhere, the regulatory commission was chosen to facilitate the recontracting process. However, its powers were much more limited than those given to the Nova Scotia or New Brunswick commissions.

The first Quebec utilities commission was established in 1909.[5] It could only determine rates where there was no contract between the utility and a municipality. As such, it was meant to provide an instrument of last resort – when a franchise contract could not be renegotiated. Perhaps more indicative of its real role was the power it was given to order a municipality to permit a utility to enter its boundaries. The inability to cut across local boundaries was one of the major problems the British had faced in establishing efficient-sized electrical units (Hannah, 1979). The Quebec regulatory commission thus had the power to overcome a problem that would have been more acute in Montreal than Toronto with its greater proliferation of municipalities and suburbs.

The impotence of the regulatory commission in Quebec continued until the 1930s. While the Quebec Public Services Commission supplanted the PUC in 1920, it too could not act on rates where there were existing contracts.[6] It was not until 1935, when the Quebec Electricity Commission was formed, that this was changed. Rates were at last to be based on the "real value of the undertaking and the capital actually and usefully invested."[7] The 1935 legislation also fully protected property rights. Investor as well as consumer interest was specified as important. Moreover, any municipality that constructed its own plant during the course of a contract with a private utility was required to compensate the latter for the unexpired portion of the franchise.

Not only did regulation by tribunal prove to be relatively ineffective before 1935, but state ownership also did not prove to be a serious threat to the industry. At about the time that the 1909 *Public Utilities Commission Act* was being passed, Montreal requested the right to build a municipal electric plant. While it received permission to do so, a condition was attached requiring it to purchase the plant of Montreal Light if it built its own plant. Because of the size and scope of the latter, serving as it did both Montreal and its suburbs, this would have been costly to the city. Montreal's finances were too precarious during this period to permit such a purchase.

Street railways were also made subject to the 1909 *Public Utilities Commission Act*, except when it came to rates. These were already regulated separately.[8] Rates were specified as 5 cents for the first three miles and 2 cents/mile thereafter. A type of sliding scale was built into the *Tramways Regulatory Act* specifying the maximum profit rate at 10 per cent; but it was based on the value of issued capital and not on the value of plant and equipment.[9] It was this provision that led to the massive refinancings that occurred over time as companies wrote up the value of their stock so as to increase their dividend payouts.

The Quebec PUC, almost immediately after its creation in 1909, had to rule on the propriety of a large new stock issue associated with the 1911 reorganization of the Montreal Street Railway Company. The commissioners approved the offering, arguing with impeccable logic that it reflected the value of the franchise. It was not within their power to act so as to reduce existing property rights granted by the original charter and franchise.

The Montreal utilities, however, did not readily accept the jurisdiction of the PUC in other areas. In 1912, the PUC began an examination of the adequacy of railway service – only to have it blocked by court action for some three years. Montreal Light challenged the right of the Commission to investigate rate complaints. As a result, new powers were granted to the Commission to investigate whether rates were "just and reasonable."[10] But the Commission never did conduct a full rate-review case (Armstrong and Nelles, 1986, p. 206). Its role was one of last resort – to be used if the municipality was unable to reach an agreement with a utility. Because of the ramifications of not doing so (lights could be turned off), this did not occur.

There were no other regulatory initiatives taken by the province with regards to electrical generation. While Quebec might have exerted control through its assignment of water rights, it chose not to. Before 1907, Quebec disposed of water rights by sale, often at very low rates. After 1907, leases were signed, but at relatively low annual rentals (Dales, 1957, pp. 30-31). Industrial growth, not the extraction of rents, was the primary objective of the province with regards to hydro development.

The Evolution of the
Montreal Tramways Contract

The one major change in the regulatory environment came in the street railway sector. It was aimed at resolving a crisis in the recontracting process brought about by the degree of franchise proliferation. Because of the number of franchises that had been consolidated under one company, renegotiation of the contracts proved to be so complex that an impasse developed. While no one municipality could hope to expropriate the system, one suburb could cause considerable chaos across the system by failing to renew a franchise.

Between 1911 and 1919, the framework governing the Montreal Street Railway changed dramatically. In 1911, the street railway, newly reorganized under E. A. Robert, applied to the provincial legislature for a new charter.[11] A charter was granted that gave a 42-year franchise, providing new agreements could be reached with individual municipalities. But Montreal was unwilling to strike a bargain with the company. It was incensed that the company had been able to go to the legislature for a new charter; besides, it was not content with the service provided. It therefore launched a request for the PUC to examine service; and when the company blocked the PUC's investigations with an appeal to the courts, the city launched a publicity campaign against the street railway (Armstrong and Nelles, 1986, pp. 249-50).

Negotiations on the new franchise were resumed in 1913 but with no success. In June 1915, the city offered a fixed-rate-of-return contract, but the company rejected it because it also contained a buyout clause that could be invoked at any time. With local negotiations stalemated, in December 1916 the province appointed a Commission with the authority to conclude a binding agreement on behalf of the city that would have a 36-year period. During the subsequent year, inflation drove up costs and net earnings plummeted. The stock price of the Montreal Tramways and Power Company, which had averaged between $40 and $41 from 1914 to 1917, fell to only $24.50 in 1918. Inflation of costs, combined with the fixed fare that the company was allowed to charge, severely eroded earnings. This provided the company with the incentive to agree to a new contract. While municipal ownership was considered, Montreal's financial condition ruled out this option (Armstrong and Nelles, 1986, p. 251).

The Commission eventually recommended in 1918 a service-at-cost contract that was accepted by the company. The provincial government established a Tramways Commission to oversee the new arrangement.[12] An independent regulatory tribunal had thus been created to oversee the operations of the street railway. The Commission conducted a detailed valuation of the company's capital stock (excluding franchise value) and then sanctioned new higher fares of 6 cents/ticket (Armstrong and Nelles, 1986, pp. 253-54). Annual fares were to be determined by a sliding-scale-service-at-cost contract. Operating expenses, depreciation, and a 6-per-cent return on capital (reproduction cost, no depreciation) were to be covered by revenues. A $500,000 annual payment to the city of Montreal replaced the percentage of gross revenue tax. An incentive of one-eighth of 1 per cent on capital was to be paid if the company met the operating cost allowance set by the Tramways Commission at the beginning of the year. Any surplus was to be shared: 30 per cent by the city, 20 per cent to the company, and 50 per cent to a tolls-reduction fund. This fund, as in the case of the Toronto gas company, was to be used to reduce fares. Finally, additional debt was not to exceed 75 per cent of new capital raised, and dividends could not exceed 10 per cent (Wilcox, 1921, pp. 456-63).

While electric tramways were therefore placed under a standard regulatory commission by the 1920s, the electric

utilities remained under the old franchise arrangement. Cities were left to regulate the former by *ex ante* contract.

Quebec City: 1929-35

Montreal was not the only city in the province of Quebec that left regulation to an *ex ante* contract. The province's capital did likewise. The history of the rate control movement in Quebec City is indicative of the relatively strong bargaining position possessed by the industry in this province as late as the 1930s.[13]

In 1923, Shawinigan consolidated the gas, light, and transit business in Quebec City under Quebec Power. In 1925, it negotiated a 10-year contract with the city for an exclusive franchise. Quebec City's rates, at least for domestic customers, were high – 5.5 cents/kwh in 1929, versus 3.25 cents for Montreal Light in Montreal, and 1.67 cent in Ontario municipalities served by Ontario Hydro.

Discontent with these rates led to a campaign, orchestrated by Hamel, a prominent dentist, for local control of electricity rates. The matter became an important issue in municipal politics. In 1930, the city appointed a special advisory committee to examine the cause of the high Quebec electric rates. This committee reported that over-capitalization had led to unduly high rates. At the same time, the Board of Trade, which had been working with Quebec Power to attract industry, released its own report and argued that only large power customers were paying too much.

The advisory committee's report outlined a set of "fair" rates that were then demanded of Quebec Power. In order to provide a credible alternative, the city engaged counsel Louis St. Laurent to advise on the legality of municipalization. When no settlement on rates was reached and the city was advised by counsel that it could set up a domestic distribution system but not an industrial one, the conflict moved to the legislature. The city asked to have its charter amended to remove any uncertainty about its ability to build its own power plant. Quebec Power tried to have its own charter amended so as to increase expropriation costs and to have the Quebec Public Services Commission apply to its operations. The latter bill was withdrawn at the urging of the Premier, whose own party members began deserting because of public outcry against the company's manoeuvres.

The threat of municipalization disappeared with the Depression. By 1932, the city's revenues were sufficiently affected by the Depression that municipalization was no longer an alternative. Not surprisingly, negotiations on new electrical rates proceeded in a desultory fashion through 1932 and 1933. In turn, Hamel moved to develop support for rate control by developing closer ties with nationalist groups working at the provincial level. As he did so, and as he came to see municipalization as the only viable control mechanism, much of the support that he enjoyed in the business community disappeared.

In 1933, Quebec City's Board of Engineers prepared a detailed report that called for domestic electrical rate reductions of 26 per cent. The Quebec and Levis Federated Trades and Labour Council demanded that Quebec City residents at least get rates equal to those in effect in Ottawa. However, the Quebec City mayor, cognizant of the city's inability to finance municipalization, negotiated only a minor change in rates for a new contract starting August 1, 1935. This contract also extended Quebec Power's franchise for another decade.

It is not insignificant that the regulatory process was avoided. The 1933 Engineer's Report had recommended that the city go to the Quebec Public Services Commission if no satisfactory result was possible. Yet no mention is made of this route being used. While various regulatory boards existed from 1909 onward, they are reported as having virtually no impact up until the late 1930s. The electric industry evolved in Quebec in an atmosphere of "unfettered private enterprise" (Dales, 1957, pp. 30-31 and 224-25).

In summary, the long-term franchise continued as the regulatory contract in Quebec City. Those who wished to redress a situation where rates appeared to be unduly high were faced with two insuperable obstacles. The first was that bargaining had been reduced to a small-numbers situation; the city had no option but to deal with the incumbents. Second, there was little support for a stricter regulatory environment. The Ontario solution of expropriation without adequate compensation was decried in Quebec. In 1934, during hearings into a new regulatory agency, the Quebec premier assured bondholders and "all others connected with the power corporations that their rights would be respected in any reforms eventually decided upon" (Dales, 1957, p. 224). Expropriation with compensation was beyond the means of the city in the 1930s.

While the consumer revolt in Quebec came to naught at the municipal level, it did set in motion greater provincial regulatory control. In 1935, the Quebec Electricity Commission created the first "modern" regulatory agency in Quebec. At the same time, the *Electricity Municipalization Act* clearly gave municipalities the right to establish their own power systems.[14] The means of controlling utilities therefore arrived; but it was very belated compared to Ontario.

Conclusion

Quebec's regulatory history during the first three decades of the twentieth century was less interventionist than most. Close rate control that required annual supervision of accounts, like that adopted by U.S. regulatory agencies, was lacking. While Quebec's regulatory framework was certainly similar to that which emerged a continent away in British Columbia, the regulatory environment in Quebec differed radically from that of her Canadian neighbour in Ontario, with whom Quebec was vying for industrial dominance.

How then can the difference between the Ontario and Quebec situations be explained? Armstrong and Nelles (1983) offer four explanations. The number of competing companies was greater in Montreal than in Toronto; municipal interests had greater sway in Toronto than in Montreal because the provincial legislature assembled in Toronto but not in Montreal; Montreal was less cohesive as a geographic area, and there were, therefore, more political divisions; waterpower resources were more numerous in Montreal, and thus, the pressure was less to control monopolies that could be overturned by entrants should they charge monopoly prices.

These arguments are not persuasive. The argument that municipal agitation had to correspond to the provincial capital for it to be effective is contradicted by events in Quebec City (Dirks, 1981). Similarly, an examination of the political divisions in southern Ontario reveals many rifts – as was the case in Montreal. Diversity of opinion on the type of regulation required existed in both provinces. Finally, the argument that Montrealers were less willing to demand regulation because of differences in market structure seems to suggest that Quebecers were more concerned with appearance than reality. The reality was that market structure in Quebec was sufficient to produce domestic or household rates well above those of Ontario. Rates for Montreal Gas as opposed to Toronto Consumers' Gas were 50 per cent higher ($1.20 v. 80¢/MCF) at the turn of the century (Gauvin, 1978, p. 19). Domestic rates for electricity in Toronto were considerably below those in Montreal – especially after Ontario Hydro began delivering power. In 1916, Montrealers faced a rate of 5 cents/kwh; Torontonians received a rate of 2.98 cents from Toronto Hydro.[15] By 1920, Montreal Light charged 4.8 cents/kwh; Ontario municipalities served by Ontario Hydro only 2.56 cents/kwh. Table 11-1 presents a more detailed comparison. It is evident that throughout this period Montreal domestic consumers paid at least 50 per cent more for energy consumed than did those in Ontario.[16]

Table 11-1

A Comparison of Ontario and Montreal Domestic Electricity Rates, 1908-33

	Montreal Light, Heat and Power Consolidated	Domestic service: all municipalities in Ontario served by Ontario Hydro
	Cents/kwh	
1908	12.75	
1909	10.00	
1910	9.00	
1911	7.50	
1912	7.00	
1913	6.40	
1914	6.00	5.08
1915	6.00	4.08
1916	5.00	3.42
1917	5.00	3.20
1918	5.00	3.00
1919	4.80	2.82
1920	4.80	2.56
1921	4.80	2.48
1922	4.80	2.26
1923	4.25	2.04
1924	4.00	1.89
1925	3.50	1.85
1926		1.81
1927		1.80
1928	3.25*	1.71
1929		1.67
1930	3.00*	1.61
1931		1.59
1932		1.57
1933		1.57

* A sliding scale starting at this rate.

SOURCE   Column 1, J. H. Dales, *Hydroelectricity and Industrial Development: Quebec, 1898-1940* (Cambridge, Mass., Harvard University Press, 1957), p. 118, and Annual Reports of Montreal Light, Heat and Power from Houston, *Annual Financial Review* (Toronto: various years); column 2, W. R. Plewman, *Adam Beck and the Ontario Hydro* (Toronto: Ryerson Press, 1947), p. 482.

By examining rates for the entire customer distribution, it is evident that not all power users paid more in Quebec. Table 11-2 does this for five classes – domestic, commercial light, small power users, large power users, and street lighting – for two years, 1933 and 1939.[17] While average revenue/kwh is less overall in Quebec than in Ontario for both years, there is only one class that benefits – the large power users, of which the pulp and paper industry was the most important. All other classes paid more in Quebec than

in Ontario for electricity. It is, therefore, difficult to argue that competition in the Quebec utility sector served generally to keep prices as low as in Ontario and to deflect consumer complaints. The small consumer was better off in Ontario than in Quebec.

It is true that the support given the drive to regulate the industry at the provincial level of government was different in the two provinces. In Ontario, Adam Beck operated at the provincial level and his influence was essential for several reasons. For one, it allowed the legislative power of the province to be used to coerce the private sector, as has already been outlined. In Quebec, no such dominant figure with the goal of a public-hydro system emerged at the provincial level. But to base an explanation of events on the personality of one man is to ignore the underlying support he generated. That support was for a rate level and structure that was clearly different from that which emerged as Quebec's choice.

To what can this political preference be ascribed? It was probably not due to economic backwardness. While Toronto was jealous of Montreal and anxious to develop, so too was Quebec City at the end of the 1920s. Yet Quebec City did not turn to municipalization. It may have been the result of the French-English schism in Quebec that caused the business community, which was primarily English, to regard municipalization as politically unpalatable because it would put an important economic segment under French control. The history of politics in both Montreal and Quebec suggests this as a plausible explanation. With the shift of control from an English to a French-speaking electorate, members of the English community dominated the "good government" movement. This group sought and received, in 1894, provincial legislation that would limit the "spendthrift" habits of those now in control. The Reform movement, with strong support in the English community, focused on preventing abuses that originated in ward politics up to 1914. When Médéric Martin defeated the candidate of the "respectable groups," Washington Stephens III, in 1914, the French-speaking electorate in the east end of Montreal once more gained control (see Gauvin, 1978, pp. 17-23). The resulting deficits forced the province to place the city under the Appointed Administrative Commission from 1918 to 1921. As a result, Montreal was in no position throughout most of this period to mount a serious threat of municipalization of electric power. Moreover, the city's administrative record in other matters did not suggest that it could have run a power company successfully – at least to the English-speaking business community.

Dirks (1981), in her history of the Quebec City movement for rate control, portrays a similar picture of business

Table 11-2

A Comparison of Ontario and Quebec Distribution of Electrical Sales and Rates by Class of Service, 1933 and 1939

	Ontario				Quebec			
	1933		1939		1933		1939	
	000 kwh	Cents/kwh	000 kwh	Cents/kwh	000 kwh	Cents/kwh	000 kwh	Cents/kwh
Domestic service	917,649	1.77	1,374,325	1.43	240,110	3.25	311,420	2.94
Commercial light	346,061	2.11	549,713	1.60	171,418	3.20	270,928	2.78
Small power users	185,450	1.89	251,480	1.65	81,988	2.69	135,274	1.89
Large power users	2,920,423	0.68	5,610,395	0.48	4,896,147	0.57	10,294,197	0.35
Street lights	91,013	2.26	98,857	2.14	36,472	3.28	39,918	3.08
Total	5,563,647	0.88	9,458,130	0.65	7,451,968	0.60	11,890,447	0.48

NOTE   The total includes line losses and free service.
SOURCE   Canada, Dominion Bureau of Statistics, *Central Electrical Stations* (Ottawa: Department of Industry, Trade and Commerce, 1933 and 1939).

sympathy for regulation, but unwillingness to consider municipalization. Indeed, as the leader of the movement for rate control, Hamel, became more strident in his demands for municipalization, the support he had in the business community for regulation also vanished.

While the Legislative Assembly in Quebec did not initiate actions that would have exerted greater control over electrical rates in the province, it would be unfair to say that it acted entirely in a one-sided fashion. For example, in 1906-07, Montreal not only extended the Montreal Gas Company's contract, but granted Royal Electric an exclusive franchise – which would have placed Montreal even more firmly in the grip of Montreal Light. Business groups petitioned the legislature and had an act passed that required a referendum of all public utility contracts of more than 10 years (Gauvin, 1978, p. 19). In 1931, Quebec Power tried to have legislation passed to change its charter. This would have very greatly increased Quebec City's expropriation costs. The Quebec premier had the company withdraw the legislation (Dirks, 1981, p. 24).

In Quebec, as in the other provinces, the cultural environment cannot be ignored. This environment consisted of more than the actions of the business community. The antistatist attitude of the Catholic Church has been commented on elsewhere (Brunet, 1964, pp. 142-59). While this did not prevent public initiatives in the education, in

the public health, and in the social security areas, it meant that more energy was expended than would otherwise have been required to obtain needed reforms in these areas, leaving less for controlling the utilities. Equally important was the attitude of the leader of the Liberal Party from 1920-36. Premier Taschereau (1920-36) believed in industrial development based on cheap hydro-electric power. Vigod (1978) has emphasized the commitment of Taschereau to this goal, and his belief that its success rested on the attraction of private capital. Indeed, so strong was his commitment to this group that when the widespread impression developed in the 1930s that there were abuses in the electricity field, Taschereau's continued public defence of the electricity industry earned him the title of a "trustard."

In the end, both nationalization and the adoption of the modern form of a regulatory tribunal were avoided in Quebec because there was no pressing demand for revision of the earliest form of franchise contract. A utility strategy of consolidation and franchise extension served to deflect the forces of civic populism and to provide a counterweight during renegotiations. Civic populism, which caused a regulatory crisis in Vancouver, Winnipeg, and Toronto, did not emerge as a strong force in Montreal and Quebec City until late in the period. Since the recontracting problem that often accompanies a small-numbers situation did not develop, no crisis resulted. The history of post-1939 Quebec is, of course, another story.

12   Conclusion

The Choice of Regulatory Instrument

This study has detailed the early evolution of the regulatory instrument used in Canada to control the utility sector. It follows the choice of contract from the mid-1800s, when the utility sector was first developing, to the 1920s, when major changes in the regulatory contract had emerged. As a study of the reasons for instrument choice, its focus is on the nature of contractual failure and the reasons for it. It recounts the problems that developed in the original contracts that were used to regulate the utility sector and the nature of society's response to these problems.

Regulation of utilities in the water, gas, electricity, and transportation sectors was not a phenomenon that suddenly emerged in the twentieth century. Regulation, via the franchise-type contract, existed almost from the beginning in each of these sectors. Demsetz (1968) was correct when he noted that regulation in its modern form is not the only way in which consumers can avoid exploitative prices when faced by natural monopolists. They can and did write *ex ante* fixed-term contracts with the monopolist. However, in most cases, these contracts proved to have inherent flaws and the *ex ante* regulatory contract was supplanted. In some cases, the replacement was a form of the modern regulatory tribunal. This instrument facilitated more frequent revisions of the terms of the contract that governed the operations of private utilities. In other cases, it was replaced, not with a regulatory tribunal, but by a sliding-cost-type contract. Finally, in some instances, transactions failure was internalized via the creation of public enterprise.

The history of changes in the choice of the regulatory instrument that has been outlined herein has focused on the contractual process between state and private capital. It has used the framework adopted by the transactions-failure literature to categorize the problems that arose with the original regulatory contracts. This literature has primarily been used to explain why contractual failure occurs during arm's-length transactions between separate firms, and to explain why internalization via the joining of these separate entities into a larger firm is the concomitant result. In this study, the same taxonomy has been used to aid our understanding of the evolution of the regulatory process.

The transactions-failure literature starts with the observation that, because of uncertainty about future events and the costliness of completely specifying what is expected of each party in the case of a large number of unpredictable contingencies, contracts will necessarily have to be renegotiated. Renegotiation may lead to contractual breakdown, especially where the option of reopening the contract with third parties disappears. Where outside options are unavailable during recontracting (where a large-numbers bargaining situation reduces to a small-numbers negotiation), the contracting process becomes difficult and fails more frequently, either because opportunistic behaviour develops or because the fairness of the contract becomes difficult to judge due to the lack of alternatives. Contractual failure is particularly costly where capital is long-lived and specialized, because the investor is held captive during the renegotiation process.

The original regulatory instrument involved a franchise contract between a public authority and the party enfranchised to provide a service. Whether it was in the water, gas, electricity, or tramways sectors, in return for being given a franchise, the utility promised to fulfil certain contractual conditions. In waterworks, it usually entailed the provision of hydrants; in gas and electricity, the provision of street lighting at an agreed-upon price; in the case of tramways, the provision of service to specified streets, paving obligations, and a fixed fare. Most of these contracts had relatively long terms – anywhere from 20 to 40 years. In some cases, a perpetual franchise was given.

At an early stage, franchise contracts with fixed terms were supplanted by alternate regulatory instruments, neither of which involved the modern regulatory tribunal. In Toronto, the gas utility voluntarily adopted a form of the sliding-scale contract. But even here, foresight was imperfect and the state had to renegotiate the terms of the contract as the profitability of the industry improved. In the case of waterworks, contractual failure resulted in internalization via the creation of public enterprise.

Despite these problems, franchise contracts continued until the turn of the century to be the norm rather than the exception, and with the emergence of electrical utilities, they were adopted as the means of regulation once again. Nonetheless, these contracts handled uncertainties in a relatively imperfect fashion. In particular, the first contracts did little to constrain the emergence of monopoly profits. Technology was sufficiently untried that the state seems to have given little thought to this objective. Service and a fixed price rather than the profit level were the overriding concerns evidenced by the early franchise specifications. This probably resulted from the existence of an alternate form of control that municipalities possessed over rates. Municipalities would renegotiate rates for hydrants or street lighting at intervals less than the length of the franchise. During these renegotiations, prices for both public and private usage were specified. At first, this was an adequate form of control; but this lasted only as long as public consumption was large relative to private consumption. As private consumption grew relative to public, the lever that the municipalities possessed diminished and the objective of general rate control required an alternate instrument.

There was a second factor that made the franchise contract a less suitable regulatory instrument. The number of options available to the public authorities at the periodic franchise renegotiations diminished substantially. When tenders were first called for gas, electricity, and tramways, municipalities generally had several parties from which they could choose. For example, in both Montreal and Toronto, the horsedrawn tramway franchises expired just as new technology promised a new generation of electric railways. When tenders were called for the new service, new firms stepped forward and succeeded in gaining the franchise in both Winnipeg and Toronto. Similarly, several gas and electric companies competed for street lighting contracts up to the twentieth century. But the degree of franchise competition decreased substantially around 1900. Whether because of economies of scale or because of a business strategy that was intended to strengthen the private sector's bargaining position, consolidation removed the alternatives available to municipalities. In Vancouver, Winnipeg, Toronto, Montreal, and Halifax, large companies emerged that jointly controlled both gas and electricity. Except for Montreal, they also owned the tramway system. In the telephone industry, Bell so successfully consolidated its position that it was able by 1900 to avoid the need to renegotiate local franchises with municipalities.

Contract renegotiations arose just as competition for the utility franchises was declining. In these circumstances, the transactions theory literature suggests that contract failure will become more widespread, and more complex forms of regulatory instruments will evolve. This is what happened in both Canada and the United States. But the two countries differed in the extent to which the modern regulatory tribunal was chosen. In the United States, a set of judicial rulings had emerged, somewhat fortuitously, that constrained the

ability of the state to act opportunistically. The judicial system offered fewer constraints on opportunistic behaviour by the state in Canada.

Opportunism in the transactions-failure literature is generally used to describe deceitful or unfair actions of one or other of the parties to the contract that occur during renegotiations. The literature has concentrated on describing the conditions where such behaviour will be particularly costly. Less attention has been paid to actions which may create the preconditions for opportunistic behaviour or the characteristics of the parties that might lead to a predilection for opportunism. This monograph points out that, where the state is a party to contract renegotiation, a problem of some importance may develop. The state possesses police powers that can be used for confiscation where judicial restraints on this behaviour are weak or do not exist. In states where little or no constitutional protection is offered to private property, the state may on occasion exercise that power in a myopic fashion because of populist pressures. If it does, internalization of contractual difficulties will lead to nationalization, because confiscation is relatively inexpensive compared to jurisdictions where constitutional guarantees are given private property.

The case studies presented here demonstrate that where the publicly owned utility was chosen to solve contractual difficulties, various Canadian jurisdictions acted in a confiscatory fashion. At the federal level, the government's regulatory agency drove the new transcontinental railways into bankruptcy by failing to allow the inflated costs of the 1917-20 wartime period to be fully passed along in price increases. A special arbitration panel failed to recognize the effects of this action in evaluating the value of the Grand Trunk's railway assets. In Ontario, the legislature specifically voided protective legislation and previous franchise clauses that protected the private utilities from competition by publicly owned utilities. In Manitoba, the province threatened Bell Canada with discriminatory taxation if it did not sell its Manitoba assets to the province.

Confiscation and opportunism were present in all three cases. But to blame the result just on myopic public officials would be misleading. In each of these cases, the actions of the private sector contributed to the impasse that developed. The consolidation of utilities turned the large-numbers bargaining process into a small-numbers adversarial contest. Whether this was an innocent reaction to the potential for exploiting scale economies or a deliberate attempt to place the state in a difficult situation when it came to recontracting, the result was the same. The state found the original franchise-type contract unworkable.

The franchise contract developed other defects by the beginning of the twentieth century that led to a search for a new regulatory instrument. Tales of corruption and bribery had tainted the public agents responsible for negotiating the franchise contract and brought the contract itself into disrepute. In addition, the jurisdiction of federal authorities over companies like Bell, which had received a charter for the general advantage of Canada, threatened the ability of municipalities and provinces to exert local regulatory control.

The case studies demonstrate that contractual failure did not lead to nationalization in all cases. In two Maritime provinces and Alberta, a regulatory instrument emerged that resembled the independent regulatory tribunal that came to be adopted in a large number of American jurisdictions after the turn of the century. Rates were set so as to yield a fair return on fair value of capital. The Nova Scotia experience shows how a PUC was able to diffuse an extremely contentious take-over that was widely interpreted as a stock-watering exercise.

In three other jurisdictions, the franchise contract was modified, not so much in response to consumer complaints about high rates, but because the original terms had become onerous for the company as a result of inflation. Before and after the end of World War I, wage and materials costs escalated dramatically. Tramways, which were governed by fixed-fare clauses in their franchises and which were characterized by a relatively high percentage of costs relating to labour, found that their operating surpluses evaporated at this time. In Vancouver, a new contract with a higher fare was negotiated, with provisions for relatively frequent renegotiations. In Montreal, a cost-of-service contract was imposed on the Montreal urban community after the squabbling constituent municipalities proved unable to reach a unified position vis-à-vis a new franchise contract. In Manitoba, a PUC which had been created for reasons other than the monitoring of private utilities, proved willing to revise fares upward after evaluating the transit system's capital stock on a reproduction cost base.

While both British Columbia and Quebec did modify the regulatory instrument when tramways were threatened, they did not embrace the regulatory tribunal in general. That a full-blown regulatory agency was not also created in British Columbia for electrical rates was more the result of a quixotic turn of fate arising from the unforeseen consequences of a federal railway bill than of calm, reasoned choice. Nevertheless, the fact remains that British Columbia continued to regulate electric rates in a very ad hoc fashion. The same was true of Quebec. Its public utilities legislation made its regulatory agency into an instrument of last resort. The contractual process between municipalities and

utilities was supplemented, not suppressed by this approach.

The history of events, then, shows a considerable diversity in Canada of the state's response to the contractual crises that developed in the utility sector. Franchise contracts were supplanted by public enterprise in some instances, were continued with minor modifications in others, and were handed over to regulatory agencies in still others. This stands in marked contrast to the United States where the regulatory tribunal was the common instrument chosen. The differences in the approaches taken both across different Canadian jurisdictions and between Canada and the United States potentially offers us the ability to discriminate among alternate theories of instrument choice.

The Theory of Instrument Choice

Economists are prone to classify theories as being normative or positive. Recent work in the theory of instrument choice for public policy has analysed the constraints facing policymakers and the factors that determine the degree of substitutability among instruments (Trebilcock, et al., 1982). That work was directed at the normative notion that instrument choice should be determined by relative technical efficiency; that is, whatever the objective of policy might be, it should be accomplished by the most efficient instrument possible.

Whether such an approach can also be used to explain why instruments are chosen in specific situations and thus provide a useful positive theory is a separate matter. In actual fact, an examination of the reason for the choice of a specific instrument, such as the public corporation, has both normative and positive aspects to it. The work of Trebilcock and Prichard (1983) focuses on the special institutional characteristics of public enterprise so as to evaluate the effectiveness of the instrument; that of Borcherding (1983) approaches the positive aspects of the choice of public enterprise. But both essentially try to infer a theory from observation of performance, and thus resemble one another in the end.

While economists attempt to understand the choice of an instrument with the aid of a simplifying conceptual framework, the historian trained in the tradition of the humanities, tends to focus on the diversity of human experience. Institutions are seen to emerge from a complex interaction of economic problems, political systems, and judicial constraints.

This work borrows heavily from both traditions. The central focus is on an economic issue – the choice of the regulatory instrument. The historical approach is used to trace the evolution of the instrument or type of contract in response to changes in technology and market structure. Judicial constraints in Canada are recognized as changing over time, and never quite so binding as in the United States.

Nevertheless, the pattern of instrument choice that emerges suggests that a theory based on economic determinism alone is less than persuasive. The economic problem was not resolved in a single simple fashion. The regulatory instrument chosen differed substantially both by industry and by jurisdiction. The taste for public enterprise was sufficiently great, or the moral-legal constraints sufficiently weak, that state ownership resulted – in railways at the federal level, in telephones in Manitoba, in the electrical field in Ontario, and in waterworks in general. Only in waterworks can we say there was general contractual failure. It is striking that in many other jurisdictions in these same fields, not only was the instrument of state ownership avoided, but so too was the modern regulatory tribunal. In British Columbia, and in Quebec, electrical and gas rates went unregulated, except by franchise contract. The transit system in these provinces came under a form of regulation only when the industry was threatened with economic collapse. This might suggest that the standard theory of regulation based on protection of consumers lacks credibility, except that franchise regulation also existed. At first glance, it could also be used to argue for a capture theory of regulation. But that too would be inadequate. The contractual revision in the regulation affecting tramways around 1919 essentially only restored the status quo that had existed under the franchise contract.

In Canada during this time, the modern form of regulatory tribunal was adopted as a general instrument only in three provincial jurisdictions: Nova Scotia, New Brunswick, and Alberta. Here, the inherent defects of political opportunism seem to have been overcome by the use of an agent whose decisions were in accord with the position taken by the American judiciary as to actions deemed to be confiscatory. Even so, this experience does not suggest a general theory for the choice of regulatory agency. In Manitoba, for example, the choice of a regulatory agency was as much related to the need to oversee the provincially owned telephone company as to control the rates of private utilities. Nor can we argue from the Maritime experience that the choice of a regulatory instrument in Canada was sufficient to resolve the recontracting problem. The federal government may have chosen a regulatory instrument for the railway and telephone sector; but since it never adopted a fair-return-on-fair-value standard, it was, therefore, also responsible for the bankruptcy and nationalization of the railway system. On the other hand, the same result did not occur in the federally regulated telephone industry. The federal experience then provides two contrasting examples and illustrates that the success of the instrument was not dependent upon the jurisdiction adopting it.

The Canadian experience provides a striking contrast to that of the United States. There, the state regulatory commission became the normal form of intervention. Troxel (1947, p. 71) notes that, following the New York and Wisconsin legislation in the first decade of the century, use of the state regulatory commission spread rapidly. By 1918, about 30 states had passed laws to control one or more local monopolies. By 1930, some 48 jurisdictions had public service commissions; 42 to 45 supervised rates of gas or electricity, or utilities of street railways (Mosher and Crawford, 1933, pp. 28-29); 32 had extensive evaluation standards for capital invested and 23 could control security issues. In Canada, by way of contrast, only three provinces had regulatory agencies that approached the United States standards – Nova Scotia, New Brunswick, and Alberta.

In other Canadian jurisdictions, one of two extremes developed. In British Columbia and Quebec, only a minimal level of regulation – in street railways – was used. Elsewhere, in Ontario, Manitoba, and in the federal railway sector, public enterprise became the chief regulatory instrument. The effect of legal constraints (or the lack thereof) on the choice of public enterprise in Ontario, Manitoba, and at the federal level has been developed at length. The results in British Columbia and Quebec can also be partially ascribed to the lack of legal or constitutional constraints to force the government to abide by fairly written contracts.

That both British Columbia and Quebec continued to leave their utility sectors unfettered by a modern regulatory tribunal can be attributed either to a preference for *laissez-faire* or to the uncertainties of the Canadian legal system. The latter is a more compelling explanation of events. While the prerequisites for successful regulation were being put in place during this period, the impact of this institution was far from certain. It took both Nova Scotia and New Brunswick over a decade before the results of the new institution could be fully appreciated. Institutional choice, like the choice of production techniques, involves learning-by-doing. The fact that the Maritime provinces led the way in American-style regulation was not unrelated to their close political and social ties to New England. Massachusetts had led the way in the United States in developing a state regulatory commission (Thompson and Smith, 1941, p. 193). The rest of Canada took longer to understand the benefits of the regulatory tribunal because the judicial decisions on what constituted acceptable behaviour were slow in developing. Hence, British Columbia and Quebec were simply being cautious in the adoption of new institutions. While taste mattered, its influence should be interpreted as affecting the timing not the desire for regulation. By 1935, Quebec had passed legislation establishing a regulatory tribunal; by 1938, British Columbia did the same.

The legal environment also helped determine the choice of public enterprise as a regulatory instrument. There are at least two hypotheses that could be used to explain why Canada has more frequently chosen to use public enterprise than has the United States. On the one hand, it could have been the result of a predilection for public enterprise because of certain socio-political ethics. On the other hand, it could have been the result of the cost of regulation being higher relative to public ownership – a relative cost effect. Both the taste and the relative cost hypotheses would predict greater frequency of public enterprise as opposed to regulation, and it is therefore difficult to discriminate between them. While it is impossible to eliminate the preference argument, historical events are compatible with the relative cost rationale.

If the relative cost argument is correct, the transition from franchise regulation to public enterprise should have been accompanied by transactions failure. In particular, the state should have acted in an opportunistic manner. In three major cases – the railways, the hydro-electric sector, and telephones – this was so. There is, of course, still the argument that the relative cost effect may have been insignificant compared to the preference effect. But since politicians in each case recognized there was some doubt that political support could be mustered for nationalization if full compensation had to be paid private capital, this suggests the participants in the process appreciated the significance of the relative cost effect.

The examples chosen to illustrate the applicability of the theory are taken from events that occurred between 1870 and 1939. The passage of time permits sufficient details to be unearthed by researchers that a reasonably complete picture of events can be reconstructed. That is not the case for more recent nationalizations, such as Hydro Quebec. The temptation to extend the examples has therefore been avoided herein. Nevertheless, it is not argued here that all recent nationalizations have also been the result of a transactions failure of the type described here. Indeed, in light of the gradual evolution in Canadian court rulings that began to set U.S. standards for the Canadian authorities, a set of nonbinding judicial constraints did develop, which should have made the institution of regulation as opposed to nationalization less costly. More recent nationalizations are therefore less likely to have been associated with opportunism.

The approach that has been adopted here does not provide an irrefutable theory to explain the choice of all Crown corporations. For one thing, this study has focused on the reason for contractual failure in only one area – that of natural monopoly. However, the focus on contractual failure is probably the appropriate one even in other situations. Of course, the reason for contractual failure may differ elsewhere. Air Canada (Trans-Canada Airlines) was not intended to be 100 per cent government owned at its inception. A partnership with the CPR was offered and rejected, probably because Canadian Pacific knew the value of its minority position depended upon government actions that might not always have profit maximization as their motive. While this was a different type of contractual failure, it is, nevertheless, closely related to the one discussed herein.

Ultimately, the importance of the approach taken here extends beyond the reinterpretation of historical events. The message contained herein is that contractual failure lies at the heart of the explanation of instrument choice. Society must solve the same problem that arose here, but in other contexts, if a varied range of policy options is to be kept open. The state has to find a way to write a "fair" contract and bind itself to the terms thereof. The regulatory process was chosen as a way to decide upon the terms of a fair contract in the utility sector. The regulatory agency's independent status and its elaborate rules were aimed at establishing its authority to decide a fair contract – one that was not unduly influenced by narrow partisan or corrupt considerations. But even so, the regulatory agency could not work until it was constrained from opportunistic behaviour – until it was forced to abide by the terms of the contract that it negotiated.

More recently, the Canadian government has embarked on a new series of initiatives that only relate peripherally to the original thrust of intervention aimed at protecting consumers from exploitation by natural monopoly. Regional development objectives, industrial strategy, energy policy, and aviation policy have all led to the establishment of public enterprises. In some instances, it may be that traditional transactions failures, relating to difficulties in auditing, information processing, and incentives, explain the entry of public enterprises. But the role of moral-hazard problems should not be discounted as the Air Canada example was meant to indicate. In most cases, the success or failure of a policy initiative depends upon other aspects of government policy. Government policy, in other areas, is sufficiently unpredictable that all contingencies cannot be carefully considered in the terms of the original contract. Recontracting will, therefore, be required and moral hazard of the sort evinced in the railway nationalization example can create problems. In most instances, no protection is available to the private parties concerned should political pressures lead to opportunistic behaviour. The establishment of a public enterprise is one of the ways in which such externalities can end up being internalized.

The ability of the government to constrain itself in these situations permits consideration of a wider range of policy instruments than just public enterprise. Where there are efficiency benefits from the organization of production in private hands, or where, as in the private sector, there are benefits from sharing risk through a franchise-type arrangement, the government may want to choose an instrument other than a public enterprise. If it cannot solve the transactions-failure problem that is associated with the moral-hazard dilemma attendant with government activity in general, it may have no choice but to use public enterprise as the instrument of government policy. If a choice of contractual arrangements is to be considered and if policy thrusts are to be considered without accompanying them with the creation of Crown corporations, the moral-hazard problem that so often accompanies government contracts must be faced directly. If it is not, then this work suggests one instrument, public enterprise, will tend to be adopted more frequently than would otherwise have been the case. Those who embrace the objectives associated with more recent policy thrusts, but are uncomfortable for political or economic reasons with the spread of public enterprises, will want to consider the type of safeguard that might allow alternate contractual arrangements to meet some of the same objectives.

Notes

CHAPTER 1

1 See P. L. Joskow and R. G. Noll (1981) for a discussion of some of the issues involved.

2 G. Stigler (1961), J. R. Baldwin (1975), and S. Peltzman (1976).

3 G. Douglas and J. Miller (1974), W. Jordan (1970), and A. F. Friedlander and R. H. Spady (1980).

4 G. Stigler and C. Friedland (1962), and G. A. Jarrell (1978).

5 See F. M. Scherer (1971), pp. 537-38, fn. 40, for an alternate interpretation of the Stigler/Friedland results.

CHAPTER 2

1 A. Kahn (1970), vol. 1, provides a good summary of the traditional view.

2 O. E. Williamson (1971, 1979, 1981*a*, 1981*b*), and Williamson *et al.* (1975).

3 See U. S. Federal Communications Commission (1939).

4 Intergenerational transfers of wealth could, of course, still occur with public ownership and thus the efficiency problem is not resolved by state ownership.

CHAPTER 3

1 The histories are taken from I. R. Barnes (1942), and C. W. Thompson and W. R. Smith (1941).

2 See Barnes, pp. 224-29, and Thompson and Smith, pp. 163-71, for a discussion of the terms of the franchises.

3 See Thompson and Smith, p. 157, and Barnes, p. 228, for a more complete description of the fees demanded.

4 This problem became particularly acute between 1910 and 1920 when price levels increased about 150 per cent.

5 For an account of the relationship between New York politics and utility franchises, see G. Myers (1974).

6 Article I, Section 10 of the Constitution, see Thompson and Smith, p. 157.

7 See Barnes, pp. 219-22, for a discussion of the three types of contracts.

8 See I. Bussing (1968) for an extensive discussion of this type of contract.

9 See Barnes, pp. 234-41, and Thompson and Smith, pp. 180-81, for a general discussion of the problems that arose with service-at-cost contracts.

10 Justice Taft in *Wolff Packing Co. v. Court of Industrial Relations of Kansas*, 262 U.S. 522 (1923), quoted in Barnes, p. 6.

11 Justice Holmes in *Tyson & Brother v. Banton*, 273 U.S. 418-456 (1927), quoted in Barnes, pp. 8 and 17.

12 *Chicago, Burlington & Quincy R. Co. v. Iowa*, 94 U.S. 155 (1877).

13 *Munn v. Illinois*, 9 U.S. 113 (1876).

14 *German Alliance Insurance Co. v. Kansas*, 233 U.S. 389 (1914).

15 *Tyson & Brother v. Banton*, 273 U.S. 418-456 (1927).

16 *Ribnik v. McBride*, 277 U.S. 350 (1928).

17 *New State Ice Co. v. Liebmann*, 285 U.S. 262 (1932).

18 *Nebbia v. New York*, 291 U.S. 502 (1934).

19 See Barnes, p. 12, see also C. F. Phillips (1965).

20 Phillips, pp. 79-80, notes that by 1940 the Court concluded that the issue of "public interest" had been discarded with the Nebbia case, and that by 1950 it no longer received any mention.

21 *Slaughter-House Cases*, 83 U.S. (16 Wall.) 36 (1873), quoted in Barnes, p. 198.

22 *Stone v. Farmers' Loan & Trust Co.*, 116 U.S. 307 (1886), quoted in Barnes, pp. 198-99.

23 *Reagan v. Farmers' Loan & Trust Co.*, 154 U.S. 362 (1894), quoted in Barnes, p. 199.

24 For a discussion of the concept of a property right in connection with use or exchange value, see J. R. Commons (1932), ch. 2.

25 *Smyth v. Ames*, 169 U.S. 466-550 (1898); see Barnes, pp. 371-78, for a discussion of the case.

26 The lower courts had ruled earlier in the 1890s on this matter. See Barnes, pp. 371-72.

27 For one of the few scholarly works devoted entirely to this issue, see N. L. Smith (1932).

28 See Barnes, pp. 523-25, who notes these points were summarized in *Bluefield W. W. & Imp. Co. v. W. Va.* 262 U.S. 679, 692 (1923).

29 Originally recognized in *Reagan v. Farmers' Loan & Trust Co.* See Barnes, pp. 199 and 525.

30 *Willcox v. Consolidated Gas Co.*, 212 U.S. 19, 48-49 (1909), quoted in Barnes, p. 524.

31 *Bluefield v. W. Va.*, quoted in Barnes, p. 524.

32 *Bluefield v. W. Va.*, quoted in Barnes, p. 525.

33 See Phillips, p. 267, quoting *Public Service Commission of Montana v. Great Northern Utilities Co.*, 289 U.S. 130, 135 (1935).

34 See Myers (1968), Chapters 10 and 11 for a description of this process in the early railway building age in Canada.

35 *Willcox v. Consolidated Gas Co.*, 212 U.S. 19 (1909), quoted in Barnes, p. 380.

36 *Newton v. Consolidated Gas Co.*, 258 U.S. 165 (1922), quoted in Barnes, p. 383.

37 *McCardle v. Indianapolis Water Co.*, 272 U.S. 400 (1926), quoted in Barnes, p. 391.

38 *Lindheimer v. Illinois Bell Telephone Co.*, 292 U.S. 151 (1934), discussed in Barnes, pp. 393-95.

39 *Federal Power Commission v. Natural Gas Pipeline Co.*, 315 U.S. 575, 586 (1942).

40 See Barnes, pp. 506-14, for a discussion of the extent to which Massachusetts' practice conformed with the prudent investment standard.

41 Jarrell, p. 270, see also C. E. Troxel (1947), pp. 70-74.

CHAPTER 4

1 See G. R. Stevens (1962), p. 474, for the comments of the Royal Commission (1916) on the importance of removing control of the Grand Trunk from British hands and returning it to Canada.

2 See L. T. Fournier (1935), pp. 40-42. Of the $294 million in funded debt of the Canadian Northern, some $211 million was guaranteed by the government. The Grand Trunk Pacific's debt, if not guaranteed by the Grand Trunk, was backed by the Dominion government.

3 See Stevens, pp. 504-05, see also A. W. Currie (1957), pp. 472-73.

4 Advances to Canadian Pacific for the Crow's Nest section were made to counter American threats to enter the area; the government's construction of the Intercolonial Railway, connecting central Canada to the Maritimes, was the result of a desire to have a connection that did not run through northern Maine as did the Canadian Pacific line; the agreement with the Grand Trunk to build the National Transcontinental (the western section to be the Grand Trunk Pacific) included a clause specifying that "the whole railway was to have a national character." See G. P. Glazebrook (1964), p. 137.

5 Land grants were also attached to other charters granted, many of which were eventually purchased by the Canadian Northern. See Stevens, pp. 22-28, and Glazebrook, p. 145.

6 See W. A. MacIntosh (1924), p. 13, for a description of Prairie resentment directed at the CPR.

7 For a discussion of the pressures placed on the government to equalize freight rates, see W. T. Jackman (1935).

8 These hearings revealed the Grand Trunk had distorted its results from 1914 onward, and particularly during the protracted negotiations for relief from its Grand Trunk Pacific obligations. See Currie (1959), p. 467.

9 For a history of railway regulation in Canada, see A. R. Wright (1963).

10 See Jackman (1935) for a discussion of the tendency of the railway regulatory commission to concentrate on rate structure rather than rate levels.

11 Jackman, pp. 239-77, as reported in Currie (1959), p. 45. See also Currie (1946), p. 148, also (1957), p. 445, and (1959), p. 32.

12 *The Western Rates Case*, Currie (1957), pp. 534-35.

13 Stevens, p. 419, and Currie (1957), p. 445.

14 Canada, House of Commons (1922), *Grand Trunk Arbitration Award*, p. 176.

15   Canada, House of Commons (1922), *Grand Trunk Arbitration Award*, p. 171.

16   The absolute guarantee was reduced to $2,292,760 when the Lake Superior line was leased to the government. See Canada. House of Commons (1922), *Grand Trunk Arbitration Award*, pp. 184-85 and 202.

17   Taft was particularly well qualified in the matter of valuation since he had been instrumental in getting the U.S. Interstate Commerce Commission to officially value the investment base of U.S. railways. See Currie (1957), p. 461.

18   Stevens, p. 242, notes that by the turn of the century, one-sixth of the eastbound traffic of the American Mid-West was carried on Grand Trunk lines.

19   See Currie (1957), pp. 310-24, for an account of the conflict between the Grand Trunk and the Canadian Pacific.

20   The data in Table 4-6 are derived by Moody's from the official accounts that are denominated in pounds sterling and translated by this financial publication to dollars using 4.86 as the exchange rate. Since the exchange rate differed from this after 1914, the gross revenue and operating expense would also differ if the actual exchange rate were used – but the trend in terms of higher operating expenses relative to gross revenues would not be affected. Fixed charges would be the same because they were partially denominated in terms of the 4.86 exchange rate (See fn. 21). Net revenues, which are just surplus plus fixed charges would not be affected because the surplus is already denominated in Canadian dollars.

21   Part of the guaranteed debt of the Grand Trunk Pacific for which the Grand Trunk was responsible was denominated in dollars, part in pounds sterling. The dollar value of the interest payments for which the Grand Trunk was responsible under its guarantee would therefore have potentially varied with the Canadian-U.K. exchange rate. Before the war, the exchange rate stood at C$4.86 to 1 pound sterling; but by 1920, the date of the arbitration board decision, the cost of 1 pound sterling had fallen to C$4.08. However, it seems to have been the practice to specify the bondholder could receive the payments either in the U.K. or in North America and that the exchange rate for any such conversion would be the 4.86 figure. This would have removed any advantage to the Grand Trunk from the appreciation of the Canadian dollar. It is difficult to determine from the Moody's and Poor's manuals whether all of the guaranteed sterling debt was given this privilege. To the extent that some was not, the ability of the Grank Trunk to cover its contractual obligations would have been even greater since the 4.86 value has been used here to calculate the amount of the interest obligations whereas the actual exchange rate is used to translate C$ earnings to pounds sterling.

22   The Prime Minister at the time is reported to have been hostile to the Grand Trunk. Stevens, p. 458, reports that

> in 1908 he [Borden] believed that the company had abandoned its political neutrality and had committed itself to the Liberal cause, whereupon he wrote testily . . . that if the Grand Trunk wanted a fight, the Conservative Party would be ready to oblige.

Yet a reading of Borden's offers to the Grand Trunk prior to the establishment of the Arbitration Board suggests no niggardliness. Whether he let this attitude influence his pressures on the regulatory agency is more difficult to evaluate.

CHAPTER 5

1   The decision of J. Riddel in *Florence Mining Co. v. Cobalt Lake Mining Co.*, 1908, 18 O.L.R. 275 at p. 279, as quoted in G. S. Challies (1963), pp. 75-76.

2   E. Jones and D. McCalla (1979), pp. 314-20; and A. F. Artibise (1975), ch. 12.

3   *Edinburgh Street Tramways Co. v. Lord Provost, etc., of Edinburgh*, 1894, A.C. 456, as quoted in Challies, p. 172.

4   *In re London County Council v. London Street Tramways Co.* L.R., 1894, 2 Q.B., 189, in Challies, p. 173.

5   *Kingston Light, Heat, and Power Co. v. Kingston*, 1904, 20 T.L.R. 448 P.C.

6   *Peterborough v. Peterborough Electric Light and Power*, 1916, 52 O.L.R. 9, in Challies, p. 196.

7   *Toronto v. Toronto Ry.*, 1925, A.C. 177; 1924, 4 D.L.R., in Challies, p. 171.

8   See Challies, p. 111, quoting cases in 1909, 1910, and 1918.

9   *In re Toronto v. Toronto Street Ry.*, 1893, A.C. 511, in Challies, p. 188.

10   *Town of Berlin v. The Berlin and Waterloo Street Ry.*, 1908, 19 O.L.R. 57; 1910, 42 S.C.R. 581, in Challies, pp. 195 and 215.

11   Nova Scotia, *Statutes*, 1912, 2 Geo. V, c. 64.

12   Halifax Electric Tramway Company Limited, *Annual Report*, 1902, in Houston, *Annual Financial Review*, 1903.

13   Nova Scotia, *Statutes*, 1895, 58 Vic., c. 107.

14   Nova Scotia, *Statutes*, 1886, 49 Vic., c. 124.

15   Nova Scotia, *Statutes*, 1890, 53 Vic., c. 193 and 1889, 52 Vic., c. 135.

16   Nova Scotia, *Statutes*, 1903-04, 3 Edw. VII, c. 26, "An Act to amend c. 33, Acts of 1903."

17   Nova Scotia, *Statutes*, 1907, 7 Edw. VII, c. 40.

18   Nova Scotia, *Statutes*, 1909, 9 Edw. VII, c. 1.

19   Nova Scotia, *Statutes*, 1912, 2 Geo.V, c. 64.

20   Nova Scotia, House of Assembly, *Journals and Proceedings*, 1913, pt. 2, Appendix 27, *Report of Board of Commissioners of Public Utilities, 1912.*

21   Nova Scotia, House of Assembly, *Journals and Proceedings*, 1919, pt. 2, Appendix 27, *Report of Board of Commissioners of Public Utilities, 1918.*

22   Nova Scotia, *Statutes*, 1917, 7-8 Geo. V, c. 56.

23   Nova Scotia, *Revised Statutes*, 1923, c. 15, s. 15.

24   Nova Scotia, House of Assembly, *Journals and Proceedings*, 1924, pt. 2, Appendix 27, *Report of Board of Commissioners of Public Utilities*; see also other years (1917-25).

25   Nova Scotia, *Statutes*, 1909, 9 Edw. VII, c. 167.

26   Nova Scotia, *Statutes*, 1910, 10 Edw. VII, c. 160.

27   See C. Armstrong and H. V. Nelles (1976), for an account of this struggle and the subsequent political controversy.

28   Nova Scotia, *Statutes*, 1912, 2 Geo. V, c. 78.

29   Nova Scotia, *Statutes*, 1913, 3 Geo. V, c. 194.

30   Nova Scotia, House of Assembly, *Journals and Proceedings*, 1914, pt. 2, Appendix 27, *Report of Board of Commissioners of Public Utilities, 1913.*

31   Nova Scotia, *Statutes*, 1914, 4 Geo. V, c. 180.

32   Nova Scotia, House of Assembly, *Journals and Proceedings*, 1917, pt. 2. Appendix 27, *Report of Board of Commissioners of Public Utilities, 1916.*

33   Nova Scotia, House of Assembly, *Journals and Proceedings*, 1919, pt. 2, Appendix 27, *Report of Board of Commissioners of Public Utilities, 1918.*

34   The decline in the realized rate in 1902-03 is the result of an increase in capitalization that took place in these two years that had not yet been reflected in earnings.

35   The debt of both Halifax Tramway and Nova Scotia Light and Power was issued with a 5 per cent coupon.

36   For the issue price, see Armstrong and Nelles (1976), p. 127; for the recapitalization of 1928, see the 1929 *Annual Report* of Nova Scotia Light and Power in Houston, *Annual Financial Review*, 1929.

37   In calculating this percentage, the discounts authorized by the PUC have been applied to the figures for debt and equity reported in the annual report of the Nova Scotia Tramways and Power Company.

38   New Brunswick, *Acts*, 1910, 10 Edw. VII, c. 5.

39   *Synoptic Report of the Proceedings of the Legislative Assembly of the Province of New Brunswick*, 1910, p. 20.

40   See Armstrong and Nelles (1986), pp. 198-200.

41   Transcript of New Brunswick Telephone hearings, January 21-June 18, 1920, p. 106, as partially quoted in Armstrong and Nelles (1986), p. 281, fn. 31.

42   New Brunswick, *Revised Statutes*, 1927, c. 127.

43   *R. v. Board of Public Utility Commissioners ex parte, Moncton Tramways, Electricity, and Gas, Limited*, quoted in Challies, p. 170.

44   *Moncton v. Moncton Tramways, Electricity, and Gas Company*, PUR 1932 B. 368, p. 373, as quoted in Challies, p. 169.

45   *R. v. Board of Commissioners of Public Utilities*, 1934, 9 M.P.R. 1, p. 8, in Challies, p. 170.

46   *King v. Rideout et al. ex parte, Moncton Electricity and Gas Company, Limited*, June 29, 1949, N.B. Supreme Court, D.L.R., vol. 4, p. 12.

47   The regulatory process got off to a shaky start when the Alberta Appelate Division ruled in 1920 that contracts made prior to 1915 were not subject to review by the regulatory agency. Subsequent rulings changed this. See H. R. Milner, p. 104.

48   In one case, because of a lack of data on actual investment, it had to hold a valuation hearing to arrive at the capital value based on replacement value of investment. See *Red Deer and Western General Electric Co. Rate Case*, in Milner (1930), p. 105.

49   *Annual Reports* of the Western Natural Gas, Light, Heat, and Power Company, 1917 and 1918, as cited in Houston, *Annual Financial Review*, 1918 and 1919.

50   *Annual Report* of the Western Natural Gas, Light, Heat, and Power Company, 1921, in Houston, *Annual Financial Review*, 1922.

51   See *Annual Report* of International Utilities Corporation, 1925, in Houston, *Annual Financial Review*, 1925.

CHAPTER 6

1   Those cities like Hamilton and Quebec that owned their own system from the outset had originally looked for private companies, but found no respondents since the rewards did not offset the risks of the enterprise in small towns. See Armstrong and Nelles (1986), pp. 31-32.

2   In 1856, only one-ninth of all houses were connected to the waterworks. See Jones and McCalla, p. 306.

3   Province of Canada, *Statutes*, 1843, 7 Vic., c. 44, as quoted in Armstrong and Nelles (1986), p. 16, fn. 10.

4   Province of Canada, *Statutes*, 1857, 20 Vic., c. 81, s. 10; see also Armstrong and Nelles (1986), p. 18.

5   Ontario, *Statutes*, 1872, 35 Vic., c. 78.

6   Since there were no meters at this time, forced connection would have resulted in the company receiving a guaranteed revenue per household. See Artibise (1975), p. 350, fn. 17.

7   In 1893, the company had provincial legislation passed that prevented Winnipeg from operating its own waterworks until the company's franchise expired in 1900. See Artibise, pp. 349-50, fn. 12.

8   Much of the history that follows can be found in Armstrong and Nelles (1986), pp. 13-29.

9   Province of Canada, *Statutes*, 1847, 10-11 Vic., c. 79.

10 The Consumer's Gas Company managed to have a restrictive clause inserted in the new charter, granted in 1853, limiting gas rates to a maximum of $2.50/MCF. See Armstrong and Nelles (1986), p. 23.

11 *Saturday Night*, January 14, 21, and 28, 1888, cited in Armstrong and Nelles (1986), p. 82, fn. 33.

12 The protection was only partial in that the state could have revoked that protection, although it chose not to do so.

13 For details of the regulatory contracts in Toronto and Montreal recited herein, see Armstrong and Nelles (1986), pp. 37-38, and 46-51.

14 For an account of the renegotiating process that took place in Europe in the 1890s, see J. P. McKay (1976). A case study of the evolution of the industry in one state of the United States can be found in E. S. Mason (1932).

15 The acts of incorporation can be found in Province of Canada, *Statutes*, 1861, 24 Vic., c. 84. An Act to Incorporate the Montreal City Passenger Railway Company and *Statutes*, 1861, 24 Vic., c. 83. An Act to Incorporate the Toronto Street Railway Company.

16 The Montreal Street Railway Company controlled this threat by acquiring these companies. See Armstrong and Nelles (1986), p. 42.

17 William Mackenzie was instrumental in utility development in Vancouver, Winnipeg, and Toronto; as well, he was the chief organizer of the Canadian Northern Railway Company.

18 In the United States various state governments took advantage of competition by granting competitive franchises. See D. F. Wilcox (1921).

19 See *Annual Report, 1910* of the Toronto Railway Company, as reported in Houston, *Annual Financial Review*, 1911. The tax was 8 per cent for revenues up to $1 million, 10 per cent up to $1.5 million, 12 per cent up to $2 million, 15 per cent to $3 million, then 20 per cent above $3 million.

20 Montreal Street Railway Company, *Annual Report, 1911*, as cited in Houston, *Annual Financial Review*, November 1911, Appendix, p. 237.

21 Montreal Street Railway Company, *Annual Report, 1902*, as published in Houston, *Annual Financial Review*, 1903.

22 Toronto Railway Company, *Annual Report, 1902*, as published in Houston, *Annual Financial Review*, 1903.

23 See chapters 7, 9, 10 and 11.

CHAPTER 7

1   British Columbia, *Public Utilities Act*, 1938, 2 Geo. VI, c. 47, s. 44.

2   For an extensive and detailed history of the BCER, see Patricia Roy's articles published in 1971, 1972, and 1973.

3   British Columbia, Legislative Assembly, *Journals*, 1894-95, Appendices, as quoted in Armstrong and Nelles (1986), p. 97, fn. 14.

4   British Columbia, Legislative Assembly, Royal Commission on Municipal Government, *Report 1912*, Victoria, King's Printer, 1913.

5   As reported in the BCER *Annual Report* for 1920; see Houston, *Annual Financial Review*, 1921. The BCER had already fought off one challenge from the company by invoking its connections with the Liberal government in Ottawa. The WCP company had challenged the rights of the BCER to the waters of Lake Coquitlam – by encouraging the city of New Westminster to oppose the BCER's rights to water from this source. The federal government had jurisdiction over these water rights as the result of a 1910 decision of the Judicial Committee of the Privy Council. It was ruled the railway belt, a strip 20 miles wide on either side of the CPR's main line, fell under federal authority. In return for a promise of BCER financial support for a new Liberal newspaper in British Columbia, the federal Cabinet ruled in the BCER's favour. See P. E. Roy (1972), pp. 240-43.

6 Report of the Royal Commission of Inquiry into the Vancouver Utilities Question (1918), Commissioner to Investigate the Economic Conditions and Operations of the British Columbia Electric Railway and Subsidiary Companies, 1918.

7 See BCER *Annual Report*, 1919, in Houston, *Annual Financial Review*, 1919.

8 British Columbia, Legislative Assembly, *Journals*, 1919, Bill 69.

9 British Columbia, Legislative Assembly, *Journals*, 1920, Bill 64.

10 Roy (1971), pp. 12-13; Armstrong and Nelles (1986), p. 261, fn. 34. Refer also to Canada, *Statutes*, 1920, 10-11 Geo. V, c. 65.

11 It proposed to do this by transferring its physical assets to its federally chartered subsidiary – the Vancouver, Fraser Valley and Southern Railways. See Roy (1971), p. 14.

12 The agreement was passed in 1922 by the province as the *British Columbia Electric Railway Passenger Rates Act*. Any municipality or the BCER could ask the Cabinet for a commission under the *Public Inquiries Act* to investigate whether rates were "unjust" or "unreasonable." See Roy (1971), p. 18.

Chapter 8

1 Province of Canada, *Statutes*, 1880, 43 Vic., c. 67, An Act to Incorporate the Bell Telephone Company of Canada, as quoted in Armstrong and Nelles (1986), p. 72, fn. 43.

2 Quebec, *Statutes*, 1881, 44-45 Vic., c. 66; Ontario, *Statutes*, 1882, 45 Vic., c. 71, as quoted in Armstrong and Nelles (1986), p. 72, fn. 44.

3 Western Union tried to obtain a seat on the Bell Board in the early 1880s, but failed and shortly thereafter sold its stock in Bell Canada. See Armstrong and Nelles (1986), p. 72, fn. 42.

4 See Canada, House of Commons, Select Committe Appointed to Inquire into the Various Telephone Systems in Canada and Elsewhere, *Report*, vol. 2 (Ottawa: King's Printer, 1905), p. 101, as quoted in Armstrong and Nelles (1986), p. 108, fn. 46.

5 A clause had been inserted in Bell's charter during an 1892 recapitalization that required Bell to seek approval from the Cabinet for any rate increase. See Province of Canada, *Statutes*, 1892, 55-56 Vic., c. 67, An Act Respecting the Bell Telephone Company.

6 PAC, RG 46, Board of Railway Commissioners, *Papers*, vols. 1 and 2, as quoted in Armstrong and Nelles (1986), p. 167, fn. 12.

7 Canada, *Statutes*, 1908, 7-8 Edw. VII, c. 61, s. 4, pp. 1-8.

8 Ontario, *Statutes*, 1907, 7 Edw. VII, 37. See Armstrong (1981), ch. 5.

9 Armstrong and Nelles (1973), pp. 172-75, and (1986), pp. 172-73.

10 Canada, *Statutes*, 1906, 6 Edw. VII, c. 42, as quoted in Armstrong and Nelles (1986), p. 174, fn. 36.

11 *City of Montreal v. Bell Telephone Co.* (1912), 15, C.R.C. 118, quoted in A. J. de Grandpré (1970), p. 30.

12 *B.C. Telephone Co. v. Vancouver* (1921), 27 C.R.C. 259, as quoted in de Grandpré (1970), p. 30.

Chapter 9

1 Bell's capital investment was $1,360,787 as of December 31, 1905. It spent about $1,000,000 in Manitoba in 1906, and about $700,000 in 1907 for a total of $3,060,787 as of the end of 1907. See J. Mavor (1917), pp. 26-27.

2 As in Ontario, the public corporation was not burdened by municipal taxes; the private firm was – see Mavor (1917), p. 59.

3 See Mavor (1917), p. 23, for testimony from the Attorney General that the lowering of farm telephone rates after nationalization was directly specified by the government.

4 See Mavor (1917), pp. 21, 58, 69, 75, 79, and 83.

5 Manitoba, *Statutes*, 1912, 2 Geo.V, c. 66.

6 Mavor (1917), pp. 123-31, reports the private power company applied for a telephone charter, but was turned down at this time.

7 See Manitoba, *Statutes*, 1892, 55 Vic., c. 56, as noted in Armstrong and Nelles (1986), p. 94, fn. 3.

8 See Manitoba, *Statutes*, 1899, 62-3 Vic., c. 25, as noted in Armstrong and Nelles (1986), p. 154, fn. 36.

9 This likelihood was greater than it might have appeared at the time. Nelles (1976), p. 470, notes both the Premier and members of his Cabinet owned shares in the private company.

10 J. E. Rea (1975), p. 85, and Nelles (1976), p. 469.

11 *In re Winnipeg Electric Co.*, PUR 1920 F. 879, at p. 893, as quoted in Challies, p. 169.

12 See Nelles (1976), pp. 472-78, for a detailed description of the Department of the Interior's objectives.

13 Armstrong and Nelles (1977a), outline how in an earlier case involving Calgary, the federal authorities chose a monopoly for development of additional waterpower supplies because it would yield greater efficiencies from shared watershed development.

14 Nelles (1976), p. 473, suggests the federal authorities preferred private to public development on ideological grounds as well as for ease of negotiations.

15 Nelles (1976), pp. 475-76. Winnipeg had to pay $17.50/kwh. See Manitoba (1939).

16 See Armstrong and Nelles (1984), for a discussion of the role of these scandals.

17 For a discussion of federal-provincial conflict in general, see Armstrong (1981), ch. 5.

Chapter 10

1 Armstrong and Nelles (1986), pp. 58-59; see also Figure 1, on page 135, for a comparison of population growth rates in Toronto and Montreal.

2 A franchise had been given to this company in 1892, but nothing came of it.

3 In 1906, the government received only $60,000.

4 J. C. Hopkins, *Canadian Annual Review*, 1907, p. 516.

5 See the *Ontario Hydro Act* of 1906 which specified the interest cost that municipalities would have to bear for investments incurred on their behalf.

6 Hopkins, *Canadian Annual Review*, 1908, p. 299 – the towns of Toronto, London, Guelph, Stratford, St. Thomas, Woodstock, Berlin, Galt, Hespeler, St. Mary's, Preston, Waterloo, New Hamburg, and Ingersoll.

7 Ontario, *Statutes*, 1906, 6 Edw. VII, c. 15, s. 11 and 12. See also Mavor (1925), p. 55.

8 See Dewar (1983), for an account of this episode.

9 Hopkins, *Canadian Annual Review*, 1906, p. 183.

10 Hopkins, *Canadian Annual Review*, 1909, p. 374.

11 Hopkins, *Canadian Annual Review*, 1913, pp. 417-18.

12 Mavor (1925), p. 138, see also Nelles (1975), p. 292.

13 Ontario, *Statutes*, 1916, 6 Geo. V, c. 20, s. 7.

14 Nelles (1975), p. 300, and Mavor (1925), p. 150.

15 Hopkins, *Canadian Annual Review*, 1916, p. 511.

16 Hopkins, *Canadian Annual Review*, 1914, p. 403.

17 Hopkins, *Canadian Annual Review*, 1914, p. 403.

Chapter 11

1 See J. H. Dales (1957), ch. 3, for a history of this period.

2 At the time of the power company consolidation, a new power contract was signed with the Montreal Street Railway Company for $25/HP for 20 years.

3 See "The effect of public competition on the rates charged by the Montreal Light, Heat, and Power Company," in *4th Annual Report* of the N.Y. Power Authority (1934), pp. 90-103, as reported in Barnes, p. 840. See also Dales, p. 225.

4 In 1923, the Montreal Public Service Corporation was renamed the Quebec-New England Hydro-Electric Corporation and was sold to a new company, the United Securities Company. This company had been jointly formed by Montreal Light and Shawinigan. United Securities was combined with Montreal Light, Heat, and Power to form a new company, Montreal Light, Heat, and Power Consolidated, in 1926.

5 Quebec, *Statutes*, 1909, 9 Edw. VII, c. 16.

6 Quebec, *Statutes*, 1920, 10 Geo. V, c. 21.

7 Quebec, *Statutes*, 1935, 25-26 Geo. V, c. 24.

8 Quebec, *Statutes*, 1904, 4 Edw. VII, c. 35.

9 Quebec, *Statutes*, 1904, 4 Edw. VII, c. 12.

10 Quebec, *Statutes*, 1911, 1 Geo. V, c. 14.

11 Quebec, *Statutes*, 1911, 1 Geo. V, c. 27.

12 Quebec, *Statutes*, 1918, 8 Geo. V, c. 811.

13 See P. Dirks (1981) for a history of the movement to reduce power rates in Quebec during this period. See also Dales, pp. 241-42.

14 Quebec, *Statutes*, 1935, 25-26 Geo. V, c. 49.

15 Dales, p. 118, see also Armstrong and Nelles (1986), p. 365, fn. 14.

16 The comparison is even more lopsided if the rates in Quebec City were used. In 1929, the domestic rate therein was 5.5 cents/kwh. See Dirks, p. 20.

17 The first year for which the breakdown is available is 1933.

List of Tables

Bibliography

ARMSTRONG, C. 1981. *The Politics of Federalism: Ontario's Relations with the Federal Government 1867-1942*. Toronto: University of Toronto Press.

ARMSTRONG, C. and H. V. NELLES. 1973. "Private property in peril: Ontario businessmen and the federal system, 1898-1911." *Business History Review* 47:158-76.

_____. 1976. "Getting your way in Nova Scotia: 'Tweaking' Halifax, 1909-1917." *Acadiensis* 5:105-31.

_____. 1977a. "Competition vs. convenience: Federal administration of Bow River waterpowers, 1906-13." In *The Canadian West: Social Change and Economic Development*, edited by Henry Klassen, pp. 163-80. Calgary: Comprint Publishing Co.

_____. 1977b. *The Revenge of the Methodist Bicycle Company: Sunday Streetcars and Municipal Reform in Toronto, 1888-1897*. Toronto: Peter Martin and Associates.

_____. 1983. "Contrasting development of the hydro-electric industry in the Montreal and Toronto regions, 1900-1930." *Journal of Canadian Studies* 18:5-27.

_____. 1984. "The rise of civic populism in Toronto, 1870-1920." In *Forging a Consensus: Historical Essays on Toronto*, edited by Victor Russel, pp. 192-237. Toronto: University of Toronto Press.

_____. 1986. *Monopoly's Moment: The Organization and Regulation of Canadian Utilities, 1830-1930*. Philadelphia: Temple University Press.

ARTIBISE, A. F. J. 1975. *Winnipeg: A Social History of Urban Growth, 1874-1914*. Montreal: McGill-Queen's University Press.

BALDWIN, J. R. 1975. *The Regulatory Agency and the Public Corporation*. Cambridge, Mass.: Ballinger.

_____. 1984. "Regulation versus public enterprise: Instrument choice in the case of natural monopoly." In *Government Enterprise: Roles and Rationales*, pp. 103-82. Paper presented at a symposium held by the Economic Council of Canada, Ottawa: Economic Council of Canada (september 1984).

BARNES, I. R. 1942. *The Economics of Public Utility Regulation*. New York: F. S. Crofts and Co.

BIGGAR, E. B. 1920. *Hydro-Electric Development in Ontario*. Toronto: Ryerson Press.

BORCHERDING, T. E. 1983. "Toward a positive theory of public sector supply arrangements." In *Crown Corporations in Canada: The Calculus of Instrument Choice*, edited by J. R. S. Prichard, pp. 99-184. Toronto: Butterworths.

BRUNET, M. 1964. *La présence anglaise et les Canadiens: Études sur l'histoire et la pensée des deux Canadas*. Montréal: Beauchemin Press.

BUCHANAN, J. and G. TULLOCK. 1965. *The Calculus of Consent, Logical Foundation of Constitutional Democracy*. Ann Arbor: University of Michigan Press.

BUSSING, I. 1968. *Public Utility Regulation and the So-Called Sliding-Scale*. New York: AMS Press (originally published in 1936) New York: Columbia University Press.

CANADA. DOMINION BUREAU OF STATISTICS. 1927. *Street Car Fares and Index Numbers*. Ottawa: Department of Industry, Trade and Commerce.

_____. 1933 and 1939. *Central Electrical Stations*. Ottawa: Department of Industry, Trade and Commerce.

_____. Public Utilities Branch. 1931. *Index Numbers of Rates for Electricity for Residence Lighting and Tables of Monthly Bills for Domestic Service*. Ottawa: Department of Industry, Trade and Commerce.

CANADA. HOUSE OF COMMONS. 1922. *Sessional Papers. Grand Trunk Arbitration Award*. Vol. LVIII, no. 6, Sessional Paper no. 20.

_____. *Railway Statistics*. Various years.

CANADA. *YEARBOOK*. Ottawa: King's Printer, various years.

CANADIAN PACIFIC RAILWAY COMPANY. 1949. *Submission to the Royal Commission on Transportation*. Appendix to Part I. Montreal, Quebec.

CHALLIES, G. S. 1963. *The Law of Expropriation*. 2nd ed. Montreal: Wilson and Lafleur.

COMMONS, J. R. 1932. *Legal Foundations of Capitalism*. New York: Macmillan.

CURRIE, A. W. 1944. "Rate control of public utilities in British Columbia." *Canadian Journal of Economics and Political Science* 10:381-90.

_____. 1946. "Rate control on Canadian public utilities." *Canadian Journal of Economics and Political Science* 12:148-58.

_____. 1957. *The Grand Trunk Railway of Canada.* Toronto: University of Toronto Press.

_____. 1959. *Economics of Canadian Transportation.* Second ed. Toronto: University of Toronto Press.

DALES, J. H. 1957. *Hydroelectricity and Industrial Development: Quebec, 1898-1940.* Cambridge, Mass.: Harvard University Press.

DAYAN, D. 1972. "Vertical integration and monopoly regulation." Ph.D. dissertation, Princeton University.

DE GRANDPRÉ, A. J. 1970. "Fair return for utilities – Concept or reality?" *McGill Law Journal* 16:19-38.

DEMSETZ, H. 1968. "Why regulate utilities?" *Journal of Law and Economics* 11: 55-65.

DEWAR, K. C. 1983. "Private electrical utilities and municipal ownership in Ontario, 1891-1900." *Urban History Review* 12, no. 1 (June):29-38.

DE ZOETE. 1985. *The de Zoete Equity Gilt Study: A Study of the Relative Performance of Equity and Fixed Interest Investment from 1919 to 1984.* 30th Annual edition. London: de Zoete and Bevan.

DIRKS, P. 1981. "The public power movement in Quebec City, 1929-1934." *Urban History Review* 10:17-30.

DOUGLAS, G. and J. MILLER. 1974. *Economic Regulation of Domestic Air Transport.* Washington: The Brookings Institution.

DOWNS, A. 1957. *An Economic Theory of Democracy.* New York: Harper and Row.

EASTERBROOK, W. T. and H. G. J. AITKEN. 1963. *Canadian Economic History.* Toronto: Macmillan.

FOURNIER, L. T. 1935. *Railway Nationalization in Canada: The Problem of Canadian National Railways.* Toronto: Macmillan.

FRIEDLANDER, A. F. and R. H. SPADY. 1980. *Surface Freight Transport: Equity, Efficiency and Competition.* Cambridge, Mass.: MIT Press.

FRISKEN, F. 1984. "A triumph for public ownership: The Toronto transportation commission 1921-53." In *Forging a Consensus: Historical Essays on Toronto,* edited by Victor Russel, pp. 128-71. Toronto: University of Toronto Press.

GAUVIN, M. 1978. "The reformer and the machine: Montreal civic politics from Raymond Préfontaine to Médéric Martin." *Journal of Canadian Studies* 13:16-27.

GLAZEBROOK, G. P. de T. 1964. *A History of Transportation in Canada,* vol. II. Toronto: Clarke, Irwin.

HALL, C. A. S. 1968. "Electrical utilities in Ontario under private ownership, 1890-1914." Ph.D. dissertation, University of Toronto.

HANNAH, L. 1979. *Electricity Before Nationalization: A Study of the Development of the Electricity Supply Industry in Britain to 1948.* London: Macmillan.

HINES, W. D. 1928. *War History of American Railroads.* New Haven: Yale University Press.

HOPKINS, J. C. *The Canadian Annual Review of Public Affairs.* Toronto: Annual Review Publishing Company. Various years.

HOUSTON, W. R. *Annual Financial Review.* Toronto: W. Briggs. Various years.

HUGHES, T. P. 1983. *Networks of Power: Electrification in Western Society, 1880-1930.* Baltimore: Johns Hopkins University Press.

JACKMAN, W. T. 1935. *Economic Principles of Transportation.* Toronto: University of Toronto Press.

JACKSON, A. B. 1964. "The determination of the fair return for public utilities." *Canadian Public Administration* 7:343-59.

JARRELL, G. A. 1978. "The demand for state regulation of the electric utility industry." *Journal of Law and Economics* 21:269-95.

JONES, E. and D. McCALLA. 1979. "Toronto waterworks, 1840-77: Continuity and change in nineteenth century Toronto politics." *Canadian Historical Review* 60:300-23.

JORDAN, W. 1970. *Airline Regulation in America.* Baltimore: Johns Hopkins University Press.

JOSKOW, P. L. and R. G. NOLL. 1981. "Regulation in theory and practice: An overview." In *Studies in Public Regulation,* edited by G. Fromm, pp. 1-78. Cambridge, Mass.: MIT Press.

KAHN, A. 1970-71. *The Economics of Regulation: Principles and Institutions,* 2 vols. New York: Wiley.

LAVALLÉE, O. S. A. 1961. *The Montreal City Passenger Railway Company.* Montreal: Canadian Railroad Historical Association.

MACAVOY, P. W. 1965. *The Economic Effects of Regulation; the Trunk-Line Railroad Cartels and the Interstate Commerce Commission before 1900.* Cambridge, Mass.: MIT Press.

MACINTOSH, W. A. 1924. *Agricultural Cooperation in Western Canada.* Toronto: Ryerson Press.

MANITOBA. 1939. *Report of the Royal Commission on the Municipal Finances and Administration of the City of Winnipeg*. Winnipeg, Manitoba.

MASON, E. S. 1932. *The Street Railway in Massachusetts: The Rise and Decline of an Industry*. Cambridge, Mass.: Harvard University Press.

MAVOR, J. 1917. *Government Telephones: The Experience of Manitoba, Canada*. Toronto: MacLean Pub. Co.

_____. 1925. *Niagara in Politics: A Critical Account of the Ontario Hydro-Electric Commission*. New York: E. P. Dutton and Company.

McCORMICK, R. L. 1981. "The discovery that business corrupts politics: A reappraisal of the origins of progressivism." *American Historical Review* 86:247-74.

McKAY, J. P. 1976. *Tramways and Trolleys: The Rise of Urban Mass Transport in Europe*. Princeton, New Jersey: Princeton University Press.

MERCER, L. J. 1972. "Taxpayers or investors: Who paid for the land-grant railroads?" *Business History Review* 50:279-91.

MILNER, H. R. 1930. "Public utility rate control in Alberta." *Canadian Bar Review* 11 (February):101-11.

MOODY'S INVESTORS' SERVICE. *Analysis of Railroad Investments*. New York. Various years.

_____. *Analyses of Investments, Steam Railroads*. New York. Various years.

MOSHER, W. E. and F. G. CRAWFORD. 1933. *Public Utility Regulation*. New York: Harper and Brothers.

MYERS, G. 1968. *History of Canadian Wealth*. New York: Argosy-Antiquarian Ltd. (First printed, 1914.)

_____. 1974. *History of Public Franchises in New York City*. Politics and People Series. New York: Arno Press.

NELLES, H. V. 1975. *The Politics of Development: Forests, Mines and Hydro-Electric Power in Ontario, 1849-1941*. Toronto: Macmillan.

_____. 1976. "Public ownership of electrical utilities in Manitoba and Ontario, 1906-30." *Canadian Historical Review* 57, no. 4 (December):461-84.

PELTZMAN, S. 1976. "Toward a more general theory of regulation." *Journal of Law and Economics* 19:211-40.

PHILLIPS, C. F. 1965. *The Economics of Regulation: Theory and Practice in the Transportation and Public Utilities Industries*. Homewood, Illinois: R. D. Irwin.

PLEWMAN, W. R. 1947. *Adam Beck and the Ontario Hydro*. Toronto: Ryerson Press.

POOR'S, *Manual of Railroads and Corporation Securities*. New York: Poor's Publishing Company. Various years.

POOR'S, *Manual of the Railroads of the United States*. New York: Poor's Publishing Company. Various years.

REA, J. E. 1975. "How Winnipeg was nearly won." In *Cities in the West*, edited by A. R. McCormack and Ian MacPherson, pp. 74-87. Ottawa: National Museums of Canada.

ROY, P. E. 1971. "Regulating the British Columbia Electric Railway: The first public utilities commission in British Columbia." *B. C. Studies* 11:3-20.

_____. 1972. "The fine arts of lobbying and persuading: The case of the B. C. Electric Railway, 1897-1917." In *Canadian Business History: Selected Studies, 1497-1971*, edited by D. S. Macmillan, pp. 239-54. Toronto: McClelland and Stewart.

_____. 1973. "Direct management from abroad: The formative years of the British Columbia Railway." *Business History Review* 48 (Summer):239-59.

SCHERER, F. M. 1971. *Industrial Market Structure and Economic Performance*. Chicago: Rand.

SHAWINIGAN WATER AND POWER COMPANY. 1926. *Twenty-Five Years of Progress: The Shawinigan Water and Power Company*. Montreal: Desbarets.

SKELTON, O. D. 1916. *The Railway Builders: A Chronicle of Overland Highways*. Toronto: Glasgow, Brook and Company.

SMITH, N. L. 1932. *The Fair Rate of Return in Public Utility Regulation*. Boston and New York: Houghton Mifflin.

STEVENS, G. R. 1962. *Canadian National Railways*. Vol. II. Toronto: Clarke, Irwin.

STIGLER, G. J. 1961. "The theory of economic regulation." *Bell Journal of Economics and Management Science* 2:3-21.

STIGLER, G. and C. FRIEDLAND. 1962. "What can regulators regulate? The case of electricity." *Journal of Law and Economics* 5:1-16.

THOMPSON, C. W. and W. R. SMITH. 1941. *Public Utility Economics*. 1st ed. New York: McGraw-Hill.

TREBILCOCK, M. J., D. G. HARTLE, J. R. S. PRICHARD, and D. N. DEWEES. 1982. *The Choice of Governing Instrument*. Ottawa: Economic Council of Canada.

TREBILCOCK, M. J. and J. R. S. PRICHARD. 1983. "Crown corporations: The calculus of instrument choice." In *Crown Corporations in Canada: The Calculus of Instrument Choice*, edited by J. R. S. Prichard, pp. 1-98. Toronto: Butterworths.

TROXEL, C. E. 1947. *Economics of Public Utilities*. New York: Rinehart.

UNITED STATES. BUREAU OF THE CENSUS. 1960. *Historical Statistics of the United States: Colonial Times to 1957*. 2 vols. Washington, D. C.: Department of Commerce.

_____. 1976. *The Statistical History of the United States from Colonial Times to the Present*. New York: Basic Books.

_____. FEDERAL COMMUNICATIONS COMMISSION. 1939. *Investigation on the Telephone Industry in the United States*. Also published as House Document no. 340, 76th Congress, 1st session (1939).

URQUHART, M. C. and K. A. H. BUCKLEY. 1965. *Historical Statistics of Canada*. 1st ed. Cambridge: Cambridge University Press.

USHER, D. 1981. *The Economic Prerequisite to Democracy*. New York: Columbia University Press.

VIGOD, B. L. 1978. "Alexandre Taschereau and the negro king hypothesis." *Journal of Canadian Studies* 13:3-15.

WALLACE, H. E. 1900. *The Manual of Statistics, Stock Exchange Handbook*. New York.

WHITE, W. A. 1981. "Toronto's reluctant entrance into the railway mania of the 1850s." *Urban History Review* 10:31-38.

WILCOX, D. F. 1910-1911. *Municipal Franchises*. 2 vols. Rochester, N. Y.: The Gervais Press, New York: Engineering News book department.

_____. 1921. *Analysis of the Electric Railway Problem*. New York: the author.

WILLIAMSON, O. E. 1971. "The vertical integration of production: Market failure considerations." *American Economic Review* 61:112-23.

_____. 1975. *Markets and Hierarchies: Analysis and Antitrust Implications*. New York: The Free Press.

_____. 1979. "Transaction cost economics: The governance of contractual relations." *Journal of Law and Economics* 22:233-61.

_____. 1981a. "The modern corporation: Origins, evolution, attributes." *Journal of Economic Literature* 19:537-70.

_____. 1981b. "The economics of organization: The transaction cost approach." *American Journal of Sociology* 87:548-77.

WILLIAMSON, O. E., M. L. WACHTER, and J. E. HARRIS. 1975. "Understanding the employment relation: The analysis of idiosyncratic exchange." *Bell Journal of Economics* 6:50-80.

WRIGHT, A. R. 1963. "An examination of the role of the Board of Transport Commissioners for Canada as a regulatory tribunal." *Canadian Public Administration* 6:349-85.